GEORGE PAYNE RAINSFORD JAMES

THE LIFE

OF

HENRY THE FOURTH

KING OF FRANCE AND NAVARRE

Volume II

Elibron Classics
www.elibron.com

Elibron Classics series.

© 2005 Adamant Media Corporation.

ISBN 1-4021-8946-X (paperback)
ISBN 1-4021-2036-2 (hardcover)

This Elibron Classics Replica Edition is an unabridged facsimile
of the edition published in 1847 by T. and W. Boone,
London.

Louis XII   1498 - 1515
Francis I   1515 - 1547
Henry II   1547 - 1559
Francis II   1559 - 1560
Charles IX   1560 - 1574
Henry III   1574 - 1589
Henry IV   1589 - 1610

Royal Quarto, on Indian Paper, price 1s. 6d.

PORTRAIT OF
MAJOR-GENERAL SIR CHARLES JAMES NAPIER,
CONQUEROR OF SCINDE.

FROM A SKETCH BY MAJOR-GENERAL W. F. P. NAPIER.

" I must say that, after giving the fullest consideration to those operations, that I have never known an instance of a general officer who has shewn to a higher degree than he has done all the requisite qualifications to enable him to conduct great operations. He has manifested the utmost discretion and prudence in the formation of his plans, the utmost activity in perfecting his preparations to ensure success; and finally the utmost zeal, gallantry, and science, in carrying those plans and preparations into execution. I must say that the march of General Napier against Emaum Ghur was one of the most extraordinary marches I ever read of; and it was, I must say, most completely successful. He marched the army through the desert, with all the heavy guns, transporting all his materiel as well, and by this extraordinary march he deprived the enemy of all means of retreat."—*Speech of the Duke of Wellington.*

" The taking of the fort of Emaum Ghur, was one of the most brilliant affairs ever undertaken and executed."—*Speech of the Earl of Ripon.*

" To the example which he set the troops—inspiring an unparalleled confidence in their commander,—we must mainly attribute the success of the actions of Meeanee and Hyderabad."—*Speech of Sir Robert Peel.*

In one volume 8vo. price 7s. boards,

REMARKS ON MILITARY LAW
AND THE PUNISHMENT OF FLOGGING.

BY MAJOR-GENERAL SIR CHARLES JAMES NAPIER, K.C.B.

" In Scinde he had an opportunity of shewing some of the greatest qualities which which could distinguish a military Commander—prompt decision, energy, undaunted bravery, consummate military skill, and, above all, that power which particularly distinguishes superior minds—the power of inspiring into all who served under his command a portion of the same spirit by which he was himself animated."—*Speech of Lord Howick.*

" He was cognisant of many transactions in which that gallant officer was concerned during the Peninsular war, and his humanity was equal to his gallantry. It was the opinion of the whole army, that to his master-mind was to be attributed that final success."—*Speech of General Sir H. Hardinge.*

" This work, we have several times taken occasion to remark, is far less known than it deserves to be, especially among the profession. It abounds in lessons of profound wisdom, delivered in the clearest language, and it is as modestly as it is ably written; nor have we often met with a more amusing book. There are to be found in it many interesting and characteristic anecdotes, and there is a vein of quiet humour that is very diverting, but which interferes not at all with the serious purpose of the author, who has left upon every page traces of a benevolent heart and sound intellect."—*Naval and Military Gazette.*

COLONIZATION:
PARTICULARLY IN SOUTHERN AUSTRALIA,
WITH SOME REMARKS ON SMALL FARMS AND OVER POPULATION.

BY MAJOR-GENERAL SIR CHARLES JAMES NAPIER, K.C.B.
Author of " The Colonies; particularly the Ionian Islands."
In 1 vol. 8vo. price 7s. boards.

" We earnestly recommend the book to all who feel an interest in the welfare of the people."—*Sun.*

Now ready, complete in 1 vol. 8vo. with Plans,

THE CONQUEST OF SCINDE,

WITH AN

ACCOUNT OF THE MILITARY TRANSACTIONS AND BATTLES OF

Major-General Sir Charles J. Napier in that Country.

BY MAJOR-GENERAL W. F. P. NAPIER,

Author of " History of the War in the Peninsula."

" We are glad General Napier has found any excuse for presenting the public with his views of the policy adopted in reference to Scinde and Affghanistan, and of the manner in which that policy was carried out. His is no common pen. He adorns and dignifies a good cause, and renders a bad one attractive. As a commentary upon some remarkable political events, and daring military achievements, this volume will rapidly find a place in every soldier's library."—*Atlas.*

" The Author is the historian of the Peninsular War, whose connection by blood with the gallant conqueror of Scinde affords a security for the authenticity of his sources of information—some of which are the letters of Sir Charles himself—and whose high character, as an author, as well as a soldier, is a guarantee for his fidelity in the use of his ample materials. We may add to the Author's other qualifications, an unflinching intrepid honesty, which makes him speak out, and utter the plain truth, without considering whether it be unpalatable."—*Asiatic Journal.*

In Two Volumes, post 8vo. price 21*s.*

COMMODORE SIR CHARLES NAPIER'S

ACCOUNT OF THE WAR IN PORTUGAL.

BETWEEN DON PEDRO AND DON MIGUEL;

WITH PLANS OF HIS ACTION OFF CAPE ST. VINCENT.

" If we read the account of that naval action in which, with a force wholly unequal, had it not been directed by the utmost skill and valour, to compete with the enemy— if we read the account of that action in which, in the space of five minutes, a signal victory was achieved. by which the glory of St. Vincent was revived—I say, if we read the records of such an action, we shall find that the commander bore the name of Napier."—*Speech of Sir Robert Peel.*

" An excellent and spirit-stirring book—plain, honest, and straight-forward—the very stuff of which the web of history alone should be composed. This is indeed an honest, fair, and impartial history."—*Morning Chronicle.*

" In spirit and in keeping, from beginning to end, Admiral Napier's ' War in Portugal,' is the happiest picture we could conceive of the battle off Cape St. Vincent— its especial excellence consisting in a regardless bluntness of manner and language that is quite admirable and delightful."—*Monthly Review.*

" It is Cæsar's Commentaries in the first person."—*Spectator.*

" Candid to a degree, and sincere as a sailor's will. This is the very stuff of which history should be composed."—*Bell's Messenger.*

" If Admiral Napier be not distinguished by the common-place facilities of authorship, he possesses the higher qualities of truth, discretion, and clear-sightedness, in no slight degree."—*Atlas.*

" In speaking of himself and his deeds, he has hit the just and difficult medium— shewing his real feelings, yet steering 'clear of affected modesty on the one hand, and of over-weening modesty on the other.'—*Tait's Magazine.*

" This is a very graphic account of the affairs in which the gallant author figured so nobly, and added fresh lustre to the name of Napier."—*News.*

The Third Edition, in one vol. post 8vo. price 10s. 6d. bds. of

ADVENTURES IN THE RIFLE BRIGADE,
IN THE
PENINSULA, FRANCE, AND THE NETHERLANDS,
FROM THE YEAR 1809 TO 1815,
BY CAPTAIN JOHN KINCAID, First Battalion.

" An admirable little book."—*Quarterly Review.*

" To those who are unacquainted with John Kincaid of the Rifles,—and few, we trow, of the old Peninsula bands are in this ignorant predicament, and to those who know him, we equally recommend the perusal of his book: it is a fac-simile of the man —a perfect reflection of his image, *veluti in speculo.* A capital Soldier, a pithy and graphic narrator, and a fellow of infinite jest. Captain Kincaid has given us, in this modest volume, the impress of his qualities, the *beau ideal* of a thorough-going Soldier of Service, and the faithful and witty history of some six years' honest and triumphant fighting.

" There is nothing extant in a Soldier's Journal, which, with so little pretension, paints with such truth and raciness the 'domestic economy' of campaigning, and the down-right business of handling the enemy.

" But we cannot follow further;—recommending every one of our readers to pursue the Author himself to his crowning scene of Waterloo, where they will find him as quaint and original as at his *début.* We assure them, it is not possible, by isolated extracts, to give a suitable impression of the spirit and originality which never flag from beginning to end of Captain Kincaid's volume; in every page of which he throws out flashes of native humour, a tithe of which would make the fortune of a Grub-street Bookmaker."—*United Service Journal.*

" His book has one fault, the rarest fault in books, it is too short."
Monthly Magazine, April.

Also, by the same Author, Second Edition, in one vol. post 8vo. price 10s. 6d.

RANDOM SHOTS FROM A RIFLEMAN.

" It is one of the most pithy, witty, soldier-like, and pleasant books in existence."
United Service Journal.

" The present volume is to the full as pleasant, and what is still more strange, as *original* as the last. Criticism would become a sinecure if many such volumes were written: all left for us is to admire and recommend."—*New Monthly Magazine.*

" The present volume is likely to add to his reputation. It is a useful Appendix to the larger works of Napier and other military commentators. It is never dull, tedious, technical, or intricate."—*Times.*

" Those who have read Captain Kincaid's Adventures in the Rifle Brigade will seize this volume with avidity, and having dashed through it, will lay it down with only one feeling of regret—that it is not longer."—*News.*

Elegantly bound in the Uniform of the Regiment, 1 vol. post 8vo. price 10s. 6d.
THE
ADVENTURES OF CAPTAIN JOHN PATTERSON,
With Notices of the Officers, &c. of the 50th, or Queen's Own Regiment,
FROM 180 TO 1821.
DEDICATED BY PERMISSION TO QUEEN ADELAIDE.

" This volume contains a well-written, yet unvarnished narrative, of the adventures of the 50th foot, (better known as the 'Dirty Half-hundred,' from their black facings), during the Peninsular war. It argues well for the bravery, as well as modesty, of Captain Patterson, that throughout his work we have but little of himself, and much of his brother officers."—*Bell's Messenger.*

" Captain Patterson's Adventures are the record of a brave soldier—of a dashing, high-minded British officer, who never fears a rival, and never knew what it was to have an enemy, or to hate any man. His descriptions are remarkable for their vividness and accuracy, and his anecdotes will bear repetition once a week for life."—*Sun.*

" Captain Patterson is one of the pleasantest of the numerous tribe of gallant officers who has done so much credit to the British name, by fighting and writing with equal spirit "—*Constitutional.*

In 2 vols. 8vo. cloth, price 24s.

HISTORICAL RECORD

OF THE

ROYAL MARINE FORCES,

From their Formation to the Present Time,

INCLUDING

AN ACCOUNT OF THEIR SERVICES IN CHINA,

BY P. H. NICOLAS,

LIEUT. ROYAL MARINES.

" Mr. Nicolas has had a wide and fertile field to work upon, and excellently has he turned his materials to account. Impelled by a sincere attachment for his old comrades, by an ardent desire for their welfare, by the very natural wish for a more minute and connected narrative of their daring career than has hitherto been given to the world, he has produced a luminous and comprehensive work, than which none can be better of its class, and which reflects equal credit upon his feelings as an officer, and his talents as a writer."—*United Service Gazette.*

" These volumes cannot fail to prove eminently acceptable to the members of the gallant corps, whose honours they record, and generally indeed to the military service of both arms."—*Naval and Military Gazette.*

" It is historical, and must interest all historical readers; it is proudly national, and speaks to the heart of every Englishman; while to the sailor, the soldier, and especially the marine, whose services it chronicles, it will prove a valuable record. It is a work, which for historical information, and clearness of arrangement, may fairly compete with any of its class."—*Literary Gazette.*

In One Volume, post 8vo. price 10s.

A BRITISH ARMY,

AS IT WAS,—IS,—AND OUGHT TO BE:

ILLUSTRATED BY EXAMPLES DURING THE PENINSULAR WAR.

With Observations upon India—the United States of America—Canada— the Boundary Line—the Navy—Steam Warfare, &c. &c.

BY LIEUT.-COLONEL JAMES CAMPBELL,

Late Brigade-Major, 3rd Division, and formerly of the 45th and 50th Regiments.

" We may safely affirm, that few military men can rise from its perusal without gratification and even benefit."—*United Service Gazette.*

" Of very considerable merit, containing many suggestions which might be adopted for the benefit of British Soldiers. The work contains much valuable information interesting to every class of readers."—*Woolwich Army Register.*

" We have in this volume much that deserves attention. The work cannot be perused by his brother officers, without interest and instruction."—*United Service Jour.*

" The author is a bold original thinker, and exercises his genius upon a subject which has seldom been examined with so much fearless acuteness."—*Atlas.*

" The Colonel was himself upon the staff of the third division, during the whole of the Peninsular war, and was one of the Duke's real working and essential officers. That the book is most practically useful, no military man can read and doubt."

Isle of Man Sur.

THE HISTORY OF THE GERMAN LEGION,

FROM THE PERIOD OF ITS ORGANIZATION IN 1803, TO THAT OF ITS
DISSOLUTION IN 1816.

Compiled from Manuscript Documents,

By N. LUDLOW BEAMISH, Esq. F.R.S., LATE MAJOR UNATTACHED.

Two vols. 8vo. complete, with Plans and Coloured Plates of Costumes, price £1. 10s.

The second volume sold separately, price 10s.

" The work is not like others we could name—a mere compilation from newspapers
and magazines.   Major Beamish has left no source of information unexplored; and
the access he obtained to manuscript journals has enabled him to intersperse his general
narrative with interesting personal anecdotes, that render this volume as delightful for
those who read for amusement, as those who read for profit."—*Athenæum.*

" We are altogether much pleased with the volume, and heartily recommend it to
the British public."—*Literary Gazette.*

In One Volume, post 8vo, price 10s. 6d. boards.

NARRATIVE OF

EVENTS IN THE SOUTH OF FRANCE,

AND OF THE ATTACK ON NEW ORLEANS IN 1814 *AND* 1815.

By CAPT. I. H. COOKE, 43rd Regt.

" This clever and fearless account of the attack on New Orleans is penned by one
of the ' occupation ;' whose soldier-like view and keen observation during the period
of the stirring events he so well relates, has enabled him to bring before the public the
ablest account that has yet been given of that ill-fated and disgraceful expedition, and
also to rescue the troops who were employed on it from those degrading reflections
which have hitherto unjustly been insinuated against them."—*Gent.'s Mag.*

" We wish earnestly to call the attention of military men to the campaign before
New Orleans.   It is fraught with a fearful interest, and fixes upon the mind reflections
of almost every hue.   Captain Cooke's relation is vivid; every evolution is made as
clear to the eye as if we had been present, and the remarks, we think, are eminently
judicious.   The book must be generally read," &c.—*Metropolitan.*

" It is full of good feeling, and it abounds with sketches of the service."
Sunday Herald.

MEMOIR BY

GENERAL SIR HEW DALRYMPLE, Bart.

OF HIS PROCEEDINGS AS CONNECTED WITH THE AFFAIRS OF SPAIN,

AND THE

COMMENCEMENT OF THE PENINSULAR WAR.

In one vol. post 8vo. price 9s. boards.

" The care bestowed upon this subject by Sir Hew Dalrymple, is evident in the publication before us, which is unquestionably the most dignified, clear, and satisfactory
vindication of Sir Hew's motives and conduct, and forms, with the documents in the
Appendix, a very valuable and authentic addition to the materials for the history of the
period in question.   Without a participation in the facts it discloses, the records of the
war, as far as regards this particular subject are, in fact, incomplete or distorted."
United Service Journal.

In 18mo. cloth, gilt leaves, price 2s. 6d. ; or, postage free, 3s., which may be sent in postage stamps,

HINTS to SUBALTERNS of the BRITISH ARMY.

By HENRY HARDBARGAIN, Late —— Regt.

Dedicated to WILLIAM HIGGINSON DUFF, ESQ., &c. &c. &c.

" *Scribimus indocti doctique.*"

Containing—Sketches of Commanding Officers—The Art of getting Leave of Absence—Military Miseries—Glossary, &c.

"I have also added, for the information of those non-military readers who may deign to peruse this small volume, a Glossary of those exclusively military terms, they might otherwise be at a loss to comprehend; and which, the profound ignorance that great part of the world are in with respect to military matters, renders it most necessary to explain :—for instance, I assure my readers, that the other night when I was dining out, an old gentleman asked me whether the officers who were on guard in London, on the day of the Derby, did not receive a compensatory pension from government; nay, so firmly convinced was he that such was the case, that I had some difficulty in persuading him that his impression on the subject was erroneous."—*Preface.*

In post 8vo. price 5s.

RECOLLECTIONS AND REFLECTIONS

RELATIVE TO THE

Duties of Troops composing the Advanced Corps of an Army,

By LIEUT.-COLONEL I. LEACH, C.B., LATE OF THE RIFLE BRIGADE,

Author of "Rough Sketches of the Life of an Old Soldier."

Also, by the same Author,

A SKETCH OF THE

SERVICES OF THE RIFLE BRIGADE,

From its Formation to the Battle of Waterloo.

In 8vo. price 2s. 6d. boards.

AN ESSAY ON THE PRINCIPLES AND CONSTRUCTION OF

MILITARY BRIDGES,

And the Passage of Rivers in Military Operations,

By GENERAL SIR HOWARD DOUGLAS, BART. K.S.C. &c. &c.

The Second Edition, containing much additional Matter and Plates.

8vo. price 20s. boards.

"Of this valuable work we expressed a very high opinion when it was first published ; and now that the able author has added much important new matter to it, we need only say that it is worthy of his own high reputation as a tactician and Military Engineer; and that no soldier in Europe can know his business thoroughly without consulting it."—*Literary Gazette.*

NAVAL EVOLUTIONS;

A MEMOIR.

By MAJOR-GENERAL SIR HOWARD DOUGLAS, BART. K.S.C. &c. &c.

Containing a Review and Refutation of the principal Essays and Arguments advocating Mr. Clerk's Claims, in relation to the Manœuvre of the 12th of April, 1782; and vindicating, by tactical Demonstration, and numerous authentic Documents, the professional skill of the British Officers chiefly concerned on that memorable occasion.

With plates, 1 vol. 8vo. price 10s. cloth boards.

Third Edition, 18mo. cloth, gilt leaves, price 2s. 6d.

SHORT WHIST,

BY F. P. WATSON, ESQ.

To which is added,

LONG WHIST,

WITH INSTRUCTIONS FOR YOUNG PLAYERS,

BY ADMIRAL JAMES BURNEY.

REVISED BY F. P. WATSON, ESQ.

Second Edition, 18mo. cloth, gilt leaves, price 3s.

HAND-BOOK to the GAME OF BILLIARDS,

ADDRESSED TO THE NOVICE AND THE PROFICIENT,

With the Laws and 44 Diagrams,

To which is added,

POOL,

BY COLONEL B * * * * *.

"This is a very useful little book, and ought to be in the hands of all beginners."
Bell's Life in London.

"All that the Billiard player can acquire from instruction, he may gain from this hand-book; and having well studied it, it will be his own fault if, by practice, he do not become a proficient in this most delightful pastime."—*Argus.*

"Every Billiard player, be he novice or proficient, will find this a manual adapted exactly to his wishes."—*Court Journal.*

Sixth Edition, 18mo. sewed, price 1s.

HINTS TO THE CHARITABLE,

BEING

PRACTICAL OBSERVATIONS ON THE PROPER REGULATION OF PRIVATE CHARITY:

CONTAINING LETTERS ON

THE COAL FUND,	THE LOAN FUND,
THE WIFE'S SOCIETY,	THE CHILDRENS' ENDOWMENT
THE PENNY CLUB,	SOCIETY,
THE BENEFIT SOCIETY,	&c. &c. &c.

BY THE HON. AND REV. S. G. OSBORNE,

Author of "Old Rainy Day," 8vo. price 3d.; "Hand-bill for the Cottage Wall," &c.

Also by the same Author, 18mo. price 1s.

HINTS

FOR THE AMELIORATION OF THE MORAL CONDITION OF

A VILLAGE POPULATION.

CONTENTS.

THE SQUIRE,	KEEPERS OF PUBLIC HOUSES,
THE FARMER,	THE LABOURER,
THE TRADESMAN,	FEMALE SERVICE,
EDUCATION, &c. &c.	

THE LIFE

OF

HENRY THE FOURTH,

KING OF FRANCE AND NAVARRE.

BY G. P. R. JAMES, ESQ.

AUTHOR OF

" THE LIFE AND TIMES OF LOUIS THE FOURTEENTH,"

" THE HISTORY OF CHARLEMAGNE,"

" THE LIFE OF EDWARD THE BLACK PRINCE,"

&c. &c.

IN THREE VOLUMES.

VOL. II.

LONDON:

T. & W. BOONE, 29, NEW BOND STREET.

MDCCCXLVII.

LIFE OF HENRY IV.

KING OF FRANCE AND NAVARRE.

BOOK V.

No doubt can exist that in the massacre, which commenced in Paris on St. Bartholomew's day, it was the intention of the court of France, not only to weaken the Huguenot party, by the loss of the distinguished Calvinists who had been collected in the capital, but actually to extirpate the Reformed religion from the land, by the slaughter of all the Protestants in the kingdom. The monarch and his counsellors, however, shewed all that vacillation and infirmity of purpose, which the perpetration of great and unheard-of crimes generally brings with it. Terror and cruelty usually go hand in hand, till long impunity in wickedness has calmed the cowardly part of tyranny ; and it is evident that the brutal assassins of the metropolis felt afraid, that the first news of the massacre might find the Protestants of the provinces better prepared to resist, and the governors less ready to execute, the work of slaughter than had been the case in Paris.

On the first or second day of the butchery,* Charles sent letters to various parts of his dominions, informing his officers that a horrible tumult had taken place in the capital, occasioned by the long existing animosity of the two houses of Guise and Chatillon, but assuring them that he was taking vigorous measures to suppress the disorder, and to punish the authors. At the same time he commanded the edict of pacification to be strictly observed, and the Catholics to remain tranquil, without molesting their Huguenot neighbours. In several instances, he represented the conspiracy as directed against his own person, the Queen, his mother, and even against the King of Navarre and the Prince of Condé. The very next day, however, messengers, on whom he could rely, were despatched with orders, in some cases verbal, in others written,† but all tending to the opposite course. The governors of the chief provincial towns were commanded to exterminate the Protestants wherever they were found; and the massacre still continued in Paris, till

---

* Some authors say, the first, some the second.

† It is evident from the replies, that some of these orders were in writing; and such is also the direct assertion of Papyrius Masso, the eulogist of Charles IX. The author of the "Dissertation sur la S. Barthelemi," who, in a manner almost ludicrous, attempts to pervert the plain facts of history to favor the Papists, admits (page 25,) that two orders were sent, one to Lyons and the other to Orleans, commanding "the officers of justice, the mayors, and the sheriffs, to take arms, and to make sure that they were the strongest in the town." What could be the result of such an order, with the example of Paris before their eyes?

it was supposed that all the leaders of the Huguenot party then in the capital, and the greater part of their followers had been slain.

The courage of the court had by this time returned; all fear of resistance, in the metropolis at least, was over; the Reformers throughout the realm were without chiefs; and it was apparent, that, " if in some parts of the kingdom, where the malady of Calvinism was excessive," (to use the words of a rancorous Papist, who has done much to fix the stigma of premeditation upon his brethren,*) "they had been able to apply the remedy as well as the Parisian physicians, the same year an end would have been put to the civil war, and a durable peace established." Charles himself, and his court, issued forth in splendid array into the reeking streets of the capital; the licentious ladies of the Queen-mother contemplated, with mirth and ribald jests, the slaughtered bodies, stripped, and piled up before the Louvre; and when, after having been treated with every horrible indignity, the headless trunk of Coligni was carried to a public gibbet at Montfaucon and hung up by the feet, the young monarch, with a train forced to attend upon him, went out to glut his eyes with the sight. Some of those who accompanied him, though afraid to express their detestation of the spectacle, endeavored to prevail upon him to retire, alleging, that the body already emitted a putrid scent. But Charles reproved them for

* Papyrius Masso.

their delicacy, exclaiming, in the words of Vitellius, that the smell of a dead enemy was always pleasant.*

On the Tuesday, the third day of the massacre, the King, having at length determined to take the responsibility of the act upon himself, proceeded to the Parliament, and held a bed of justice, in which he recanted all the statements that he had previously made, and terminated a course of the basest perfidy, by branding himself openly with the name of liar. It was no longer asserted, that the horrible slaughter of the Huguenots had been caused by the ancient quarrels of the houses of Guise and Chatillon; the act was no longer imputed to popular fury; no indignation was any longer feigned against the perpetrators of the deed; but the King of France, in the face of his people, and the world, contradicted all his former assertions, and acknowledged, that, by his order, a large body of his subjects, confiding in his princely word, trusting to the most specious appearances of favor and forgiveness, had been massacred in cold blood, in his capital, in his palace, and in his presence.†

There can be no doubt that this public avowal was made by the advice of Catherine de Medicis, who was too acute to hope that the fact could be concealed, and too politic not to know that, if it could be so, it would be imprudent to shew that the royal authority was so weak as not to be able to prevent

* Brantome.   † Aubigné.   Davila.

the commission of such a crime, or to punish its perpetrators. It was necessary, however, to put forward some sufficient motive for the act, in order to di·minish the load of infamy which rested on all concerned ; and, accordingly, the King informed the assembled court, that he had, "as if by a miracle," discovered that Coligni and his party were engaged in a conspiracy against his own life and that of all his family, including even the King of Navarre. This was the cause assigned for the wholesale assassination, which he admitted he had commanded ; but though the parliament of Paris proceeded solemnly to inquire into the facts, to bring the dead to trial, to justify the King, and to condemn several prisoners for crimes of which they had never dreamed, the stream of time, which generally separates truth from falsehood, however intimately mingled at first, has not left even the shadow of suspicion upon those whom he accused.

The order was given, in the course of the same day, to suspend the massacre ; but for the purpose of judicially confirming the King's statements in the eyes of horrified Europe, the parliament proceeded against the memory of Coligni, sentenced him to be hung in effigy, ordered his arms to be dragged through the towns of France, at the heels of a horse, his castle of Chatillon-sur-Loing to be razed to the ground and never rebuilt, the plantations, of which he was so fond, to be cut down, his land to be sown with salt, his portraits and statues to be destroyed, wherever they were found, his children to lose their nobility, a column to be erected to commemorate his sentence, and his goods and estates to be confiscated to the use of the crown.   Two distinguished Protestants, Cavagnes and Bricquemaut, who had been found in the town, were subsequently condemned to a horrible death; and the King and court enjoyed the spectacle of their execution by torchlight.*

The sanguinary orders sent by the King to the provinces were strictly obeyed in most of the principal towns. The Rhone, the Seine, and the Loire, ran with blood, and putrified with corpses; carnage spread over the whole face of France, and crimes enough were committed, in the space of a few weeks, to blacken the history of a century.

There were some examples of virtue, however; and the names of Chabot-Charni, Gordes, Tanneguile-veneur, Matignon, Villeneuve, and Mandelot, are distinguished, as having resisted, in different degrees, the royal command to massacre. The Bishop of Lisieux, also contrived, in the true spirit of Christian charity, to save the Protestants of that town. St. Heran, the governor of Auvergne, replied to the King's letter in the following words : " Sire, I have received an order, under your majesty's seal, to put all the Protestants of this province to death. I respect your majesty too much not to believe that this letter is a forgery; and if, which God forbid, the order be genuine, I respect your majesty still too much to obey you." The Viscount of Orthez, too, the

---

* Brantome.

King's lieutenant at Bayonne, made answer : "Sire, I have communicated the commands of your majesty to the inhabitants of the town, and the soldiers of the garrison, and I have found good citizens and brave soldiers, but not one executioner; on which account, they and I humbly beseech you to employ our arms and our lives in things we can effect. However perilous they may be, we will willingly shed therein the last drop of our blood." The noble-minded man, however, who made this reply, and the Count de Tendes, who also refused to obey the King's order, died shortly after, not without a suspicion that their virtue had met the reward which at that period usually followed honorable opposition to the royal will.

In the midst of all the crimes and horrors which Paris presented during the massacre, several instances of generous humanity are recorded ; and one case demands notice from the singular circumstances attending it. Monsieur de Vessins,* one of the most fierce and irritable men in France, had filled the post of Lieutenant of the King in Querci, where the Protestant forces, during the last war, had been commanded by Monsieur de Regnier. A private quarrel had added to the virulence of party strife ; and after peace had apparently been restored in 1570, the two gentlemen sought each other in Paris to satisfy their angry feelings by a

* This name is very differently written by the various contemporaries who mention this anecdote. I find it spelt Vessins, Veseins, Vezins, and Voisin.

duel. In the midst of the massacre Regnier, while at prayers, with his servant, heard the door of his house broken open, and turning with the expectation of immediate death, beheld Vessins enter with a countenance as red as fire. Instantly offering his throat, the Protestant gentleman exclaimed, " You will have an easy victory." Vessins' only reply was an order to the valet to seek his master's cloak and sword, and then making him descend into the street, he mounted him on a powerful horse, and with fifteen armed men, escorted him safe into Querci, without exchanging with him a single word. When they reached a little wood, however, within a short distance of Regnier's chateau, he bade him dismount, saying, " Do not think I seek your friendship by what I have done. All I wish is to take your life honorably."

" My life is yours," replied Regnier, " and you may employ it against whom you like."

" Will you be so base," demanded Vessins, in return, " as not to resent the perfidy you have experienced?" meaning probably the late massacre. Regnier answered, that he could never forget what he owed to him ; and Vessins, exclaiming, " Well, bold friends or bold enemies !" left him, making him a present of the horse on which he rode.

The number of the Protestants who fell in the massacre of St. Bartholomew and in the tumults which followed in various parts of France is uncertain ; almost every different author who wrote upon the subject, near the time, having fixed it at a different amount, from one hundred thousand* to about twenty thousand.† Papyrius Masso, indeed, reduces it still lower, namely to twelve thousand, but his account only includes those who were slaughtered in the provincial towns, immediately after the receipt of the King's orders.‡ Sully states, that seventy thousand were murdered, and De Thou reduces the slain to "nearly thirty thousand;" in which probably he was as accurate as any one could be, in judging from the vague statements of those who buried the dead. But the number of victims does not in any degree diminish the criminality of the assassins, whose object, it is admitted, was to exterminate the French Calvinists, wherever they could be found.

However well concerted had been the plot against the Huguenots, however complete the fraud, a considerable number of distinguished Protestants escaped. Several, as we have seen, had left the capital with well founded doubts of the King's sincerity, and others, from various motives, had taken up their abode in the suburbs. The Vidame of Chartres and the Count of Montgomery, with a large party of gentlemen, were lodged in the Faubourg St. Ger-

---

* Perefix.   † La Popeliniere.

‡ The bad faith of the author of the Dissertation, is made evident by his quoting Papyrius Masso, as authority on this point, but omitting to mention that he distinctly states the massacre in the provinces to have been perpetrated in consequence of written orders from the King.

main; and so completely had many of them been deceived by the King's affected apprehensions of a rising on the part of the house of Guise, that when the tocsin and the outcry of the butchery was first heard, they imagined that Charles was attacked in the Louvre, and hastened to the bank of the river, with a view of going over to give him succor. They were seen there when day broke, waiting for boats; and the Duke of Guise lost no time in crossing to destroy them; but various accidental circumstances saved their lives. The sight of the troops approaching, and the impatience of the King, who himself fired at them from the windows of the Louvre, warned them how cruelly they had been betrayed; a mistake regarding the keys delayed the Duke of Guise; and they had time to mount their horses and fly towards Montfort, pursued in vain for many leagues by their bloodthirsty enemies. Several others lay concealed till the massacre ceased, and then made their escape into the country.

It may be expected, that, after having stated the facts of this most horrible event, and having commented upon the statements made by different parties, regarding the question of premeditation, the author should express some opinion upon the latter point, which certainly greatly affects the degree of guilt chargeable upon the King and his counsellors. We have seen, that, beyond all doubt, at the meeting of the courts of France and Spain, in Bayonne, Catherine de Medicis was advised by Alva to strike at the leaders of the Protestant party. We have also seen, that during three successive civil wars, in which the whole authority of the crown was employed, no progress had been made towards the suppression of the Reformed religion. We have likewise found, that in the course of these wars, acts had been committed by the Huguenot chiefs, which Charles IX. had sworn he would never forgive.* We moreover learn, from good authority, that it was an ordinary maxim at the monarch's court, that all edicts of pacification were merely voluntary acts of the King's grace, which might be recalled at pleasure, and that Charles himself, in several of his declarations, made upon any infringement of the treaties, sanctioned the doctrine. It was usual also for his courtiers to maintain, that princes were not in any degree bound to keep faith with rebels;† and some of the best informed and noblest of the monarch's friends and kindred, amongst others the Duke of Montpensier, openly avowed that they did not consider it in any degree necessary to observe engagements contracted with heretics. We have learned, too, that, in the midst of a furious contest, and after denunciations of the most vengeful character, Charles, exhausted by civil war, suddenly made peace with the insurgent Protestants, affected the greatest

* Brantome.

† Memoires de Castelnau. The gentleman who states this fact, was always himself honorably opposed to such a doctrine.

esteem and love for their leaders, preferred them to the friends of his youth, granted them every favor they could demand, gave his sister in marriage to one of their chiefs; and by these measures gathered all the principal nobility of the party together in Paris, and even reassured the timid, by an ostentatious display of care for their safety. At the same time, we find from the account of several contemporaries of good authority, that in a moment of indiscretion, he asked his mother if he did not play his part well; that the Bishop of Valence warned several of his friends to look to their safety; and that letters were even at the time* reported to be written by Cardinal Pelevé to the Cardinal of Lorraine, in which he assured that prelate, that the King was still resolute, that he played his part well, and that the enterprise was never forgotten, whatever might be the appearances to the contrary. We have remarked, that the Cardinal of Lorraine himself, the unceasing persecutor of the Calvinists, was the person who obtained a papal dispensation for the marriage of the Protestant King of Navarre with Marguerite of Valois; we find that troops were collected, money raised, and fleets equipped, upon pretence of a war against Spain, which was never commenced; and we shall hereafter discover that those preparations were employed against the Huguenots who escaped the massacre. We have also seen, that as soon as the greatest possible

* Sully.   Memoires de Coligni.   Papyrius Masso.

number of Calvinists were assembled in the capital, the regiment of guards was introduced into Paris; that after the Admiral was wounded all the leading Protestants were gathered together into one quarter of the town; and a guard much larger than was necessary for his security against personal foes, was placed over the house of Coligni. It is proved, beyond a doubt, that during the last two days preceding the massacre, Charles acted with the utmost duplicity; caressing those whose destruction was already determined, and affecting fears of the house of Guise, with which he was in secret communication, and that by these means he lulled the Huguenots into that fatal security, which rendered them an easy prey when attacked in the night. He is admitted by those who eulogise his character, and applaud the act, to have been false and deceitful in the highest degree; and he is shewn during the massacre to have denied all participation in it; to have accused the house of Guise of the deed, affecting the greatest concern for that which had taken place;* and immediately after to have acknowledged that the crime was committed by his express orders, and to have

---

* See his letter to M. de Joyeuse in the Dissertation sur la S. Barthelemi. I have not mentioned a proclamation made by the King on the 24th to stop the massacre, as the fact of such a proclamation having been ordered is very doubtful; and it is clear that the butchery continued with the King's countenance, and under his direction to the afternoon of the third day.

justified it by another falsehood, sealed by a judicial murder. It is also proved, that in the awful butchery itself, he displayed a degree of wild ferocity, only to be accounted for by a long repressed thirst for vengeance, in a heart naturally brutal and sanguinary. With these facts before us, and with the concurrent opinion of Aubigné, Sully, and all contemporary Protestant authors, on the one hand, and De Thou, Davila, Pierre Mathieu, Perefix, Papyrius Masso, Muratori, and various Roman Catholics, on the other,* it is impossible not to conclude that the design of luring the Huguenots to Paris, and crushing them for ever by one decisive blow, was entertained by Charles and the whole French court, from the termination of the third civil war.

It is possible, and indeed probable, that the idea of such a sanguinary and indiscriminate massacre, as that which eventually took place, did not at first suggest itself to the minds of the conspirators, that

---

* The authority of La Popeliniere is of no weight, except in the eyes of the Abbe Caveyrac. He was first a Protestant, but was afterwards converted to Popery; and it is evident from many parts of his work, as well as from the dedication to the Queen-mother, that he wrote in the spirit of a renegade. Various passages can be shewn, in which he has perverted or concealed notorious facts, with a want of candor only equal to that of Caveyrac himself, who represents this author throughout as a Protestant writer. It is not necessary to say any thing of Dr. Lingard's feeble imitation of Caveyrac.

the death of the more obnoxious chiefs, and the imprisonment of the rest, was the original limit of the design, and that circumstances of various kinds, fears, difficulties, apprehensions, offences, jealousies, combined to give it the terrible scope to which it was at length extended. It is even possible, that Charles, on discovering the high qualities of many of those whom his mother's policy and the fanatical spirit of his religious doctrines, had alienated from his court and driven into rebellion, wavered in his resolution, and that his very indecision alarmed the Queen-mother for the duration of her influence, and hurried her on to the horrible excess which stained her name, and that of her son, with the blackest crime in history.

But that the death of many, and the extinction of the Protestant faith in France, by the combination of fraud and force, was devised long before, that that object was pursued with every art of perfidy and falsehood, and that on the King, on Catherine, on the Duke of Anjou, and their principal advisers, rests the additional guilt of long premeditation, no one, I feel convinced, who studies the facts with an impartial mind, can doubt.

That either Catherine or her son were actuated solely by sincere religious convictions, however, I do not believe. They looked upon the Huguenots more as rebels than as heretics, more as enemies than opponents of their faith, more as advocates of liberty in general than as claimants alone of freedom of conscience ; and they made use, as an excuse to others, and probably to themselves also, of a religion which has unhappily at all times, since the fall of the Roman Church from the purity of the Catholic faith, sanctioned falsehood and justified crime. Many of the actors in the tragedy, however, were undoubtedly imbued with the spirit of fanatical intolerance, and superstitious persecution. The leaders avowed it in the midst of blood and carnage in the streets of Paris; the populace proclaimed it each fresh victim that they slew; the writers of the same faith display it in every page; and the Romish Church by the voice of her supreme Pontiff, set her seal upon the deed, and announced it as her own.*

The expectations entertained by Charles IX. and his politic mother, regarding the results of the massacre of St. Bartholomew's day, were frustrated, and the more zealous Catholics were equally disappointed by the events which followed. Rebellion

* At Rome the rejoicings on the news of the massacre were frightful and indecent. The messenger was richly rewarded by the Cardinal of Lorraine, who questioned him, Anquetil himself declares, "en homme instruit d'avance." Cardinal Alexandrini exulted, "that the King of France had kept his word." The cannon of St. Angelo were fired as for a victory. A solemn mass and Te Deum were celebrated by Gregory XIII.; and a medal was struck, giving a representation of the destroying angel smiting the Protestants, and an inscription bearing the words "Huguenotorum Strages, 1572." The motto was simply barbarous; but an allegory which represented the most brutal passions of men under the holy attribute of almighty justice was surely a terrible blasphemy.

was by no means crushed by this sanguinary execution; and, though fear might produce apparent converts, persecution, with its invariable effect, strengthened and augmented the suffering party.　When the time allowed to the young King of Navarre and the Prince de Condé, for consideration and instruction, had expired, they were summoned to the presence of the King, and once more commanded to abjure the Protestant faith.　Henry yielded with little resistance, but his cousin shewed a firmer spirit; and though the furious monarch, who had already butchered so many of his noblest subjects, exclaimed with passionate imprecations, "Death, the Bastille, or the Mass," he still struggled for freedom of belief, till a Protestant minister, who had himself given up his religion under the influence of terror,* was brought to satisfy the conscience of Condé, when the scruples of the Prince were at length overcome, but not without hesitation and regret.

The greater facility displayed by the King of Navarre, is not unworthy of more particular notice, as it first brings to light a trait of his character, which though not to be admired, is visible throughout his life; and one of the historians of the time remarks, that he shewed more of the easy and indifferent disposition of his father, on religious

* His name was De Rosier; and he was employed by the court to work other conversions in the Provinces.　Having been afterwards sent, however, to Sedan, to convert the Duchess of Bouillon, he made his escape to Heidelberg, where he recanted and published a work acknowledging his weakness, and begging forgiveness of those whom he had been instrumental in perverting.

points, than the stern and uncompromising mind of his mother. All her talents he possessed, all her decision and determination in worldly concerns, but his religious convictions were never so strong, and in him the severity of her character was tempered with a degree of mildness, which she seldom evinced.

The first effect of the massacre of the Protestants was to spread dismay and confusion amongst them. Nothing but flight was thought of; and England, Switzerland, and the Palatinate, received the fugitives. A number, however, sought refuge in the difficult passes of the Cevennes, and within the walls of the cities which had been given as places of security by the treaty of St. Germain ; and there they soon began to recover from the terror which had seized them. Indignation took the place of fear, and despair lent its own peculiar courage. Nought seemed left but voluntary exile, or resistance to the knife; and a multitude preferred the latter to the abandonment of home, and to banishment from all the associations of their native land. Their enemies, too, did not follow up the terrible blow they had struck, with the same energy of determination which had prompted the massacre. They seemed awed by the enormity of their own crime ; and the roar of horror which burst from almost every quarter of outraged Europe, startled and intimidated them, while from England and Germany, messages of comfort and condolence, and promises of assistance and support, reassured the Huguenots and confirmed their resolution.

The first open resistance was made by the towns of Rochelle and Sancerre, around which Strozzi had been hovering with an army, ever since the Admiral had visited the court. The port, too, of the former city, had been watched by the royal flotilla, and many efforts had been made to bring over a part of the inhabitants to the views of the crown. A number of gentlemen and about nine hundred soldiers, having escaped the massacre, cast themselves into Rochelle in the beginning of September; and the Baron de Biron, known to be favorable to the Protestants, and who had only avoided falling a victim, during the proscription in Paris, by preparations for vigorous resistance, was sent by Charles to take upon himself the government of the town, in the belief that his reputation would induce the citizens to submit to him more willingly than to any other. The young King of Navarre, who, acting under severe compulsion, had been forced to pronounce the abolition of the Protestant religion in his hereditary dominions, was also driven to write to the people of Rochelle, desiring them to receive Biron within their walls; and many of the more wealthy inhabitants were induced to listen to the proposals and promises of the court. But the great mass of the population refused to yield to the wishes of the more timid; the gentlemen who had sought refuge in the place pointed out the impossibility of trusting to engagements so often broken; letters were intercepted, shewing the real views of their opponents; and a party of Italian

c 2

and French engineers, having approached the port in two gallies, for the purpose of reconnoitring the defences, though under pretence of negotiating, were attacked by the Protestant boats, and after a desperate resistance, one of their ships, together with their leader, was taken and carried into Rochelle. This act determined the wavering citizens, and all overtures on the part of the court were rejected.

It now became necessary for the King's council to determine upon its course. Nothing but weakness and imbecility, however, was displayed; and the most extraordinary scheme that perhaps ever suggested itself to a body of experienced and politic men, was adopted. The famous La Noue, who during the period of the Admiral's apparent favour with the King, had been sent with Genlis to aid the Protestants of the Low Countries, in their struggle against Alva, had seen his efforts frustrated, as it is supposed, by secret intelligence conveyed to the enemy by the agents of the French monarch, and had returned to Paris, after the slaughter of the Huguenots had ceased in that city. To him Charles now applied to bring the inhabitants of Rochelle to obedience; and finding himself at the mercy of the court, he undertook to make the attempt, upon the promise that nothing contrary to his faith and honor should be exacted from him. The Rochellois however refused to admit him ; and when a party of their deputies went out to confer with their old comrade, he had the mortification to hear them exclaim, "We thought to find La Noue here ; and we do not see him. This man is like him, but the La Noue we remember played a very different personage, and we are sure that this is not the same."

Concealing his grief, that great officer argued with the deputation, and so far succeeded in persuading them of his sincerity, that they admitted him at length within the walls; and there, after long deliberation, convinced of his faith and honor, they offered him a choice of three courses : to remain with them as a private individual, in which case they offered to supply him with the best entertainment they could afford : to take the command of the city during the approaching siege, on which condition they assured him of the obedience of the nobility and citizens : or to go to England, for which purpose they promised to furnish him with a vessel. After consulting with the Abbé Guadagni, who had been sent with him by the court as a spy upon his actions, La Noue accepted the command of the town; and this strange mission of a steady Protestant and old insurgent, to the citizens of Rochelle, was followed by the still more strange result of his directing the defence of the town, with the royal consent, against the King's own forces, and yet giving not the slightest occasion for suspicion to the inhabitants, nor the slightest cause for reproach to the monarch.

No movement of any great importance was made on the part of the royal army before the end of the year, though Biron advanced towards the town with a considerable force, burned the mills in the neigh-bourhood, cut off a part of the canal which supplied the place with water, and endeavored to prevent the inhabitants from obtaining a sufficient supply of provisions to enable them to protract their resistance.

In the mean time, in Guienne and Languedoc the Protestants recovered gradually from their first consternation; a number of noblemen, who had escaped the massacre, took the field with a few followers; town after town declared for the Huguenot party; and throughout the south, the hydra heads of rebellion seemed but to multiply as they were stricken down. Many strong, though small fortresses were surprised through the enterprising zeal of the Reformers; and activity and exertion once more displayed itself through the dispirited ranks of the Calvinists.

More vigorous measures on the part of the court marked the commencement of the year 1573; a large and well equipped force was brought into the field; the siege of Rochelle was commenced on a more regular plan; and the Duke of Anjou, putting himself at the head of the attacking force, announced to the insurgents, that unless they submitted within three days, he would exercise the utmost severity against the place.* All the chivalry of the Roman Catholic party accompanied the Prince; and the young King of Navarre, with the Prince de Condé, was dragged unwillingly to take part in the operations against a city, which had in former times been his refuge, and the rallying point of his friends.

* Aubigné.

It would be equally tedious and uninstructive to follow all the proceedings of the besiegers, and the efforts of the besieged. Attacks and negotiations followed each other day after day; and La Noue in the council always advocated submission on advantageous terms, while at the head of his men he displayed a degree of valor which reached the point of rashness, and caused it to be surmised, that wearied of his unsatisfactory position, he was seeking death as a relief. Nothing could be more skilful, nothing more successful, than his defence of the place, and while sickness began to waste away the forces of the Duke of Anjou, and to shake their resolution, the incessant sallies of the Rochellois, and the tremendous fire they kept up against the assailants, swept away multitudes, amongst whom were several persons distinguished both by rank and military renown. The Duke of Aumale was killed early in the siege; De Retz, Nevers, Mayenne, Clermont, Du Guast were severely wounded; Cosseins, who mounted guard over the Admiral on the night of his murder, was killed; and though several attempts were made to storm, the citizens, men, women, children, and clergy, rushed to the ruined walls wherever the attacking force presented itself, and repulsed the enemy with terrible slaughter.

In the beginning of March, the court, finding that the measures of La Noue for the defence of the town were more successful than his efforts to induce the inhabitants to capitulate upon the terms offered, summoned him to keep a promise which he had made, to quit the place when all hope of peace was at an end. That great commander made one more attempt to bring about a treaty, and in the council strongly exhorted the leaders of the Rochellois to listen at least to the royal proposals. But he found all argument ineffectual; and so greatly irritated were the citizens at the course he pursued, that a minister named La Place, followed him from the town-house to his own dwelling, covering him with abuse, and ended by striking him in the face. Several of the general's attendants seized him, in order to punish the act upon the spot, but La Noue stopped them, and calmly ordered the old man to be carried back to his wife, with a recommendation that she should take care of him. He then, in fulfilment of his promise, resigned his command in the town, and retired from Rochelle, leaving the people more resolute than ever to sustain the siege to the last.

Towards the end of April the Count of Montgomery, who had been seeking aid from England, appeared off the port with fifty-three small vessels, ill-armed and scantily provided; but the wind changed before he could reach Rochelle; the entrance was difficult, and commanded by forts raised by the royal army; and the expectations of the inhabitants were disappointed, by the sight of the long hoped for succor bearing away for Belleisle.

Other causes, however, were producing in their favor far greater results than could have been effected by the ill-equipped fleet of Montgomery. Dysentery had spread rapidly in the army of the court; the plague was soon added; the wounded soldiers were neglected and left to die; daily desertions took place; and though a reinforcement of Swiss troops enabled the Duke of Anjou to keep his ground, his men were dispirited, and he himself anxious to abandon the siege upon any pretence. The number of malcontents, too, in his camp was immense, and they were headed by his own brother, the wild, rash, furious Duke of Alençon, who, in the midst of follies, vices, and crimes, displayed some of the qualities and feelings of a great man. Brave, but irresolute, filled with ambition unguided by reason or experience, turbulent and intriguing, but without caution or art, he had been suspected in his boyhood of a tendency towards insanity;* and yet, on more than one occasion, he evinced a soundness of judgment, which is hardly to be reconciled with the other traits of character that contemporaries have transmitted to us, and the acts he is known to have committed. From a very early period he had conceived the highest veneration for the Admiral de Coligni : he admired his great military talents ; and what is indeed extraordinary, he appreciated also his high integrity and moral and religious firmness. During the residence of Coligni at the court, the young Duke sought every opportunity of being with him, and of testifying his regard for his person ; he hung upon his words ; he seemed to hope that he might acquire some share of

* Mem. de Nevers.

his wisdom from his conversation. After the murder
of the Admiral, he boldly blamed the act; and
when, to reconcile him to Coligni's destruction, a memoir was shewn him which had been found amongst
the papers of the dead man, advising the King
strongly to be cautious in assigning an appanage to
his brothers, lest he should render them too powerful
for the safety of the state, he displayed no anger.
" See what counsel your good friend bestows upon
the King," exclaimed his mother, after the contents
had been read to him in her presence. But the
young Prince replied, " I know not whether he
loved me ; but I do know that such advice could
only be given by a man faithful to his majesty, and
zealous for the good of the state."

Under the walls of Rochelle, the Duke ceased
not to regret the persecution of the Huguenots ; but
he joined to such honorable feelings, wild and whir-
ling aspirations for his own personal aggrandizement,
for military distinction, and for political power.
Surrounded by a body of young men full of talent
and ambition, he conceived a scheme for rendering
himself the head of a party in the state ; and, in the
spirit of the times, he saw no dishonor in revolting
against his brother, and breaking his solemn allegiance to his King. The plot has been represented as impracticable and absurd, and certainly,
considering the rashness and inexperience of the
Prince himself, it is probable that it would have
failed, even had he attempted to carry it into execution ; but had his character been different, and

his mind of a more powerful and well regulated complexion, it might have produced results which would have altered the whole face of history. Between himself, the young Viscount of Turenne, and a few of their most intimate companions, was formed a design for quitting the army with their attendants, seizing upon some strong place in the neighbourhood, proclaiming the Duke the Protector of the insurgents, and calling the whole Protestant party to his standard. But their plans continually varied; one proposed to cast themselves into Rochelle; another to make themselves masters of the fleet; a third to raise a party in the camp, and with one body of the royal army attack the other. It was suggested too, that England would open her arms to them in case of defeat; and the young King of Navarre and the Prince de Condé were expected to join the malcontents, and take a share in their schemes.*

Without absolutely discouraging a project which was likely to weaken and divide the forces of those who had persecuted them, and to relieve the besieged city, those two Princes held aloof from the dangerous councils of the Duke of Alençon, who continued to meditate treason against his brother, till at length, some difference of opinion arising amongst the conspirators themselves, the advice of La Noue was sought; and that able commander, after hearing

* I find in the Lettres Missives only three letters from Henry during the siege of Rochelle, and those not of a character to throw any light upon these events.

all their designs, suggested difficulties that they had not foreseen, and induced them to abandon their intentions.

The diseases which manifested themselves in his camp, the loss of twenty-four thousand men,* the indomitable courage of the Rochellois, the defection of his soldiers, the discontent in his own army, the arrival of a vessel charged with powder in the port, and the unexpected appearance of large quantities of shell-fish in the harbour, where they had never been seen before, delivering the citizens from the apprehension of famine, which had previously been imminent, all induced the Duke of Anjou to desire peace on any terms that might save him from actual disgrace.   But a still more powerful motive was called into operation, towards the end of May, by the announcement of his election to the vacant throne of Poland ; and though he kept up the appearance of continuing the siege till the negotiations for peace were concluded, he made no really vigorous effort after he received intelligence of his new dignity. Deputies from Rochelle, Montauban, and Nismes, were brought into conference with a body of the most distinguished Roman Catholics of the royal army; La Noue acted as moderator between the parties; and at length a treaty of twenty-five clauses was drawn up, in which the Rochellois secured for themselves, and, in consequence of their determined resistance, for the inhabitants of the two towns above named, the free exercise of religion within their walls, a general am-

* Millot.

nesty for all the Huguenots who had taken part in the late war, the private profession of the Protestant faith without molestation for all French Calvinists, the maintenance of the ancient privileges of the town of Rochelle, the guard and possession of the town free from a royal garrison, and a number of other advantages; upon the sole condition of receiving a governor appointed by the King, without any force which could render his residence amongst them dangerous to that liberty for which they had so resolutely fought.*

One French author† has reproached the Duke of Anjou with carrying on the siege of Rochelle with languor and indifference; but such is not the account of contemporaries; and the justice of the accusation will best appear when it is stated, that nine general assaults were attempted, one of which was renewed five times in the day, that two months before the siege terminated, fourteen thousand seven hundred and forty-five cannon shots had been discharged against the defences, that innumerable mines had been sprung under the walls and towers, and that the whole curtain was one mass of ruins.

The town of Sancerre held out after Rochelle had obtained such glorious terms, and was ungenerously omitted in the treaty concluded by the deputies. The most horrible famine at length compelled the inhabitants to surrender, but they also stipulated for liberty of conscience, and obtained a recognition of that inestimable right, after enduring a siege of seven months.

* Aubigné.   † Anquetil.

The election of the Duke of Anjou to the throne of Poland, had not been obtained without great difficulty, notwithstanding the renown acquired by his military services against the Protestants of France. The jealousy which existed between himself and his brother Charles, and which had been fostered by the representations of the Admiral, rendered Catherine de Medicis not unwilling to part with her favorite son, in order at once to place a crown upon his head, and to calm if possible the animosity which the King entertained towards him.*   It is probable indeed, that, when the negotiations regarding his election were brought to an end by the skill and perseverance of the Bishop of Valence, and Catherine saw her scheme successful, the tenderness of the mother might, as has been asserted, produce some regret, that she might wish the work she had undertaken undone, and strive to delay his departure, till the impetuous Charles declared that either he himself or his brother should go to Poland ; but it is impossible to agree with Le Laboureur in believing, that the Queen-mother labored so strenuously to obtain the Duke's elevation to the Polish throne as we know she did, employed the most skilful negotiators in the realm to ensure success, spared neither money, promises nor falsehood, to arrive at that object, merely to deceive the young King, and with the hope of being frustrated.

After many delays, however, and much hesitation, the newly created monarch set out for his dominions

* Le Laboureur.

in the north, accompanied as far as Lorraine by his
mother, who testified the most lively grief at their
separation, and it is said uttered words at parting
which marked in a somewhat scandalous manner her
anticipations of her eldest son's speedy death: "Go,"
she said after many tears and embraces, " Go, you
will not be long there."

The young King of France hardly affected to conceal his satisfaction at his brother's departure ; but
no joy accompanied Henry on his way. He was
aware that amongst the electors of his new kingdom,
doubt and suspicion had been spread by the part
which he had played in the massacre of St. Bartholomew, and that it had cost infinite labor and skill on
the part of the Bishop of Valence, to purchase or
persuade a majority to concur in his elevation to
the throne. His reception in the German courts
was cold and repulsive ; the memory of the horrible
deed in which he had borne so great a share hung
round him in every court; the countenances of French
Protestants driven into exile, and bewailing the
murder of friends and relations assassinated by his
orders, or with his connivance, met him at every
turn ; and in the palace of the Elector Palatine* he
beheld raised to a place of honor, the portrait of
the slaughtered Coligni, while beneath appeared the
words,

" Talis erat quondam vultu Colignius heros
Quam verè illustrem vitaque, morsque facit."†

The Elector himself is said to have pointed out the

* Mem. de l'Etoile. † Auvigny.

picture to the young King, and asked him, if he
knew the man. Henry replied that he did, and
named him ; on which the German Prince replied,
" He was the most honest man, the wisest and the
greatest Captain of Europe, whose children I keep
with me, lest the dogs of France should tear them
as their father has been torn."

The newly made King pursued his journey into
Poland, and was there crowned, though not without
remonstrance on the part of those who had learned
to fear from the past, his conduct for the future :
but in France he left behind him the seeds of evil,
which afterwards rose up and produced fruits to
trouble the whole course of his own existence. Nor
were they long in germinating ; instead of the dread
and submission which had been expected to spread
throughout the Protestant party, in consequence of the
slaughter of so many of its leaders, the court found
increased resistance ; and the bold and successful defence of Rochelle, did more to revive the drooping
spirits of the Huguenots, than the terrible massacre
of St. Bartholomew had done towards paralyzing
their powers.

In the summer of 1573, shortly before the departure of the King of Poland, the first decided
symptoms appeared in Charles IX. of that disease,
which, ere long, carried him to the grave. He became sad, and irresolute, as well as impetuous, stern,
severe, and unapproachable ;* and a low continued
fever hung upon him, during which his imagination,

* Brantome.

disordered by the scenes he had witnessed, and in which he had taken part, filled his ear with the dying groans the screams and cries of the murdered, and the loud tongues of the assassins.* Lonely, melancholy, full of dark remorse, suspicious of his friends, hated and feared by his family, accused of weakness, by those at whose persuasions he had sullied his soul with the darkest of all stains; doubted, suspected, accused by his Protestant subjects; seeing his kingdom given up to anarchy, without order, security, or safety, knowing no one on whom he could rely, abhorring and abhorred by all but a few devoted followers, Charles dragged on the few weary hours that remained of existence in lonely splendour, striving to divert his mind and silence the voice of conscience by the excitement of the chase, or to lose the remembrance of the past in the arms of his concubine.

Though shunning the tediousness of business, and but little able, by mental or corporeal health, to take an active part in supporting the burdens of royalty, still the painful subject of his people's revolt, was pressed upon him. The towns of Montauban and Nismes, with the Huguenot nobility of Guienne and Languedoc, refused to receive the terms agreed upon under the walls of Rochelle, and far

* Aubigné declares that he heard these facts from Henry IV. himself, in the presence of persons still living when he wrote. Sully reports the same state of mind from the account of Ambrose Paré, the King's surgeon.

from yielding to the influence of apprehension, roused
themselves to demand more than had ever been
required before. The very act which had been
intended to crush them, was cited as affording proof
of the absolute necessity of further securities for
their safety; and concessions were required, which
not only implied entire liberty of conscience through
the whole realm, but impugned the very existence
of a predominant religion in connexion with the
state. Well might the Queen-mother exclaim,
that if Louis of Condé had been still alive, with
seventy thousand horse and foot at his command,
he would not have made one half of the demands
which were now put forth by a small body of Protestants, scattered over various provinces of France.[*]
Yet Charles was advised to elude these bold applications, rather than to meet them with a direct
negative ; and the sickness which was gradually
creeping over him, debilitating both mind and body,
rendered him not unwilling to avoid any new collision with his Huguenot subjects. He accordingly
appointed deputies to confer with the Protestant
leaders ; but his last hours were not destined to pass
away in peace ; and a new conspiracy, in the heart
of his court, disturbed a death-bed already rendered
doubly terrible by remorse.

The ill-regulated ambition of his brother, Francis
Duke of Alençon; the vanity, folly, and debauchery
of that Prince's favorites ; the discontent of the
King of Navarre and the Prince de Condé, and

* Aubigné. Vol. II. liv. II.

the vengeful feelings of the Protestants throughout the realm, combined to produce new troubles early in 1574. The Duke openly aspired to the office of Lieutenant-General, which had been held by the King of Poland before his election; but his incapacity was properly considered as a bar against his promotion to a post which his birth gave him a right to expect; and while he was amused with vague hopes of commanding an army in Flanders, and of obtaining the hand of the Queen of England, the Duke of Lorraine, his brother-in-law, was entrusted with the authority he coveted.

Amongst his favorites were two gentlemen of the most corrupt and shameless character, the one named La Mole, a Frenchman, and the other, the Count de Coconas, an Italian adventurer. Both of these personages were detested by the King, the one for having the insolence to carry on an intrigue with his sister Marguerite, under his own eyes, in the Louvre; the other for exceeding himself in the cruelties perpetrated on the day of St. Bartholomew.* His hatred of La Mole had indeed been carried so far, as to induce him to lay a plan for assassinating that gentleman in the Louvre, as he descended from the apartments of the Duchess of Nevers;† and it is not

* Such is the account given by L'Etoile, who declares that the King himself stated, that Coconas had admitted having bought as many as thirty Huguenots from their captors, in order to have the pleasure of inducing them to renounce their religion, and of then putting them to a lingering death.

† L'Etoile.

improbable, that the Duke of Alençon's favorite, after escaping by a mere accident, became aware of the fate which had been prepared for him, and determined to take vengeance.

The situation of the King of Navare at the court of France was too painful to be endured a moment after the slightest prospect of escape presented itself. Not merely a prisoner, he was forced to conceal his religious convictions, to sanction acts the most repugnant to his feelings, to restrain his subjects in the exercise of those very rights for which he himself had fought, and to take part in proceedings, against which he would willingly have raised his voice and drawn his sword. He himself was treated with contempt and indignity, often refused admission to the court, and jested at as a lackey or a page.* All his movements were watched, and his very thoughts were put under restraint; while his young wife, over whom he could exercise no control, appeared upon the scene as a common prostitute, destitute of even the decency which society has a right to exact. Too young to view with the horror which they deserved, the vices and debauchery that reigned around him, prompted by passion and temperament to take part in the licentiousness in which every one indulged, the moral sense might become weakened, and undoubtedly did do so, under the contagious influence of bad example. Yet it is not possible to suppose that he could quite forget the warning letters which his

* L'Etoile.

mother had written to him from Blois, when first
the utter depravity of the whole court met her eyes.
" I would not for the world," she says in one of
them, " that you should come here to remain. For
which reason, I much desire that you should marry
and retire with your wife from this corruption ; for
though I always believed it to be very great, I find
it is still greater . . . . If you were here, you
would never escape but by the great grace of God."

The Protestants of France though bold and resolute, though confident in the weakness and disunion of the court, and in their own courage, were
nevertheless well aware, that they could make no
great effort to obtain religious freedom for which
they had so long struggled, without a leader of some
weight and consequence in the state ; and although
it is impossible now, to discover how, or with whom
the conspiracy begun, the result was a determination on the part of the Duke of Alençon, to escape
from the court, with his attendants and the King of
Navarre, and to put himself at the head of a fresh
insurrection against his dying brother. Several
of the most distinguished Protestant leaders were
engaged in the conspiracy ; La Noue himself now
took part therein, the plan was arranged for seizing
upon several towns as places of retreat, and the
whole family of Montmorenci,* with a great body

---

* It is doubtful, whether the Montmorencies, who, according
to Aubigné and others, attributed their exemption from slaughter
on the night of St. Bartholomew, solely to the absence of the
head of the family from Paris, did or did not give the first idea of

of gentlemen, in whose favour was revived the old name of Politics or Malcontents, either supported the design, or suggested it to the Duke and his counsellors.

La Noue put himself secretly at the head of the movement in Poitou ; Languedoc, part of Provence, Bearn, and a considerable portion of Guienne, were already in arms; and a general rising was appointed for Shrove Tuesday, which, far from failing, as Anquetil asserts, at every point, was eminently successful in almost all.   The part of the conspiracy that failed, indeed, was that in which success was most desirable, as upon it depended the stability and consolidation of the party.   An immense number of small towns and castles were captured at once by the Protestants.   La Noue directed the operations in Poitou ; Montgomery carried on the war in Normandy;   and nothing was wanting but the presence of the Duke of Alençon, at the head of the Huguenot forces, to ensure success to one of the most extensive conspiracies which had been formed during the civil wars of religion.   But the Duke hesitated, refused to quit St. Germain till Mantes was in the hands of the insurgents, and though all was prepared for escorting him and his companions to a place of safety, he delayed till, either from vanity or fear, La Mole divulged the secret to the Queen-

this plot to the Duke of Alençon. The young King of Navarre, who is very guarded in his declaration on this subject, does not attribute to that family anything but apprehensions for their own safety.—*Lettres Missives*, Tom. I. page 60.

mother, assuring her, that no attempt against the life or person of the King was intended.*

The real object of the conspiracy is not indeed clearly ascertained, but there can be no doubt, that no intention of injuring Charles entered into the minds of the conspirators, if we except La Mole and Co-conas, on whom suspicion still rests; and the greater part of the contemporary writers agree, that the design of the Duke of Alençon, and the family of Montmorenci, was simply to obtain a greater share of authority for the Duke, and to exclude the King of Poland from the throne of France, on the death of the reigning monarch, which all men perceived to be approaching.†

On Shrove Tuesday, the escort which was to accompany the Princes who proposed to retire from the court, appeared in the neighbourhood of St. Germain, and spread consternation amongst the council; but even in the midst of unfeigned terror, Catherine de Medicis took immediate advantage of the very circumstances which alarmed her, to secure her favorite son against the designs of his enemies. The indecision of the Duke of Alençon, and the folly of La Mole, placed the whole party at the mercy of their enemies,

* Aubigné.

† L'Etoile, Aubigné, Davila. The Queen of Navarre in her Memoirs, declares, that her brother of Alençon, had sworn and bound himself in writing, to seek revenge for the death of Coligni. Gomberville hints, that the first intimation which the Queen-mother received of the designs of the conspirators, was given by Montmorenci, who became alarmed at the foolish boastings of La Mole.

and the escort was obliged to retire without those whom it had been sent to guard. The court instantly determined to fly from St. Germain; Alençon and the King of Navarre were placed in a carriage, and conveyed under a sure guard to the capital, while the King, taken from his sick bed, in the middle of the night, was carried in a litter to Vincennes, where the royal prisoners were subsequently brought. The rest of the court fled in confusion, some in boats, some on horseback; and Aubigné relates, that he and the other friends of the young King of Navarre, who had prepared themselves for a different result, met the Cardinals of Bourbon, Lorraine, and Guise, with the Chancellor Birague, and several other lawyers and statesmen, galloping towards Paris, mounted upon Italian coursers, or great Spanish horses, holding on with both hands by the pommels, and more frightened by their chargers than by the enemy. The Prince de Condé is reported, by some authors, to have been absent at the time, by others, to have been arrested with the rest,* but it is certain that he made his escape and took refuge in a foreign country.

No sooner was the first effect of terror over, than Catherine applied herself to improve her advantage to the utmost, and beyond all doubt, she displayed a degree of skill, in making the faults of her enemies promote her own purposes, worthy of her

* Aubigné in one place comprises the Prince amongst the prisoners, but afterwards represents him as escaping from Amiens. Tom. II. liv. ii. edition 1618.

reputation as a politician. Her first object was to persuade the young King, that the designs of the conspirators were directed against his own life, in order to justify the measures which she was about to take, with the view of securing the throne, when it became vacant, to the King of Poland. While she divided the royal forces into three corps, and despatched them against the scattered bodies of insurgents in Normandy, Poitou, and Languedoc, she caused Coconas and La Mole to be brought to trial. A number of other persons were also arrested, amongst whom were the Duke of Montmorenci, and Marshal Cossé, with several of their relations and friends; and shortly after the interrogatories had commenced, in the case of La Mole and Coconas, Cosmo Bianchi or Ruggieri, was apprehended, charged with having made for La Mole an image of wax to represent the King, which being wounded with daggers, and subjected to other superstitious ceremonies, was supposed to have affected the monarch's health.

From the letters of Catherine to the Attorney-General, we find that she affected to put implicit faith in the power of this man's enchantments, and that she labored to induce him to reverse his charms, in order, perhaps, the more completely to induce a belief in Charles IX. that his life had been attempted by the conspirators, although we must not forget that the Queen-mother gave many proofs, throughout her life, of her credulity in regard to magic and witchcraft. The two favorites of the Duke

of Alençon, were condemned to death, and suffered
the penalty of their crimes, Coconas dying with
courageous indifference, La Mole displaying the
most lamentable cowardice. Their severed heads
were carried off by the Queen of Navarre, and the
young Duchess of Nevers, as memorials of their
lovers, and another barbarous scandal was added to
the many which disgraced the court.

The young King of Navarre being interrogated
on the part he had taken in the designs of the conspirators, boldly acknowledged that his intention had
been to escape from a state of captivity which was
insupportable; and the Duke of Alençon made a
wild and rambling confession, in which his real
objects were studiously concealed. Both were kept
under strict guard during the rest of the King's
life, and Montmorenci and Cossé remained
in the Bastille without being actually brought to
trial. Cosmo Ruggieri was treated by the judges as
an impostor, and sent to the gallies, from which he
contrived to escape, probably not without the connivance of persons in authority, and appeared upon
the scene more than once afterwards, in transactions
not less dark than those in which he had hitherto
figured.*

Every one who could have opposed successfully
the accession of the King of Poland to the throne
of France, on the approaching death of his brother,
was now in the hands of the Queen-mother,

* For the after life and end of this miserable villain, see the
letters of Nicolas Pasquier, liv. 3, let. 10.

and she soon had the satisfaction of seeing the Count of Montgomery, by whose hand her husband had been accidentally slain, brought to Paris as a prisoner. He was taken by Matignon, who had been sent to disperse the forces he had collected in Normandy, and his trial for high treason ended justly in condemnation, though private revenge on the part of Catherine was gratified by the sentence, that assigned to him a punishment from which others equally guilty were exempt. He was executed shortly after the death of the King, shewing the greatest firmness and magnanimity, and complaining of nothing but of having been cruelly put to the torture, after having acknowledged every act he had committed. His address to the people from the scaffold, was full of candor, boldness and good sense. He pointed out that his real crime in the eyes of his enemies, was not that for which he nominally suffered; he declared that if his children had not sufficient virtue to do honor to their birth, he consented to that part of the sentence which deprived them of nobility ; and clearing by his dying declaration the Marshals Montmorenci and Cossé of all part in the revolt, he refused to have his eyes covered, and met the blow of the executioner with a countenance serene and calm.

On the first news of Montgomery's capture, Catherine de Medicis hastened to the sick chamber of her son, to communicate the intelligence ; but the dying Prince paid no attention, and replied that he cared little for that or ought else ; and from that

moment Catherine perceived that his term of life
would be but short.* The fever which hung upon
him varied from day to day, but the sweat of blood
with which he was afflicted, continued without inter-
mission; and the remorse which he felt for his share
in the massacre of the preceding year, aggravated
the malady, and made his death-bed horrible.† He
groaned and wept over the memory of the deeds he
had committed, exclaiming, "Oh what blood! Oh
what murders! Ah why did I follow such evil counsel!" On the day before his death he seemed somewhat better; but on the morning of Whitsunday the
30th May, 1574, it became evident to all that his last
hour was at hand. He lay for some time without
speaking to any one, as if he was asleep, but then
suddenly turning, he exclaimed, "Call my brother."
The Queen-mother, who was sitting by him, immediately sent for the Duke of Alençon, but after that
Prince had arrived the young monarch turned away,
saying, "Let them bring my brother;" and on
farther question added angrily, "My brother the
King of Navarre, I mean."

Catherine then gave directions that Henry should
be called; but in order it would seem to intimidate
him, and prevent him from speaking boldly to her
dying son, she commanded him to be brought through
the vaults of the castle, between a double line of
armed guards. Henry on being summoned was
seized with fear, under the impression that he was

* Brantome.   † L'Etoile.

about to be murdered, and at first refused to go ; but the Queen having sent to assure him that no evil should happen to him, and the Viscount d'Auchy having pledged his word for his safety, he advanced to the mouth of the vaults. When he beheld the guards, however, arrayed in arms, he again hesitated, and would have drawn back ; but, d'Auchy again assuring him that he would be safe, and the guards saluting him as soon as he appeared, he was induced to go on to the King's chamber, where Charles received him with every expression of affection, and embraced him as he knelt by his bed.

"My brother," he said, "you lose a good master and a good friend : I know that you are not the cause of the trouble that has come upon me. If I would have believed all that they wished, you would not now have been in life. But I have always loved you ; and I confide in you solely for the safety of my wife and my daughter, whom I commend to your care. Do not trust to —— But God will protect you." Being interrupted by his mother, he added more words to the same effect.* He designated however the King of Poland as the lawful successor to his throne, and besought his brother Francis and the King of Navarre to make no effort to trouble the repose of the kingdom. Henry remained with

* Such is the statement of Cayet, in a work dedicated to Henry IV. himself, in which he frequently appeals to the account given by that monarch of the events of his early life, of which the author was, in many instances, an eye-witness.

him till he was at the point of death; and a few minutes after he quitted the chamber, the unhappy Charles terminated an existence, which the double policy of his mother, the ambition of his nobles, the bigotry of his church, and his own weakness and intemperance had not only rendered miserable and anxious, but in the end had darkened by the most terrible remorse.

He must however have possessed some better qualities: the love of letters was mingled with the passion for robust exercises, and a fondness for music shewed some taste for the softer arts. Though his morals were by no means pure, they might appear even severe when compared with the frightful licentiousness of his family and his court; and we do not find him accused of those horrible and disgusting vices, which in the early ages, brought down the fiery wrath of God upon the cities of the plain, but which were tolerated in his capital, soiled the lives of his principal nobles, and counted a royal votary during the reign of his brother. The depth and sincerity of the monarch's friendship we are assured was equal to the fierceness and implacability of his hatred; and that he had the power of gaining affection in return is shewn by the grief of some of his attendants for the loss of their master, which hurried them to the grave shortly after his death.*

Catherine de Medicis did not trust to the effect of her dead son's exhortations to restrain the King

* Brantome, Papyrius Masso.

of Navarre and the Duke of Alençon from pursuing the designs of which they were suspected. Both those Princes still remained in captivity, while messengers were despatched with the utmost speed to recall the King of Poland to France. It was not, indeed, that any great affection existed between the imprisoned Princes; for though sometimes united for a time by political interests, they were more frequently at open enmity; and we find, both from the memoirs of Marguerite de Valois, and from other authors, that in their intrigues with ladies of the court, they were often involved in very serious misunderstandings, which, on one occasion, by the kind offices of the Queen-mother, had nearly been fostered into an appeal to the sword.* Marguerite, on the contrary, acted as a peace-maker between them; and, perfectly contented with the liberty her husband allowed her, extended her forgiveness to his frailties, with the utmost placability.

The facility of Henry's disposition, as well as his susceptibility of that which has been very generally called the tender passion, but which has led men to as many brutal excesses as ill-regulated ambition, hatred, or revenge, rendered the court of France the most dangerous school in which his early years could be passed; but yet there was not wanting a degree of firmness that withheld him from falling into any of the darker vices with which that evil place abounded; and, although he forgot the injuries he himself had suffered, the persecution of the faith in

* Perefix.

which he had been educated, and the murder of his
friends, so far as to renew his early intimacy with
the Duke of Guise, we find no base or unworthy
friendships formed by a Prince already distinguished
by his clear insight in human character, nor any
corrupt favorites hanging upon his footsteps, and
perverting the course of his actions.

The rigor of the young King's imprisonment was
somewhat abated after the death of Charles.
Catherine, by the dead monarch's will, had been
appointed regent till the return of the legitimate
successor to the throne ; and, as speedily as pos-
ble, letters were received from Poland, confirming
the Queen-mother in that office.   Left to govern
with undivided authority, she displayed greater
vigor and determination than had characterized
her actions while she was embarrassed by the
task of ruling her son, as well as directing the
affairs of state.   A large body of German troops
were brought into the country to give support
to the royal authority ; the operations of Matignon were pressed eagerly in Normandy ; the
Duke of Montpensier was enabled to hold La
Noue in check ; and although his son, called the
Prince Dauphin, made no great progress in Languedoc, yet his presence in that quarter was
sufficient to prevent Marshal D'Amville, who was
at the head of the malcontents in the south, from
executing any project of importance.   All the approaches to the Louvre were kept in a state of

defence, and every precaution was taken to prevent any fresh attempt on the part of the factions which existed in the capital and in the country.

To rule had now become a passion with Catherine; through her favorite son, whom she had always guided at her will, she hoped to do so still; and with admirable presence of mind and ability she prepared the way for his return to the dominions which had now fallen to him by inheritance. Difficulties and dangers, however, existed beyond the confines of France, which Catherine could not remove. The Poles were unwilling to part with their monarch; and Henry was obliged to make his escape from Cracow by night, to avoid the somewhat stringent proofs of affection that were preparing for him. The German Princes on the Rhine had shewn too little reverence for his character, and too much indignation at some of his actions, to be safely trusted as he returned. The Prince de Condé was not only a well received guest at their courts, but was raising men with hostile demonstrations against his native country; and it was by no means impossible, that the Protestant Sovereigns of Germany might look upon the person of a King of France, as a good security in their hands for toleration towards the Huguenots. Two brothers of the imprisoned Duke of Montmorenci, named Thoré and Meru, were exiles on the frontiers of Switzerland, and ready to take any step which might ensure the safety of their relation. With all these perils on

the path before him, Henry determined upon taking
a circuitous road on his return; and passing by the
dominions of the Emperor, the King reached Venice
in the beginning of August.   He thence proceeded
to Turin, where he was visited by Marshal
Damville, who excused his conduct as well as
circumstances permitted, but took care not to
put himself in the power of a Prince, whom he knew
to be perfidious as well as cruel.

As soon as Catherine learned that her son was
approaching his own territories, she set out from
Paris to meet him with a large escort, accompanied
by the Duke of Alençon, and Henry of Navarre, to
whom she now granted a farther increase of liberty.
From Lyons she sent the two Princes forward,
—not without tried attendants to watch and restrain
their proceedings,— to welcome the new monarch at
Pont Beauvoisin.   Henry III., it would appear, had
by this time repented of the harsh and unfruitful
course he had instigated in others and pursued
himself, towards his discontented subjects; and he
seems to have now resolved to employ mildness as well
as force, though the capricious character of his
mind, and the dominion which his vices had obtained over him, as well as the difficulty of the position in which he was placed, and the evil counsels of
his mother, prevented him from executing this
resolution with that perseverance and activity, which,
joined to the abilities and courage he undoubtedly
possessed, would have insured success.

He received his brother and the King of Navarre with tenderness and kindness. Immediately on their arrival at Lyons, he removed all the painful restraints to which they had been subjected; he affected to treat them with open and marked distinction; and in the ceremonies of the court, and the reception of foreign ambassadors, he called them to the place of honor at his side. To confirm the friendship which they mutually professed, the three Princes took the sacrament together, on the first of November; and on that occasion the Duke of Alençon and the King of Navarre solemnly swore to be faithful and obedient to their new sovereign. About the same period, Henry III. wrote to Montmorenci in Paris, commanding him to require of his brothers, Damville, Thoré, and Meru, to lay down their arms, and return to obedience; and he also despatched letters to Rochelle—which, at the instigation of La Noue, had again displayed the banner of resistance—offering security and the maintenance of all its privileges, on its immediate submission. Montmorenci replied with humility and professions of loyalty; but the answer of Rochelle was bold and threatening.

It is probable that Henry would have proceeded at once to assert the dignity of his crown by a great military effort; but the royal treasury did not afford the means; and so terrible was the want of money in the court, that, during a journey to Avignon, made by the King and his family in the middle of

November, the pages were obliged to sell their
cloaks to obtain a bare subsistence.

The war against the scattered bodies of Protestants
was on this account carried on but feebly; and,
though the Duke of Montpensier, shortly after the
King's return to France, took the town of Fontenoy
le Comte by surprise, while the inhabitants were
treating for a capitulation, committed the most horrible butchery, and then proceeded to besiege Lusignan, his son, who still commanded in Dauphiné, saw
himself frustrated in his attempts to obtain possession of the small town of Livron, which he attacked, after having captured Pousin and Allex.*
During the stay of the King at Avignon, Marshal
Bellegarde was ordered to renew the siege of Livron;
and as Henry returned towards Lyons, he visited
the camp, in order to encourage the soldiery by
his presence. But the garrison and inhabitants
of the town saluted the court with execrations and
reproaches, from their battlements; and, after
having witnessed an attempt to take the place by
storm, which was repulsed with great slaughter the
monarch retired and the siege was raised.

An event, however, more important to France
than even the defeat of the royal army, occurred
while the King was at Avignon. The Cardinal
of Lorraine, after having walked barefoot with
Henry and the rest of the court, in a procession of
flagellants, (for the easy combination of the grossest

* Aubigné. L'Etoile. A town on the Drome.

superstition with the most detestable crimes and most
degrading vices, was displayed throughout the whole
of the reign of the last monarch of the house of
Valois,) was seized with fever, of which he died
shortly after, in a state of delirium, uttering the
most fearful blasphemies and obscenities, jested upon
by his relations during his illness, and censured after
his decease by those whom he had alternately ruled
and served.*   His death caused little regret in
France ; but though it was attributed to poison, there
is every reason to believe that the report was without
any precise foundation ; for in an age, when such
means were too frequently employed to remove those
who were odious or dangerous, a general suspicion
existed, that every great man who left the world suddenly, had fallen a victim to the arts of his enemies.

After the unsuccessful attempt upon Livron,
Henry pursued his way towards Rheims, where
the ceremony of his coronation was performed without many of the usual honors ; and the next day he
espoused the unhappy lady who was destined to be
his wife, Louisa of Lorraine, daughter of the Count
de Vaudemont.   She is only known in history by
those calm and tranquil virtues, which would probably have rendered her the happy wife of a private
man, and which doubtless soothed the sorrows of her

* His nephew, hearing him utter some foul expressions in the
wandering of delirium, declared, with a laugh, that he saw no
reason why his uncle should not recover, as he had all his natural
ways and language ; and Catherine de Medicis observed, when
informed of his death, that the wickedest man in France had
died that day.—L'Etoile, Vol. i. p. 112, 114.

union with a monarch equally unfortunate, criminal, and depraved.

On the road to Rheims, however, Henry encountered one of the greatest dangers which he had hitherto met with. The animosity of his brother the Duke of Alençon, far from being mitigated, had only been augmented by the kindness and confidence which the King had shewn him since his return. In private he always called him the robber of his crown; and with the Duke's knowledge and consent, a plan was laid for attacking the carriage of the monarch on the road from St. Marcoul to Rheims, and putting him to death. At the head of this conspiracy were La Nocle, La Fin, Beaujeu, and La Vergne, most of whom had taken part in previous plots of a similar kind. On the point of execution, as usual, the Duke of Alençon hesitated, which gave time for Fervaques, who had taken some share in the design, to repent and hasten with the news to Henry III., whom he found at Chaumont. Doubts were entertained of the truth of his intelligence; and Monsieur de Barat was sent with him to a meeting of the conspirators, which took place by night in the neighbourhood of Langres. Being introduced to them as a person in the confidence of the Duke of Alençon, he heard their whole plan detailed, and carried back full information to the King, who, after hesitating whether he should not put his brother to death, at length called him to his presence, and reproached him with his perfidy and ingratitude.

The Duke at once cast himself at his sovereign's

feet, confessed that such a scheme had been communicated to him, but with tears and oaths declared that he had given no consent, and was only criminal in having listened to the overtures of the conspirators.* Henry generously pardoned him, and even at his intercession suspended all proceedings against his guilty confederates; but no mercy touched the heart of Alençon; and the same designs against his brother's life were still meditated without remorse.

It is not at all impossible, indeed, that the doubts of the King, once raised, always cast a shadow upon the actions of the Duke, and that he entertained suspicions that were not fully justified. But the hatred that existed between them daily increased, and the mind of Henry was fully possessed with the idea that the Duke intended to reach his crown by the short road of poison. An illness with which he was seized, in the end of May, 1675, and which at first assumed the character of that which had carried off Francis II. was attributed by him to the machinations of his brother, whom he accused of having bribed one of his valets to wound him in the neck with a poisoned pin, while fastening his ruff; and nothing could remove the impression.

* The whole of this statement is derived from the account of Pierre Matthieu, whose sincerity is undoubted, and who declares that he received his information from Henry IV., from Monsieur de Barat, and Monsieur de Souvray, who took a part in discovering the conspiracy.

For some days, the pain in the ear from which he suffered, gave him no rest ; and, while the heir presumptive looked upon the throne as already his, and assumed an air of haughtiness and pride, which only served to render him at once odious and contemptible, the other members of the court assembled in the ante-chamber, looked with painful anxiety for an event, that would have cast the country into disasters more terrible than those with which France was already overwhelmed. Amongst the rest, the King of Navarre and the Duke of Guise, between whom an intimate friendship now existed, watched the course of the King's malady, and revolved in their own minds the result. On one occasion, Henry of Navarre is said to have observed to Guise, "Our man is very ill ;" to which the other replied, "It will be nothing." Shortly after, Henry perceiving that the disease had become more severe, repeated the same words to his companion, when the answer was, "We must think about it ;" and that Prince having again made a similar remark, with an inquiring look, the Duke laid his hand upon the pommel of his sword, saying, "I understand you, Sir. This is at your service."

The apprehensions of the monarch's friends at length reached the highest point, and the suspicions of all, with those of the King himself, turned towards the Duke of Alençon, whose open exultation in a degree justified their doubts. At length, believing his fate sealed, Henry III. called the King of Navarre to his bedside, and pouring forth bitter invectives against the Duke of Alençon, he endeavored to persuade his brother-in-law to put him to death, and take possession of the throne as soon as it was vacant. He pointed out to him the ease with which the deed could be accomplished ; he shewed him that the Duke of Guise, who loved him and hated the Duke, would offer no opposition ; and he even sent for the Prevôt des Marchands, and ordered him to obey the commands of the Navarrese Prince in all things. But that monarch, to use the words of Millot, was incapable of such a crime, and refused to have a share in it, though, as he afterwards remarked to the historian from whom we derive the anecdote, if ambition had been as strong in his breast as hatred was in the bosom of the King of France, but few words were wanting to excite Henry III. to cause his design to be executed on the spot. While this scene was taking place, the Duke of Alençon himself passed through the room, towards the cabinet of the Queen-mother; and, though most of the great personages of the realm were there assembled, he saluted no one.

The King, however, recovered, much to his brother's disappointment ; and Henry acknowledged that the first thing that did him good, was the false intelligence brought to the court, on the eighth of June, that Marshal Damville was dead or dying. The menacing position of that nobleman had alone hitherto saved the lives of his brother Montmorenci and Marshal Cossé; and as soon as this rumor reached the Queen-mother, orders were given for depriving the former of all his attendants, and confining him closely to his chamber. The determination was then formed of murdering him secretly in prison.* Miron the King's physician was employed to visit him, and to spread a report, that from the effects of close confinement and anxiety upon his peculiar constitution, he was likely to die suddenly; and Souvray is said to have been actually commanded by Henry to take four of the soldiers of the guard, and strangle Montmorenci and Cossé with fine napkins. Souvray remonstrated, and declined the task; and Montmorenci himself clearly perceiving the designs entertained against him, sent a message to the Queen-mother, telling her that he understood her purpose, in regard to which no such ceremonies were necessary. "She has only to send me," he added, " the Chancellor's apothecary, and I will take whatever he gives me."† But before the meditated deed was committed, the falsehood of the report of Damville's death was ascertained, and the policy of the court was altered.

The state of France at this period presents a curious but frightful picture. Civil war was raging in most of the provinces; no such thing as law or justice existed; the passions of the monarch, his mother, or his minions, decided the life or death of all persons brought to trial even for ordinary

* De Thou. Pierre Matthieu.   † L'Etoile.

crimes ;* private assassination was so common that scarcely a day passed without the chroniclers of the time having to record some new tragedy amongst the nobles of the land ; poison was employed on the slightest occasion ; prisoners were strangled in their dungeons for the purpose of bestowing their estates upon the favorites of the court ;† the King and his brother meditated the destruction of each other with very little secrecy ; Catherine de Medicis entertained designs against the life of her son-in-law, the King of Navarre ; ‡ the monarch and his mother took pleasure in witnessing the execution of criminals ; female chastity was almost unknown ; every sort of immorality was tolerated and practised ; and, with all these horrors, was mingled the external signs of devotion and piety, processions, vows, fasts, prayers, and sacraments. The King himself set the example, by running barefoot through the streets reciting his orisons, and by murmuring paternosters at his table, and in the very midst of the most frightful debaucheries ; while, to render the scene more disgusting, jests, merriment, and repartee, not only enlivened the dullest sensuality,

* An extraordinary instance of this is to be found in the case of William du Prat, Baron de Viteaux, one of the most atrocious murderers of the time, who, after full conviction, was sentenced by the Parliament to a fine.

† Such was the case with Lomenie, secretary to Charles IX., who was strangled by order of Catherine to obtain his estate of Versigny for De Retz.

‡ This fact is admitted by Marguerite herself in her Memoires.

but interrupted the proceedings of the council-table, disturbed the gravity of the court of justice, and hovered round the scaffold and the block. The human heart, when it revolts entirely to the side of vice, has no other arms against virtue than a laugh.

The daring and impetuous spirit of the Duke of Alençon could not long endure an enforced resi-dence in a court where he was viewed with just suspicion, treated with some contempt and some injustice, kept in a state of dependence, and con-scious of being detested by many. His partizans were numerous, however; a large body of malcon-tents regarded him as their destined leader; and thousands of armed insurgents called upon him to put himself at their head. After some hesitation, some delay, and many impediments, he determined upon making his escape from the court; and, when once attempted, the design was executed without much difficulty. Taking counsel with his sister Mar-guerite, he submitted to be reconciled to the King of Navarre, of whom he entertained the same con-suming jealousy that affected him towards his bro-ther; and, having given notice of his intention to his friends without, he proceeded to execute his scheme. Wrapping himself in a large mantle, he issued forth alone from the Louvre, about six o'clock in the evening of the 15th of September, passed through the porte St. Honoré, where a carriage was in waiting, and gained the open country. A quarter of a league from the town he mounted a horse which had been prepared for him, and two leagues farther on the road found an escort of three hundred men, with whom he made his way direct to Dreux.

It was not till nine o'clock the next morning that the Duke's escape was discovered at the court, and Henry was terribly agitated by the prospect of all the evils which such an event might bring about.* For a short time, his apes, his parrots, his little dogs, even his minions were forgotten; and with the utmost eagerness he applied himself to cut off his brother from a junction with the Huguenot forces in Poitou and Saintonge, and compel him to return. Letter after letter was despatched to the governors of the provinces, informing them of the flight of the Prince, and calling upon them not only to prevent his passage through the districts in which they commanded, but, taking arms for the defence of the throne, to join the King in Paris with all the friends they could collect by the eighth of October following.

In the mean time the Duke addressed a letter to his brother, and a manifesto to the country, setting forth his causes of complaint; and it is evident from the terms he uses, that the design which the King had entertained of putting him to death had reached his ears. He wrote also to the Prince de Condé, begging him to hasten forward with his German levies, and to the leaders of the malcontents through-

* Mem. de la Reine Marguerite.   Mem. de Nevers.

out the realm, giving them notice of his escape and declaring himself ready to put himself at their head, for the public good; from which expression the hostilities that followed obtained the name of " the war of the public good."

From Dreux the Prince proceeded to Poitou, where he was joined by La Noue and a number of other noblemen, the Duke of Montpensier himself, as well as most of the King's officers, having openly refused to act against him. Vast efforts were now made by the exiles in the different German courts to bring a sufficient body of troops into the field. The Elector Palatine furnished an army of reiters and lanzknechts to the Prince de Condé, under his son John Casimir, exacting, it is true, somewhat hard conditions; and Thoré, the brother of Mont-morenci, entered France with a force of two thousand men.* The Queen-mother, in order to deter him from proceeding to the support of the Duke of Alençon, gave him notice, that if he advanced she would send him the heads of his brother and Mar-shal Cossé; but Thoré made a bold reply, and con-tinued his march. To oppose him in arms, the Duke of Guise was ordered to take the command of the royal army in Champagne; and between Da-mery and Dormans, Thoré found himself in the presence of a greatly superior force.† Thoré, how-ever, determined to fight rather than suffer the dis-grace of a forced retreat at the very opening of the

* L'Etoile.   † Duchat.

campaign; and a combat took place in which it is generally admitted that he was defeated. Nevertheless, though some eight hundred of his men were slain, or surrendered, he contrived to cut his way through the enemy at the head of twelve hundred, and effected his object of joining the Duke of Alençon at Vatan, between the Cher and the Indre. The Duke of Guise was severely wounded in the face during the combat, and was marked during the rest of his life by a deep scar, from which he derived the appellation of the Balafré—a name of which he was always proud.

The position of the court was now most critical. The brother of the King was at the head of a formidable party in the centre of France; he was supported not only by the Protestants, but also by a large body of Catholics, not only by the politics, or malcontents, under the house of Montmorenci, but by his cousin the Duke of Montpensier, who had ever shewn himself one of the firmest adherents of the crown, and the most implacable enemy of the Huguenots. The Prince de Condé, with a powerful German force, menaced the eastern frontier; Damville was in arms in the south; and Rochelle appeared in open resistance to the royal authority. Very shortly after the escape of the Duke, Catherine had once more tried the means of negotiation, and in the beginning of October had obtained a conference with her son at Chambord, but Alençon refused to treat till Mont-

morenci and Cossé were at liberty, and those noblemen were consequently set free immediately.* A
suspicion, however, that his mother meant to entrap
and arrest him, caused Alençon to retire precipi-
tately; but Catherine pursued her point; and after
vain attempts to bring about a treaty of peace,
she contented herself with a truce of seven months,
which was signed by the King in the end of November.

The strait to which the court was reduced is
evident from every line of the treaty, which was as
favorable to the insurgents as it could have been,
had they gained a great victory. By the various
clauses the King promised six important towns as
security to his adversaries, the payment of five
hundred thousand livres to the German auxiliaries,
the discharge of all his own foreign troops, except
the Swiss guard and five hundred Corsicans, and
also made several concessions to the Huguenots on
points of religious toleration. In return, he only
demanded that the army of the Duke, as well as his
own, should be disbanded, with the exception of
two thousand foot, and a small body of horse, which
he himself consented to pay, and that the troops
raised by Condé should retire behind the Rhine,
and not recross that river during the truce. It was
also agreed that negotiators should be appointed to

* Anquetil gives a version of all these affairs completely erroneous. It was in consequence of the refusal of the Duke to
treat, not of the threats of Thoré, that the Marshals were
liberated.

carry on conferences, with the object of arriving at a stable and permanent peace.*   Henry III. was delighted with the result of his mother's negotiations, which promised him a period of that repose and indulgence of which he was so fond ; but the difficulty of obtaining money to discharge the pay of the German troops, and the refusal of several of the towns, mentioned in the convention, to open their gates to the Duke of Alençon, produced results which justified the malcontents in carrying on the war ; and Condé, at the head of his reiters, raised contributions in the eastern provinces of the kingdom, and advanced towards Auxerre and Montargis.†

The court of France was not destined to remain at ease ; and the King had yet to learn that tranquillity is the result of vigor, not of weakness—repose the reward of activity, not of indolence. In October, shortly before the signature of the treaty, Du Guast, one of the most insolent of the minions of Henry III. was assassinated in his own house, with two of his servants, by a party of masked murderers, at the instigation of Marguerite, Queen of Navarre ; and on the 25th of January following, another of the distinguished personages who had been so long kept in a sort of splendid captivity at the court, effected his escape and hurried to join the insurgents.

The affection with which Catherine de Medicis had at one time regarded the young King of Navarre, had

* Memoires de Nevers.   † Aubigné.

naturally been changed to hatred, by the evils which she had inflicted upon him ; and it is certain, that not only he himself, but his wife and the greater part of the court, were fully convinced that she entertained a design upon his life.* Her son-in-law had insinuated that she entertained such a purpose, when examined before the council. Marguerite admits the fact; and Henry of Navarre, afterwards, expressed to those who accompanied him in his flight, his firm belief that she had long determined to effect her object by any means. He was detained at the court under such strict watch, however, that it was difficult for him even to find opportunity of speaking with those on whom he could most rely. The guards, which had been given to him as a mark of honor, were, in fact, gaolers under another name ; the whole of them were zealous Papists, and most of them had dipped their hands in the blood of his friends upon the day of St. Bartholomew. At the same time the Queen-mother strove to enthral his mind as she had imprisoned his body; and well knowing his characteristic weakness, entangled him in intrigues with the licentious girls who surrounded her, while she held out to his ambition the prospect of the post of Lieutenant-General.

Still Henry of Navarre sighed for liberty, though he did not venture to open his purposes to any of those around him, till at length Aubigné, one of the few who remained attached to his person, took an opportunity of speaking boldly of his escape, and Fervaques, now one of the officers of the King of

* Memoires de Marguerite.   L'Etoile.

France, disgusted with the want of gratitude which had been shewn to him by the reigning monarch, made an offer of his services to the Navarrese Prince. His good faith and honor were by no means above suspicion, but Henry of Bourbon willingly listened to his overtures, and between him, Aubigné, and four others, the whole plan of that monarch's deliverance was arranged.

It was agreed that some of his friends should take measures for seizing upon several towns in Normandy and Maine, in order to secure his retreat towards Guienne; that the King himself should pretend to go upon a hunting party, in the direction of Senlis, accompanied by a small body of attendants in whose fidelity he could most surely trust, and by one only of the persons who were in the secret. The rest were to follow him to Senlis, with fresh horses and men, in sufficient number to overpower any resistance on the part of those who had been placed about his person by the King of France.

Several days were required to make all the necessary preparations; but, in the meantime, Henry conducted himself with great dexterity and self-command, meeting every difficulty and danger, with that promptitude and decision which he afterwards displayed in a wider field. He affected, in the first place, to feel sure of obtaining the office of Lieutenant-General, and taking advantage of his intimacy with the Duke of Guise, he entertained him for a whole hour, one morning in his bed-chamber, with the plans and purposes which he pretended to have formed for his behaviour, when invested with that dignity. The Duke, who was well aware that Henry III. only sought to amuse his brother-in-law with the hopes of a high command, carried the whole conversation to the French monarch, which produced much laughter at the expense of the Navarrese Prince; and the whole court remained convinced that he was fully occupied with idle expectations.*

Two days before the time fixed for his departure, however, a rumor got abroad that he had fled, and a great deal of anxiety and confusion was the result; but no sooner was Henry of Navarre himself informed of the report, than he hastened laughing to the King and the Queen-mother, and told them that he had brought them the person who had caused them so much alarm.† The very day too on which he set out, he visited the fair of St. Germain with the Duke of Guise, and even attempted to persuade his friend to go with him to hunt. He then took his departure, accompanied by two of the King's officers, named St. Martin and Spalonge, and arrived at Senlis, where he slept, on the 3rd of February, 1576.

The same night, however, Fervaques was observed by Aubigné speaking long and eagerly to Henry III., and the Huguenot, having waited for his treacherous confederate by moonlight, till he quitted the palace, suddenly seized him by the arm, and accused him of having betrayed the secret. Fer-

* Aubigné.   † L'Etoile.

vaques did not deny the fact, but told him in haste to save his master.

Aubigné ran at once to the stables, where the horses had been kept ready, and sent them off to Luzarches, giving, at the same time, a hint to Roquelaure, one of the conspirators, to hasten post to the King of Navarre, at Senlis, without having an opportunity of affording him farther information. The grooms and horses only passed the gates a few minutes before an order came to guard them strictly ; but Roquelaure reached Senlis in safety ; and he and Aubigné who followed immediately, with the few attendants whom they had been able to bring with them, were soon joined by Henry of Bourbon. As soon as he could speak to them in private, he inquired what news they brought. Their reply instantly decided his conduct ; and the only question was, what should be done with the two officers of the King of France. Some proposed to put them to death, but Henry, with his usual humanity, would not permit such an act, and made an excuse to send them back separately to Paris, charging them with messages to the King, which they undertook to carry without hesitation, probably perceiving that resistance would be vain.

The King of Navarre and his companions then mounted fresh horses, passed the Seine at Poissy, and reached Chateauneuf; whence, after obtaining some money from the farmers on his estates in that neighbourhood, he hurried on with all speed to Alençon ; having ridden, during part of this journey, twenty leagues without drawing a rein.* So great was his apprehension of being stopped, that, we are told, he did not utter a word till he found himself in security,† when, drawing a deep sigh, he thanked God for his deliverance.

At Alençon, where he remained several days, a multitude of partisans flocked round the young King of Navarre; and here also he was rejoined by Fervaques, who, when reproached with the perfidy he had committed, did not deny that he had given intimation of the plot to the French monarch; but declared that he had done so for his own security, on finding that Madame de Carnavalet had revealed the secret in the first place. Nor is it at all improbable that Henry had the weakness to communicate the scheme on which his safety depended to a beautiful woman, if we may judge of his conduct when he was a mere youth, from his actions when he had reached a period of life which should have brought caution with experience; Henry, at all events, was satisfied with the excuse, although Aubigné declares that Fervaques only quitted the court of France, because he found that the King was as

* This must have been on the 5th February, when he left St. Prix, not far from Senlis, in the morning, and reached Chateauneuf en Thimerais the same night, having accomplished a journey of thirty-four leagues in one day. See Lettres Missives.

† L'Etoile says, he was told by a gentleman who accompanied him, that he did not speak till he had passed the Loire, which is evidently an exaggeration, as he remained some time at Alençon, summoned his farmers at La Fere to pay the money that they owed, and performed various other acts, implying the use of language, long before he crossed the Loire, which he did not do for three weeks after he had quitted the court of France.

much disgusted with his treachery as he was dis-
pleased with the tardy intelligence he afforded.*
One of the first acts of Henry, after his arrival at
Alençon, was to stand godfather, in the Protestant
Church, to the child of his physician Caillard, when
it was remarked that the Psalm, in order for the day,
commenced with the words, " The King shall rejoice
in his deliverance, O Lord." He did not, however, at
this time make any open renunciation of the Roman
Catholic faith, urged, it is supposed, to refrain from
so doing by the Duke of Alençon. That Prince was
by no means well satisfied with the escape of his
fellow-prisoner, fearing that the authority which he
had obtained amongst the Protestants would be lost
by the presence of one so much better qualified for
the office of their leader. Thus the two Princes
remained separate, though holding frequent communication in regard to the negotiations for peace
which were still proceeding, and ready at any moment
to unite their forces, which now amounted in the
whole to more than fifty thousand men.†

While the Duke of Alençon fixed his principal
residence at Moulins, whence he could keep up his
correspondence with Damville, and the Prince de
Condé with his reiters advanced as far as Auxerre,
Henry of Navarre levied an army on the banks of
the Loire, and every day saw fresh parties of Pro-

* It is to be remarked that, although upon the closest in-
spection of facts, Aubigné will be found very accurate as to the
general march of events, yet when he censures others, he is not
so much to be depended upon, for he wrote under disappointment, and was always famed for malice.   † Sully.

testants join his standard. Shortly after his arrival at Thouars* he despatched Sully, who had accompanied him in his flight, with Fervaques, to demand his sister Catherine at the hands of the King. No opposition was made to her removal from Paris, and no sooner had she quitted the capital, to rejoin her brother, than she resumed the exercise of the Protestant religion. Beauvais la Nocles was also sent to Paris by the confederate Princes to propose their demands to Henry III. who, without money, without armies, and without energy, was apparently at the mercy of his revolted subjects.

Their pretensions were as great as their power. The Duke of Alençon demanded a vast augmentation of his appanage. The Prince de Condé, the government of Picardy, and the town of Boulogne, with payment for his German troops, and a new company of men-at-arms for his brother the Prince de Conti. The King of Navarre required payment of his wife's dowry, and right of remaining in his territories of Bearn, with his wife, the real and not the nominal government of Guienne, a renewal of the league between the crown of France and his ancestors, for the recovery of that part of Navarre which had been dissevered by the kings of Spain, and sovereign power in all his territories. Such demands menaced the very throne of Henry III.; and yet, as I have said, he was without power to resist, had

* This name is written Tours in most historians; but I do not find that Henry made any stay in that town, whereas his letters and household accounts prove that he remained at Thouars, or in the neighbourhood, during a great part of April and May, 1576.

the confederates remained constant to their objects
and united in their counsels. But Catherine came
to the aid of her son, and having learned and practised the art of ruling by dividing, she determined,
at any price, to detach the Duke of Alençon from the
malcontents. She was by this time well aware that
the escape of Henry of Navarre, had introduced the
elements of discord into the camp of the insurgents.
" All his followers and all the Princes of his house,"
says Pierre Matthieu, in his simple manner, " had
rallied round him. The Duke of Alençon was
annoyed, and seeing himself alone with his Catholics,
had recourse to the favor of the King." The Queen-
mother took upon herself the conduct of the negotiation, and at length, in May, 1576, a treaty of
peace was signed, consisting of sixty-three articles,*
by which, vast concessions were made to the Duke
of Alençon, and specious promises given to all the
rest of the confederates. But the only parties who
really gained, were the Duke and the court; and,
as to the others, to use the expression of Duchat,
" she reserved to herself the pleasure of breaking
her word."

A few of the stipulations agreed to by this document
must be mentioned here, as upon the breach of
almost all the promises made, turned the renewal of
the war, and the establishment, as a recognized body,
of that famous League, the foundation of which had
been laid from the time of the last meeting of
the Council of Trent. By the royal edict then
which confirmed the treaty, the full and free ex-

* Memoires de Nevers, where the edict is given at length.

ercise of the Protestant religion was guaranteed in every part of France, except in the capital and a circle of two leagues around it ; every Protestant who had abjured his faith was freed from all oaths or engagements to remain attached to the doctrine of Rome; the establishment of a court, composed of Protestants and Papists, in equal numbers, to judge of causes in which parties of the two religions were engaged, was promised; which court was to sit ordinarily with the Parliament in Paris, but was to be sent to hold its sessions for three months each year, in Poitou and Angoumois ; similar chambers were to be erected in the other Parliaments of the realm ; all sentences against Protestants and Catholics, on account of their participation in the civil wars, from the time of the death of Henry II. were reversed, and the children of the condemned were restored to their rank and inheritance, the Admiral de Coligni, Montgomery, and other leaders being specified by name ; a general amnesty was granted; all prisoners detained for offences against the state, were declared free ; perfect equality, in the eye of the law, was established between Calvinists and Papists; a convocation of the States General to be held in the town of Blois within six months, was promised; and eight towns were given to the confederates as security.* Besides these articles,

* Anquetil, with his usual inaccuracy, declares that the confederates, with the exception of Alençon, Condé, and Casimir, "yielded without conditions better or worse than before. There was only an edict, which extended a little the privileges of the Reformers ;" whereas, in fact, had the terms been fulfilled, they assured to the Protestants all they could reasonably demand.

stipulated by the edict of the King, the convention
on which it was founded conceded to the Duke of
Alençon, as an augmentation of his appanage, the
three important provinces of Anjou, Berri, and
Touraine, with almost sovereign power therein, and
a pension of one hundred thousand crowns. The
government of Picardy was granted to the Prince
de Condé, with the strong town of Peronne for
his residence, and Angouleme as another place of
refuge. The King of Navarre would seem to be
the only one whose interests were entirely neglected ;
but as the promises to all the rest, except the Duke,
were made merely to deceive, he lost little by not
having obtained concessions, which would only have
ended in disappointment.

The Duke of Alençon now took the title of
Duke of Anjou, and separated himself from the
party of the Huguenots, committing, as Sully justly
observes, one of the greatest mistakes into which
it was possible for an ambitious prince to fall.
He shewed, however, the same false and deceitful
disposition which characterized his whole family, by
endeavoring to obtain from the Rochellois a large
sum of money, before his negotiations with the
court were known ; and the feelings entertained by
himself and his friends towards their late allies
were so evident, that the Prince de Condé refused
to accompany him on his entrance into Bourges,
saying that, amongst so many people, some rogue
might be found who would send a bullet through his
head. " The rogue would be hanged, I know," he

added; " but the Prince de Condé would be dead. I will not give you occasion, my Lord, to hang rogues for love of me."* He accordingly left the Prince in the middle of July, and, accompanied by fifty horse, went on to join the King of Navarre, who was slowly proceeding towards Guienne.

Henry of Bourbon and his sister first turned their steps to La Rochelle, where some difficulty was made by the citizens to admit the young King, on account of the bad reputation of several of his companions, especially of Fervaques, and of Jean Louis de Nogaret de la Valette,† afterwards better known as the Duke of Epernon, a brave and skilful, but unprincipled man, who subsequently became distinguished, first as one of the minions of Henry III., and afterwards as an officer in the wars of the League. It has been supposed that the King of Navarre himself, wishing to cast off a number of the licentious nobles who had either accompanied him from Paris, or joined him on the way, suggested to the Rochellois the objections which they urged against his companions ;‡ but whether this was the case or not, and it is very doubtful, the inhabitants refused to receive within their walls, any of those persons who had taken part in the massacre of St. Bartholomew's day. Henry, yielding to their representations, agreed to leave all those whom they

* L'Etoile. Aubigné.　　　† Sully.

‡ Perefix. Henry's letters to the Rochellois, at this period, give no confirmation of this assertion. It is to be remarked that Aunis, and consequently Rochelle, was at this time considered part of Guienne, of which Henry was governor.

specified at Surgeres, which gave so much offence to several of his followers, that they left him, either at once or shortly after. Such was the case with La Valette, who immediately cast himself into the opposite party, and became one of the bitterest enemies of his former master.*

Having shewn this wise acquiescence in the wishes of the people of Rochelle, Henry was received in the town with royal honors, and he and his sister renounced in the most public manner the Roman Catholic faith, declared that their feigned adoption of that religion had been produced by force alone, and performed penance for the sin that they had been compelled to commit.† After a short stay at Rochelle, the King of Navarre proceeded towards Perigord, and was in general welcomed with great respect by the various towns through which he had occasion to pass; but the Prince de Condé, who soon joined him, found the gates of Angouleme shut against him, and also against the commissioners sent by the King of France to give him possession of the town, according to the tenor of the treaty. To complain of this conduct, he sent his Lieutenant to the court, but his remonstrances obtained nothing but laughter for a reply, with a promise of St. Jean d'Angeli as an equivalent for Angouleme, which the Governor Ruffec positively refused

* The writer of the life of the Duke declares that he quitted Henry because he renounced the Catholic faith; but his religious principles are not generally reported to have been so strict as to induce the reader to give much credit to the statement.

† Aubigné.

to yield. Having consulted with his cousin the King
of Navarre, and foreseeing that the same insult might
be offered to him at St. Jean, the Prince, by Henry's
advice, secretly marched several bodies of men to
that town, and without any demand for admission,
made himself master of it by surprise.   Not long
after, Bordeaux, the principal city of Guienne, at
the instigation of Marshal Villars, refused to open
its gates to the King of Navarre, attempting to
cover its open disobedience by plausible excuses.
Henry had no force, however, to compel the inhabitants to submit; and merely bidding them remember that Montmorenci had entered by a breach in
their walls, and that he might some day do the
same, he retired to the Agenois, where, before the
end of the year, he made himself master of Agen
and Villeneuve, by a stratagem similar to that
which Condé had employed against St. Jean.

The intention of the court to amuse and deceive
the Protestants once more, was evident to all.   The
Duke of Alençon, having been detached from their
party, and the link between them and the malcontent
Catholics broken, Catherine in a degree threw off the
mask, though she did not seek to discover her full
purposes at that moment.   Casimir and his reiters
were not paid, and hovered on the frontiers, pillaging the neighbouring country, and sending remonstrances to Paris; the royal governors, in many
instances, boldly refused to obey the King's injunctions in favor of the Huguenots, and were
honored for their disobedience; the mixed courts
of justice were not established; the Calvinists were

unsettled and maltreated in many places, with the sanction and in the presence of the monarch's officers; Henry of Navarre was nearly powerless in his government of Guienne; the Prince de Condé did not receive the government of Picardy so long and so often promised; the town of Peronne positively refused to give admission to him and to his troops; and in the beginning of December, 1576, Pont St. Esprit was taken by the Roman Catholics, and Montmorenci Thoré was arrested.

We have, in the preceding pages of this work, shewn the early traces of a design on the part of certain bodies of Papists to unite themselves into a general confederation for the suppression of the Protestant faith, and the persecution of those who professed its doctrines; but those traces were merely as the lines of a sketch, which was now about to be filled up as a finished picture. The first hint of the massacre of St. Bartholomew's day was given at Bayonne, during the interview between Catherine and the Duke of Alva. The first principles of that famous association, called "The League," were laid down during the progress of Charles IX. towards the meeting of the courts of France and Spain. Neither the suggestion of Alva nor the plan of the Popish conspiracy was acted upon at the time; but both were pondered, borne in mind, and developed in their season. In each of these cases the Roman Catholics were grossly criminal; in each they were the persecuting party; in each the selfish passions of the house of Guise had a great share in moving secretly the feebler agents, before they themselves came forward to lead and perpetrate. Nevertheless, we must not blind our eyes to the fact, that in neither instance were the Protestants without their part of the culpability, by holding up to the Papists examples of deeds and practices which were by them again carried to a horrible excess, and turned against their opponents. If the Catholics shewed themselves cruel and relentless in the civil strifes that convulsed the land, the Huguenots were not unsullied by massacres, murders, and vindictive barbarities. If the Papists had a Montpensier, and a Montluc, a De Retz, and a Tavannes, the Protestants could not boast of the humanity of a Montgomery, a Briquemaut, a Des Adrets. Cruelty was shewn upon both parts; and if many of the Romanists held that no faith was to be kept with heretics, and that no king was to be bound by promises made to his rebellious subjects,* ministers of a church pretending to greater purity, were found to maintain publicly, that it was lawful to use any means to destroy a tyrant; while on both sides the word of God was perverted to justify the workings of the most detestable of human passions.

The difference between the two parties and the two religions, is principally shewn in the fact, that the great majority of the leading Protestants reprobated and lamented the crimes and wickedness of the few, while the great body of the Catholics applauded or took part in the deeds which the few condemned. The commendation which has been bestowed upon

* Castelnau. Brantome.

the Duke of Guise for saving some of the Protestants on St. Bartholomew's eve, is in itself the
most frightful censure that could be passed upon the
whole party to which he belonged.

Again, in regard to the League, the Protestants
had set the example of leaguing together, under the
pretence of serving the King, but, in reality, to offer
armed resistance to his authority.   Could we believe,
indeed, that they were, in all instances, moved by
zeal for the freedom of conscience ; could we suppose
that they acted solely in self-defence, we might ex-
culpate them of all crime, and leave the Papists the
honor or the shame of having devised a confederacy inconsistent with the safety of the state, in-
compatible with the royal authority, subversive of
all law and order, and destructive to the tranquillity and prosperity of France.   But such was not
the case.   In several striking instances, personal
ambition, and many less noble and elevating motives also, are to be discovered in the actions
of the persons engaged; and levity, avarice, a
spirit of faction, may be safely attributed to more
than one great man upon the side of the Calvinists.
Coligni, perhaps, acted solely from conscientious
conviction ; but we cannot admit that such was the
case with the Prince de Condé, however gallant and
chivalrous might be his conduct in the field.   Had
the Huguenot body been purely a religious party,
and not a political one, it would have more fully
commanded our respect and engaged our sympathy.

Here again, however, the distinction between the two contending bodies is to be seen, not in the actions, or motives of individuals, but in the general principles and views of the whole. On the part of the Roman Catholic League, ambition, faction, and intolerance, were the grand moving powers, they were written on every banner, they were found in almost every heart. Amongst the members of the Huguenot Confederation, there might be some who aimed at individual objects of an unworthy kind, but the great end proposed by the whole, was freedom of conscience, with personal security. They leagued together to secure tolerance and equity; the Catholics for the purposes of persecution and oppression.

A single town on the very verge of the French territory, was destined first to give operative effect to the often suggested plan, of a Catholic League. The city of Peronne had, as we have seen, been promised to the Prince de Condé, as a place of retreat; but Peronne refused to receive him, or to admit the garrison which he was entitled to introduce. Thus, the first act of a body, which pretended to be more loyal than the King himself, was resistance to his published will. It is generally supposed, that Monsieur de Humières, governor of Peronne, inimical from private pique to the Prince de Condé, as well as unwilling to see a superior in that fortress, was the first to propose to the Catholic nobility of the city and the neighbourhood, the League which spread rapidly to every part of France. But, in truth, we know nothing of the origin of the confederation in its details: all that we find from authentic records is, that Peronne refused to receive the Prince, and that immediately after, a document appeared, setting forth certain declarations, regulations, and an oath, which, without any material change, remained the constitution of the Catholic League, till its decline after the abjuration of Henry IV. It will be necessary to give the particulars of this famous instrument in full, though it is not improbable, that, in all the copies which have come down to us, some slight variations may have been made from the original. But, before we proceed to state the pretensions of the League of Peronne, it may be as well to give the terms of an agreement, signed by the nobility and clergy of Champagne, in the year 1568, in order that the reader may be enabled to convince himself of the connection between the two conspiracies, which has been doubted, and even denied by many writers; and it will be remarked, that, in the passages about to be cited from this paper, reference is made to a League already existing, which in all probability, was the confederation we have had occasion to speak of in noticing the progress of the court through the eastern provinces of France, in the year 1564.*

* This document is furnished by the valuable collection of papers at the end of the Journal de l'Etoile, Vol. 3, page 31, and a note upon it states, that it is copied from the original, amongst

" League of Troyes.

" We, the undersigned, desiring, on account of our duty and christian vocation, to maintain the true Roman Catholic church of God, in which we have been baptized, according to the ancient traditions, from the times of the apostles to the present day. Desiring, also, according to the fidelity which we bear towards the Crown of France, to maintain that crown in the house of Valois, for all the obligations which we and our ancestors have and hold of the said house, so that in all security and liberty we can accomplish the duties of our offices, in all that concerns the service of God, and of his church, both in the administration of his word, holy sacraments, and prayers, and in the other functions to which we are called and bounden.

" Also seeing that it has pleased the King's Lieutenant* in these countries of Champagne and Brie, to associate us to the royal League and Association of the nobility and states of this Government, here above inserted, to enjoy the same according to its form and tenor, by which the said Lord-Lieutenant, with our said Lords, the nobility of his government, and other associates, promise to employ themselves, their persons, lives, and goods, for the maintenance of the said Church and Crown, so far and so long as it shall please God that we shall be governed by them, in our said Roman and Apostolical religion, to

the Seguier manuscripts, in the Bibliotheque de St. Germain, des pres. vol. 1483.

* Henry Duke of Guise, then between 17 and 18 years of age.

succor and aid us, as well by counsel and person, as by forces, and to the utmost of their power, for the preservation of our lives, liberties, and goods, against all persons without any exception, but the persons of the said Lord our King, his children, and brothers, and the Queen his mother, and that without comprising any relationship or alliance, however near it may be, on account of such relationship or alliance.* We declare, that we will succor and aid each other, as the other allies and persons comprised in this society, of whatsoever state and condition they may be, in all our affairs and *actions*† proceeding on account of this society or undertaking, which may be brought against us or our goods, by our opposites, enemies, and adversaries of the present society, and of our said Roman Catholic religion, and that immediately, and without delay. We have sworn and promised, and do swear and promise, by the most Holy and incomprehensible Name of God the Father, the Son, and the Holy Ghost, in which name we have been baptized, that to aid, entertain, and keep up the present league, society, and fraternity, we will tax ourselves, every one according to his means, for the mainte-

---

* These words, according to the construction of the French language, can only refer to the Queen-mother, and must have been intended to exclude the Princes of the House of Bourbon. The terms are " — et la Royne leur mere, et ce sans acceptation d'aucun parentage ou alliance, quelque prochaine qu'elle puisse être, pour lesquels parentage ou alliance." The construction is very confused but the meaning evident.

† The word used in the original is "plainctes."

nance of the said company and society, out of our goods, every time and inasmuch as enterprises shall be made for the maintenance of the present alliance and society, In doing which shall be promised us and kept up for us, the association, friendship, and fraternity of all the denominations of the present Holy League, as well of the nobles as others, to aid us and defend us against all those of the opposite party, who would do us wrong, to us or to our goods, and in all affairs into which we may fall : which aid shall be given at the expense of those of the present society, who bear arms by the authority and command of the said Lord-Lieutenant. All under the good pleasure of our said Lord the King our Sovereign Lord, and our Lords his Lieutenants, in witness of which we have signed these presents with our hands : The twenty-fifth day of June, 1568.''

Such is the first complete form of association which I find amongst the Roman Catholics of France against their Protestant fellow-subjects ; but it is to be remembered that it refers, as I have before pointed out, to a League already existing, and that it was itself signed eight years before that more famous document was produced, which is known as the League of Peronne. To it I shall now turn, and on comparing the two, it will be found that the one was but the type of the other.*

---

* I give this document from Pierre Mathieu who had access to the very best authorities, and most accurate copies, and whose sincerity has never been doubted.

" THE LEAGUE OF PERONNE.

" In the name of the Holy Trinity, Father, Son, and Holy Ghost, our only true God, to whom be glory and honor. The association of Catholic Princes, Lords, and Gentlemen, ought to be, and shall be instituted, to re-establish the entire law of God, to restore and retain his holy service according to the form and manner of the Holy Catholic Apostolical and Roman Church, renouncing and abjuring the errors to the contrary. Secondly, to preserve the King Henry, third of the name, by the grace of God, and his *predecessors*,* most Christian kings, in the state, splendor, authority, duty, service, and obedience which are due to him by his subjects, according to the contents of the Articles which will be presented to him at the States, which he swears and promises to keep at his consecration and coronation, with protestation not to undertake any thing which shall prejudice that which may be enacted by the said States. Thirdly, to restore to the Provinces of this Kingdom and State, the ancient rights, pre-eminence, franchises, and liberties, such as they were in the time of Clovis, first Christian king, and even better and more profitable, if they may be found under the above named protection. In case there should be impediment, opposition, or rebellion against the above, by whom and from whatsoever part it may proceed, the said associates shall be held and obliged to employ all their goods and means, even their own persons unto death,

---

* I find it so written.

to punish, chastise, and hunt down those who shall seek to restrain or prevent it, and to give a hand that all the above mentioned things shall be really and actually carried into execution. In case that any of the associates, their subjects, friends, and confederates shall be molested, oppressed, or prosecuted for the matters above named, by whomsoever it may be, the said associates shall be bound to employ their bodies, goods, and means to obtain vengeance upon those who shall have caused the said oppression and molestation, either by the way of justice or by arms, without any exception of persons. If it should happen that any of the associates, after having taken an oath to the above association, retire or depart therefrom, on any pretext whatever, which God forbid, the said persons refractory after consent, shall be injured in body and goods, in every manner which can be devised, as enemies of God, rebels, and disturbers of the public peace, without the said associates being disquieted or pursued on that account in public or in private. The said associates shall all swear prompt obedience and service to the chief who shall be appointed, shall follow and give him counsel, comfort, and aid in the keeping up and preservation of the said association, as well as in the ruin of those who shall oppose it, without favor or exception of persons. And the persons falling off and retiring shall be punished by the authority of the chief, and according to his ordinance, to which the said associates shall submit. All Catholic bodies of towns and villages, shall be informed and summoned secretly by their several Governors to enter into the said association, to duly furnish arms and men for its execution, according to the power and ability of each. That those who will not enter into the said association, shall be reported as its enemies, and shall be pursuable by all sorts of injury and molestation; and the associates shall be forbidden to enter into disputes or quarrels one with the other, without the permission of the chief, according to whose arbitration the disobedient shall be punished, either for the reparation of honor or any other matter. If for the strengthening or for the greater security of the associates, any convention shall be entered into with the provinces of this kingdom, it shall be done in the form above, and on the same conditions, whether the association be proposed to the said towns, or be by them demanded, unless it shall be otherwise decided by the chiefs."

FORM OF OATH.

" I swear, by God the Creator, touching the Evangelists, and upon pain of anathema and eternal damnation, that I have entered into this Holy Catholic Association, according to the form of the treaty which has been just read to me, loyally and sincerely, either to command, to obey, or to serve therein; and I promise upon my life and honor, to remain therein to the last drop of my blood, without opposing or retiring, upon any command, pretext, excuse, or occasion whatsoever."

Such was the frightful constitution of the League of Peronne, and such the oath which confirmed it; a confederation the most dangerous in its principles, the most horrible in its proposed objects, the most criminal in the prescribed means, the most anarchical in its tendency, and the most lamentable in its results, that the world has ever seen; an oath the most unprincipled and lawless that could be propounded to man.

According to the course of proceeding fixed by the bond, the first progress of the association was made in secret. It was long before the chief to whom the document referred, appeared upon the stage as its leader, and perhaps, it was long before he was formally nominated; but all eyes turned towards the Duke of Guise, as the existence of the League was whispered about. Every one remembered the services and death of his father, every one called to mind his own gallant acts against the Protestants, and many still living had been parties to the former confederation established in the heart of his government. It has been asserted by Protestant writers,* that even from the beginning the Jesuits took an active part in forming and directing the League; and it is not improbable that such was the case, for the peculiar cunning and duplicity which characterizes all the acts of that body, soon became apparent in its proceedings, as we shall now go on to shew.

Throughout almost every town of France,

* Aubigné.

through the streets of the capital, in public places, and in private houses, the secret emissaries of the League spread themselves in haste.* It was in vain that the first lawyers in the realm shewed the danger and illegality of such acts; it was in vain that the King exhorted the governors of the provinces to put a stop to them :† the people entered wildly into the association; the nobility and clergy gave it their countenance; and Henry III. saw his authority and character openly attacked by libels and pasquinades issuing from the store-houses of the League. Nor was this all, the new party which was rapidly forming in his dominions, found persons to deny the title of his family to the crown, and to point out the house of Guise as the rightful successors of Charlemagne.‡ This absurdity did some harm to the cause it was intended to advocate; but the King, far from rousing himself to resist vigorously the faction which already menaced the throne with overthrow, and the country with anarchy, gave way to his old animosity towards the Protestants, though too idle and luxurious even to pursue a wrong course of policy with energy. When told that the Archbishop of Rouen had driven the Huguenots out of that town with his crozier, he contented himself with a jest, ex-

* Pierre Mathieu.

† The King's letter to the Duke of Montpensier is preserved in the Memoires de Nevers.

‡ Memoires de la Ligue. Mem. de l'Etoile, in which see note upon the advocate David.

claiming, " Would that we could drive them out of France as easily, even adding the benitier." He suffered the Protestants of Paris to be stoned, and otherwise maltreated, in returning from one of their assemblies, held at the prescribed distance from the court : and a plot was discovered to murder La Noue, in regard to which suspicion attached to the monarch and his mother.

Yielding to the tide which pressed upon him, instead of resisting its current firmly, between the month of August, in which he wrote to Montpensier to suppress by all means the first efforts of the League, and the beginning of December, when the meeting of the States promised by the Edict of Pacification, took place at Blois, Henry had completely changed his views, had determined to suppress the Protestant religion, to break the treaty which he had lately concluded, with the same scandalous disregard of faith and honor which had characterized the proceedings of his predecessors towards the Reformers, and to rely upon the forces of the League which he had condemned, to support him in a new struggle with his Huguenot subjects. When visited by the Duke of Nevers on the second of December, he was found fully prepared to renew the war.* He had written into all the provinces, to encourage that formidable association, he had demanded returns of the troops which each town and district could furnish, and his only remaining hesitation seemed to be in regard to the nomination

* Journal des Etats de Blois, par M. le Duc de Nevers.

of the officers, which the members of the League boldly claimed to themselves, and which the King wished to retain in his own hands.

Some indications of his intentions had made themselves manifest, notwithstanding every effort to conceal them; and the Protestants in general feared to trust themselves in Blois, although the town had been dismantled to satisfy them. They had before their eyes the massacre of St. Bartholomew's day.

The opening of the States, though appointed for the 3rd, was put off till the 6th of the month, in order that the great hall which was in preparation might be completed; and messengers from the King were sent into Guienne to entreat that his cousin of Navarre would be present. Henry of Bourbon, however, was now too wise to visit the court of France; and he accordingly besought the King to excuse him, promising to send deputies, which he subsequently did. But no inducement could persuade him to appear at the States in person; and the Prince de Condé followed the same course, as well as the principal members of the house of Montmorenci.

In the mean while, in the absence of all the leading Protestants, nothing but intrigues took place at Blois, for the purpose of gaining over to the views of the League those deputies who were inclined to maintain peace; and the King, the Queen-mother, the Cardinals of Bourbon and Guise, the Dukes of Nevers

and Montpensier, did not hesitate to have recourse
to every base manœuvre to accomplish their object.
The Duke of Guise himself seems to have played
his game apart; and in the journal of Nevers, we
find him mentioned principally, as giving and receiving dinners, until the twenty-second of December, when he first appears as taking part in the
management of the League of Peronne. On that
day he represented to the King that his government
of Champagne and Brie would not enter into the
association, unless he was present to urge upon the
nobles the necessity thereof; and in order to meet
the King's apprehensions, regarding the chief to be
appointed to command the League, he proposed that
the names of three persons, of which he himself was
to be one, should be laid before Henry by the principal members, for his choice. But the monarch naturally disapproved of a plan which could only result
in the nomination of Guise himself. He doubtless felt
in some degree, the difficulty of the position in which
he had placed himself, by suffering a monster that
threatened the whole state, to grow up under his own
eyes. It was now too late, however, to try to suppress
it; the confidence of the Protestants was gone; the
family of Montmorenci remained alienated from the
court; and a great part of the nobility of the realm
had taken the oath which bound them to the League
for life; so that nothing was left for the King but to
yield to the current, and endeavor to render the
association as little dangerous to himself as possible.

The Monarch's first step was to induce the States to demand the establishment of one sole religion for the whole country, without appearing to suggest or desire such a course himself; and not only were the deputies tampered with, as I have mentioned, but in many cases, confidential messengers were sent off to the provinces, for the purpose of exciting the people to instruct their representatives to require the suppression of the Reformed religion. Great difficulties were encountered however; the bulk of the nobles and clergy were undoubtedly desirous of peace, and the menacing attitude assumed by the King of Navarre, the Prince de Condé, and Marshal Damville, shewed clearly that a breach of the treaty would be followed by an instant appeal to arms. To detach Damville with his relations and adherents from the opposing party, new intrigues were formed, and the King and his council vacillated from day to day, as to what measures were to be adopted with regard to the King of Navarre. Now, it was proposed to send friendly envoys to him to endeavor to pacify him and bring him to the States; now, to proceed against him in arms; now, to march under the pretence of peace, but with forces sufficient to take possession of the strong towns of his government, while he was engaged in negotiating. Levies were made; plans of the campaign were drawn up; Biron was instructed to prepare the artillery; and at length, on the twenty-ninth of December, the King made a solemn declaration in his council, by which he promised to re-establish the Roman Catholic faith as the sole religion in France; boldly asserting that he had signed the treaty of peace merely for the purpose of regaining his brother and expelling the foreign troops from France, and giving notice that he would never enter into any compromise upon the essential point of religion. By this act, we are told, he hoped to detach from the Protestant cause, all those who wavered between the two parties; but many persons clearly perceived, that such a declaration, which admitted the most scandalous breach of faith and forewarned the Reformers that they had no resource but arms, must tend to consolidate and invigorate a party which had already proved itself too strong to be crushed by any force that the crown could bring into the field.*

On the 1st of January, 1577, Henry III. announced publicly, that, on the 12th of December, he had signed and authorized the Holy Catholic League, and recommended it to the States and his people.† By putting himself at the head of the association, he expected to out-manœuvre the Duke of Guise; but in this, as in all other cases, the bold and active politician obtained the advantage of the timid and inactive monarch. The form which the King signed and justified‡ was very different from that to which

* The above particulars are taken from the Journal of the Duke of Nevers, which can be perfectly relied upon.

† L'Etoile.

‡ It is to be found in the first volume of the Memoirs of Nevers, page 114.

a great part of the nobility and people had sworn;
and by authorizing it with his name, Henry only descended from the character and dignity of a king, to
take up the position of a party leader, without
obtaining even the confidence of the faction he
countenanced, or the power over its proceedings
which he sought.

None of these manœuvres were wholly concealed
from Henry of Navarre; and step by step, with the
same wisdom and decision which was henceforth
apparent through his whole career, he took measures
to guard against the consequences of his enemies'
acts as they came to his knowledge.

The means employed by the Catholics to influence
the election of the deputies had not escaped his
notice, and he consequently, as the first counter movement, declared the States illegally constituted, refusing to take part in their proceedings. The
surprise of Pont St. Esprit by the Catholics justified
further steps; and while the States continued sitting
at Blois, the partisans of the King of Navarre and
the Prince de Condé made themselves masters of a
number of places in Guienne and Poitou, complaining more and more loudly, till the revocation of the
King's edict of pacification, the appearance of an
army in the field, the raising of large sums for carrying on the war, and the movement of troops against
the confederates, afforded sufficient justification
for an open resumption of hostilities, which commenced with a declaration on the part of the Prince

de Condé as Lieutenant of the King of Navarre.* In this document he openly accused the deputies assembled at Blois, of being suborned and corrupted by the enemies of France; he skilfully mixed the cause of the family of Montmorenci and other Roman Catholic adherents with that of the Protestants; he insinuated that the League was set on foot by foreigners, for the purpose of effecting divisions and civil wars in the kingdom; he alluded to the sums levied in France to the heavy oppression of the people, at the suggestion of Italians; and he pledged himself not to lay down his arms, till he had restored the kingdom to its ancient splendor and dignity, given freedom to the States-General, and re-established the validity of those edicts which had been promulgated for the alleviation of the evils under which the nation had so long suffered.

A counter-league was also negotiated between the insurgents, the Queen of England, the Kings of Denmark and Sweden, and the Protestant Princes of Germany; but little assistance was derived by the French Protestants from cold and distant allies. Casimir, son of the Elector Palatine, indeed, equally deceived and injured with the confederates, by the faithless conduct of the King of France, did not put the slightest restraint upon the expression of his indignation; and his envoy boldly reproached Henry III., in the presence of his council, with the fraud he had committed, saying, that he would assu-

* Pierre Matthieu.

redly blush if he were to hear detailed all the promises he had made and broken.*

Towards the close of the States, those parties who
had not actually bound themselves to the extreme
measures of the League, began to take alarm at its
proceedings.   The Parisians, very willing to crush
the Protestants, but unwilling to bear their share in
the expenses of a war, repudiated the doctrines laid
down by the deputy Versoris, who had spoken for
the Tiers Etat, and urged the necessity of employing gentler means to reclaim the heretics.† Several
Catholic towns refused to accept the League, and
drove out, ignominiously, those who strove to force it
upon them.   Montpensier shewed himself cold in
pursuing the measures of the court; and the States
themselves insisted upon sending deputies to the
King of Navarre and the Prince de Condé, in order
to reconcile them to the sacrifice of that freedom of
conscience which had been guaranteed by the last
edict of pacification.

Henry of Navarre, when the deputation arrived,
was in arms before Marmande; but he returned to
Agen to receive it, and displayed his usual courtesy
and kindness. He protested against the constitution
of the States, declared that though he loved peace,
he would never purchase it at the expense of his
honor; and adding, that he prayed God daily, if he
was in the right way to keep him therein, but if
in the wrong to shew him his error, he dismissed
the deputies without suffering himself to be shaken

* Journal du Duc de Nevers.   † l'Etoile.

H 2

in his purpose by all the eloquence of the Archbishop of Vienne.

From the Prince de Condé, the deputies sent to him, headed by the Bishop of Autun, met with a colder and sterner reception. He would not even receive the letters addressed to him by the States, declaring that he did not recognize the assembly at Blois as anything but a mass of corruption.* Three times the bishop tendered his despatches, and was three times refused in the same decided manner. Nor were the envoys sent to Damville more successful, although that officer had been carrying on for some time secret negotiations with the court, with a view to his own personal advantage.†

The court was disquieted by the failure of these efforts, and by the difference of opinion which existed in the States and in the council. Messenger after messenger was sent off to the King of Navarre; he was visited by Montpensier, Biron, and Villeroy; while every exertion was used to detach Damville from the Huguenot party, by offers of advancement and emolument which the Protestants could not equal. With him the negotiations were ultimately successful: but with the King of Navarre they remained unfruitful; that Prince always making the same answer, moderate yet firm, and by his gentleness, frankness, and determination, still gaining so much upon the envoys of the King, that Montpensier, the most furious enemy of the Reformers, became the strongest advocate for peace, and Biron and Villeroy,

* Aubigné.

† Nevers. Mezeray insinuates that the secretaries of Damville had been bribed to influence him.

though they neglected not the cause in which they
were employed, yielded insensibly to his views.

The Protestants, however, were shaken by dissensions in their councils and reverses in the field,
during the rest of the year 1577, when a new treaty
of peace was concluded; and I shall now turn to
the military events of that period, premising that
some of the proceedings I am about to mention
took place during the session of the States of
Blois, which continued sitting till the end of March.
The forces of the court were divided into three or
four different corps; but the two principal bodies
were placed under the orders of the Duke of Anjou
and the young Duke of Mayenne, brother of the
Duke of Guise. The operations of the latter were
directed against the Protestant party commanded by
Condé in Poitou and Sainctonge; those of the former, against the towns held by the confederation on
the Loire and Allier. Villars, in Guienne, made
head against the King of Navarre with a small force;
and Damville, who had not only abandoned, but
turned against his late allies, was opposed in Languedoc by his brother Montmorenci Thoré and the
youthful Chatillon, supported by a very considerable force.

The army of the Duke of Anjou, under whom
served the Duke of Guise and the well known
La Chatre, marched rapidly upon La Charité, the
governor and the inhabitants of which place would
not believe that a Prince, who had so lately pledged
himself to protect the Protestants, was advancing
towards them with hostile intentions, till the artillery,

with which his force was amply provided, were thundering against the walls. No preparation had been made for resistance ; the garrison was small and ill provided ; three practicable breaches were soon effected ; and Deslandes,* who commanded in the place, was glad to obtain an honorable capitulation. The Duke of Guise displayed his high and chivalrous spirit in preventing the infringement of the terms and the massacre of the garrison, for which the Italian soldiery were fully prepared and the Duke of Anjou not unwilling.† Issoire was afterwards taken by storm, and the cruelties which usually disgrace armies under such circumstances were perpetrated on the inhabitants. The Duke of Guise then left the army ; and the Duke of Anjou finished his campaign by committing frightful ravages in the neighbouring country, and slaughtering the unresisting peasantry.

While these events occurred in the central districts, the Duke of Mayenne displayed all those military talents at Sainctonge, which afterwards distinguished him as the General of the League. It is true his army was superior in equipment to any in the service of the court, comprised the best and most experienced soldiers, and was far more numerous than that of Condé, in which nothing but divisions and quarrels existed, while money and arms were scarce, and no artillery was to be found.

At first, the Duke shewed all the rigor which had rendered the last civil wars so destructive ; and

* I find this officer named elsewhere Jacques de Morogues.
† Aubigné.

after capturing Bouteville and Tonnay Charente, he turned the prisoners over to the executioner. The fear of reprisals, however, induced some of his officers to remonstrate; and a more humane course was subsequently pursued. Rochefort was then taken; and advancing rapidly, without suffering himself to be tempted by the inclination of his officers to attack St. Jean d'Angeli, Mayenne hastened on to Marans, whence he could menace either Rochelle or Brouage. That small place was abandoned to his troops; and new dissensions broke out amongst the Rochellois in consequence. A skirmish, in which the forces of the Prince de Condé had some advantage, checked in a degree the progress of the Roman Catholic army; but Mayenne's farther efforts were still more impeded by want of assistance from the court, in which no money could be found to carry on this unjust and ill-considered war.

It was determined, at length, in the council of the King, to recall the army of the Duke of Anjou, to despatch immediately a strong reinforcement to Mayenne, and to support this first succor, by the whole force from Issoire, with the King's brother himself at its head. The general belief in both armies, seems to have been, that this course was devised in order to cause divisions between the Duke of Anjou and the family of Guise, to whom he had become closely attached since the commencement of the campaign on the Loire and Allier, and to mortify Mayenne, by giving him a superior, at the same moment that he received sufficient forces to secure the full success of his operations. But

Mayenne adroitly parried the blow, hastened on the
siege of Brouage, as soon as the first reinforcements
arrived, carried forward his works with skill and
determination, and granted the garrison an honorable capitulation, at the very moment that the
Duke of Anjou was about to supersede him in
command.

I must now turn to events which were being
enacted on a different stage, and give more in detail
the proceedings of Henry of Navarre, who, with a
very small force, was keeping the field in Guienne,
alternately striking some blows at the enemy, and
carrying on negotiations for a peace. In both
courses he was more impeded by the dissensions
which existed in his army, than by the smallness of
his force; for, accompanied as he was by a number
of distinguished Roman Catholics, while the great
body of his adherents were of a different religion,
he was often obliged to undertake operations, and
command enterprises, in which the forces employed
were led by persons hating each other with all the
virulence of religious animosity, and by no means
disposed to obey the orders of their general. After
having taken La Reole, he saw a small body of his
troops repulsed with terrible loss, in an attempt to
surprise the town of St. Macary. Villefranche in Perigord, however, was captured by John Beaumanoir
de Lavardin, a Catholic officer of high merit, who
had attached himself to Henry Quatre; but the
same gentleman having undertaken the siege of
Marmande, a strong town on the right bank of the
Garonne, contrary to the opinion of La Noue, and

to the wishes of the King,* Henry felt himself called upon to support him, and not having sufficient forces to invest the place completely, was in danger of being repulsed with disgrace.

In the course of this siege an incident occurred, which displayed in a striking manner, the daring and chivalrous character that always distinguished the monarch through life.   Having thrown forward a small party of arquebusiers to take possession of a hollow way, a large body of the enemy unexpectedly poured upon them, and cut them off from the army. They defended themselves gallantly however ; till Henry seeing their danger, hurried down in person, half armed, to their deliverance.   He did not abandon the combat till night-fall, and not only saved his detachment, but enabled them to effect the object for which they had been sent. The siege itself proved hopeless, and the King was upon the point of retiring, when the arrival of envoys sent from Blois to open negotiations, and the conclusion of a truce for that purpose, saved the honor of his arms.

One of his numerous gallantries then carried Henry to Bearn, where he spent the time of the suspension of arms, in the society of his sister, and of Mademoiselle de Tignonville, the daughter of the Princess's governess, for whom he had conceived a temporary passion ; but before the truce had expired, he was again in the field to reduce the small

* Sully marks this fact distinctly, though Aubigné blames Henry for the enterprise.

town of Eauze,* which had revolted against his
authority.   For this purpose, he gave a rendezvous
to a part of his forces, ordering his principal
attendants to conceal their arms, under the common
habiliments of the chase, and having met them at
the place appointed, he advanced with fifteen or
sixteen gentlemen, a little before the head of the
troop, in order to gain possession of the gate by
surprise.   He was suffered to enter unopposed, but
the moment he had passed with three or four of his
immediate followers, the portcullis fell, the tocsin
was rung, and he found himself attacked by a body
of fifty men, while other parties were hurrying up
from different quarters of the town.   The cry of.
" Fire at the white plume and the scarlet tunic, for
that is the King of Navarre," was immediately heard
amongst the assailants; but Henry did not lose his
presence of mind; and, ordering his followers not to
discharge their pistols till each man was sure of his
aim, he advanced against the mutineers, and dispersed
the first party without difficulty.   The same was the
case with several other bodies which came running
up; but the numbers at length increased so greatly,
that the King was driven back under a gateway.   He
there, however, presented a firm face to the enemy,
while one of his companions was ordered to get into
the belfry, and make signs to the forces without to
break open the gate. The drawbridge, fortunately,
had not been raised, and his orders were promptly

* This place is called Euse, by Henry in his letters, and is
situated in the department of Gers, within the actual territory
of the King of Navarre.

obeyed, while the well-disposed part of the inhabitants, recovered from the state of dread in which they
had been held by the mutineers, hastened to attack
the King's assailants in the rear. The gate was soon
forced and the town filled with Henry's soldiers, who
were about to exercise summary vengeance upon the
insurgents; but they were stopped by order of the
King, who contented himself with directing four of
the ringleaders to be hung, an act of severity which
appeared too lenient in the eyes of his enraged
followers.*

From this town, Henry hurried forward to
Mirande, in the hope of delivering one of his officers
named St. Cricq, who, after having obtained possession of it by stratagem, found himself unable to
maintain his ground against the opposite party in
the place, and was forced into a large donjon
tower, where he continued to hold out, refusing all
capitulation. The news of his situation reached
the King of Navarre at Eauze; but, ere Henry
with the utmost diligence could reach Mirande, the

* The author of the life of De Mornay, gives a somewhat different account, and states that De Mornay was present; but I have
preferred the statements of Sully, as those of an eye-witness,
having many doubts as to De Mornay having been with the King
at this time. Many authors place the event in 1576, but from
the manuscript accounts of Henry's household I do not find that
he was in the neighbourhood of Eauze during the latter part of
that year, while on the contrary those accounts shew that he was at
Nogarot or Aire, within a few miles of that place, from the 8th
to the 13th April, 1577; and therefore it is probable that Sully
placed the attack on Eauze rightly, after the siege of Marmande
and the truce.

donjon had been fired by the assailants; and St. Cricq and his companions were burnt therein.

The garrison of the town finding themselves stronger than the little army which the Protestant monarch had brought against them, determined to lay a snare for him; and as soon as his lances were seen approaching, they began to sound their trumpets and beat their drums in the neighbourhood of the spot where the gallant St. Cricq had perished. Henry was deceived; and supposing that the sounds he heard were intended to testify the joy of his own officer at the sight of his forces, he was marching straight towards the town, when a Protestant soldier escaping over the walls, brought him intelligence of the enemy's stratagem. He had advanced too far for his retreat to be effected in safety; but no other resource was left; and he consequently retired, attacked by the garrison in his retrograde movement, and suffering some loss in the skirmish which ensued.

A few days after, while the King of Navarre was still at Jegun, to which place he had retreated from Mirande, the army of the court under Villars, who had become Admiral on the death of Coligni, presented itself to offer battle. The superiority of that general's force, however, prevented Henry from risking an engagement; and the strong ground occupied by the young King deterred the enemy from attempting to force his position. Thus, after several challenges, given by gentlemen on either part to their adversaries, to strike a blow for the honor of their

ladies, and several combats with the lance, in presence of the two armies, Villars and Henry withdrew
their forces, and pursued those small and unfruitful
enterprises for which Aubigné has justly condemned
the policy of his master, as tending to teach his
enemies the art of war without producing any advantage to himself.

The partisan warfare now carried on, though very
destructive to both parties, would afford little interest to the reader were I to enter into the details.
Two incidents, however, are worthy of mention, as
illustrative of the military customs of the time, and
the character of some of the persons engaged. The
Viscount de Montclar, having been thrown forward
before the army of Henry, which was moving towards Bergerac, for the purpose of uniting with the
forces of the Prince de Condé, in order to raise the
siege of Brouage, overtook the Baron de Bonrepos
on his march to join Villars, who was manœuvring
upon the left of the King of Navarre. Bonrepos,
finding himself inferior in numbers, took post
upon a bridge; and there he defended the passage
with great gallantry against all the efforts of Montclar's arquebusiers. At length the Viscount put
himself at the head of a small body of cavalry and
charged the enemy, who, however, held their ground,
till unable, on account of the narrow space, to bring
into action any of his men but the few immediately
in front, Montclar caused those who were behind to
send forward their pistols from hand to hand, so as
to enable him to keep up an uninterrupted fire upon

his adversaries, who were thus forced to give way
and fly at full speed.

Nearly at the time that the above skirmish occurred, a party consisting of twenty Catholic light
horse from Bayonne, and a small body of irregular
horse and foot levied at that city and at Dax
on the Adour, were on their march, guarding
three young ladies who had been condemned to
death by the fanatical parliament of Bordeaux,
where their immediate execution was to take
place. This force, however, was encountered in a
wide plain covered with broken woods and heath,
by the Captain of Castel-jaloux and a body of Protestant horse and arquebusiers. The Catholics,
finding that they could not avoid the combat, placed
their infantry in a small wood, to gall the Huguenots in their advance, while the cavalry drew up in
line to meet the shock of the men-at-arms.

The citizens, however, could not resist the charge
of the veteran soldiers of the Protestant party; and
thrown instantly into confusion, they cast down their
arms and demanded quarter. The Captain of
Castel-jaloux, however, remembering that on the
fatal occasion of the massacre of St. Bartholomew's
day, the citizens of Dax had butchered the Protestants without mercy, caused all the prisoners who
belonged to that town to be separated from the
rest, and put them to the sword to a man. He
then restored their arms and horses to the people
of Bayonne, gave them their liberty, in memory of
the refusal of their city to share in the butchery of

1572, and bade them return home and tell their companions the different treatment he shewed to soldiers and executioners.

The three poor girls who were on the way to death, were brought in triumph to Castillon, where their relations resided; and eight days after, a trumpet from Bayonne arrived at Castel-jaloux, bringing an embroidered scarf and handkerchief to each of the soldiers who had fought on the Protestant side.

I cannot conclude my account of this event, without adding an anecdote which is appended to it by Aubigné. Some time before the peace was concluded, he tells us, Henry of Navarre, moved by his light-hearted humor, resolved to go into Bayonne with only six companions, to be present at a fête given in the town. The whole company, well aware of his quality, surrounded the table at which he was placed, with dances, music, and presents, led by La Hillieres the governor; and having discovered that the Captain of Castel-jaloux was one of the seven Protestant guests, they loaded him with thanks and applause for his courtesy.

The news from Rochelle and Brouage, and the danger of the Protestants of Languedoc and Provence, shewed Henry, before the middle of the year 1577, the necessity of striking some decisive blow to check the progress of the royal arms. He determined then to cross the Garonne at once with all the forces he could collect; and at the same time he sent messengers into Quercy and the Limousin, requiring the Huguenot leaders in those districts to raise all the troops that could by any means be induced to follow them, and to march for Bergerac without loss of time. The Prince de Condé, the Duke of Rohan, Turenne, and La Rochefoucault, were also summoned to the rendezvous; but disunion, jealousy, and open hatred, had spread widely amongst the Protestant leaders. Violent disputes took place between Henry and Condé at Pons. The Prince, attributing the misunderstanding between himself and his cousin to the Viscount de Turenne, sought to draw the latter into a duel; and the designs of the King of Navarre were thus frustrated by the intrigues and dissensions of his party, till Brouage fell before the arms of Mayenne.

The conduct of Henry of Bourbon, during the campaign of 1577, has been severely blamed by writers of the Protestant party, and not without some show of reason; but the difficulties which surrounded him have not had the weight attached to them which they deserve. It would appear that he was never able to bring into the field more than five thousand men, and seldom even that number, a force considerably less than that which Villars the Admiral had at his command in Guienne. A considerable body of those who served under the young monarch's banner were Roman Catholics, of whom the Protestants were so jealous, that it was scarcely possible to induce the two parties to act together. Many strong towns of Guienne were in the hands of the League; and Villars, though frustrated in almost all his enterprises by the military skill of his opponent, lay watching his proceedings, ready to take advantage of any false step that Henry might commit. The views of the Prince de Condé, the license that he tolerated in his army, and the dissensions which had arisen between him and the King of Navarre, gave but little prospect of their being able to effect any great object, if their forces were united; and it was absolutely necessary, too, that the latter should maintain a communication with the Protestants of Languedoc and Provence, which the march of his small force into Sainctonge, at an earlier period of the year must have interrupted, as such a movement would have left the whole country behind him open to the operations of the Admiral. It must also be remembered, that the army of Mayenne was composed of the best disciplined troops in France; that it had been reinforced by a strong body of Swiss; that it was well provided with artillery; and that it was already greatly superior in number to any that the two Princes could bring against it. All these considerations, with others, probably, of which we are not aware, influenced the conduct of Henry of Navarre, and induced him to remain on the defensive in Guienne during the early part of 1577, gaining various small advantages over the enemy, in the neighbourhood of his own dominions, and each day assuming a more formidable aspect while he continued to negotiate for peace, rather than join his forces to those of Condé, and attempt a great effort against a superior army, in which he could not anticipate success.

Whatever might be his motives, the result was much more favorable to the Protestant party than was generally expected; and Henry at length obtained a treaty of peace, which the smallness of the confederate forces, the defection of Damville, and the advantages gained by the Dukes of Anjou and Mayenne almost placed beyond hope. In the month of July, the King of France advanced to Poitiers, while Biron, Villeroy, and the Duke of Montpensier renewed at Bergerac the negotiations for peace, which had already been so frequently commenced and broken off. The fall of Brouage, the success of the royal fleet against the armament of Rochelle, the desertion of many of the Huguenot soldiers, and a great inferiority in cavalry, caused the Prince de Condé to long for peace even more eagerly than Henry of Navarre. Leaving La Rochelle with three hundred horse, he hastened toward Pons, where he was joined by the Count of Rochefoucault with a small reinforcement; but being pursued by the whole cavalry of the Duke of Mayenne's army, and threatened with siege in a place of no great strength, he left it to be defended by the ordinary garrison, and hastened towards Bergerac, at which place the King of Navarre had already arrived. The terms of pacification were now nearly agreed upon between Henry of Bourbon and Montpensier; but, nevertheless, Henry shewed as great a degree of firmness under the disadvantageous circumstances in which the Protestants were placed, as he had previously displayed of moderation while the result

of the struggle was unknown.   He suffered not the
fall of Brouage, the inactivity of the Rochellois, or
the disunion of the Protestant party to dismay him.
But calculating upon the weakness of the French
Government, upon the jealousies that existed at the
court of France, and upon the total want of money in
the enemy's treasury to carry on the war, he adhered
to all his reasonable demands, making a forward
movement towards Montguyon, as an indication of
his resolution to succor Rochelle at any risk, should
it be attacked.

At length, on the sixteenth of September, a
general truce was proclaimed ; and, on the twenty-
eighth of the same month, the treaty of peace was
concluded, which was confirmed by a royal decree,
known as the Edict of Poitiers.   Both parties disbanded their forces immediately after the signature
of the truce ; and so rejoiced was Condé at the
news of peace, that he caused the treaty, which
reached him at night, to be read by torchlight in
the streets.

La Noue instantly set out for Languedoc, to carry
the intelligence to the belligerents in that province.
On his arrival he found the Protestant army under
Chatillon and Montmorenci Thoré, drawn up in
battle array against the forces of Damville, the
brother of the latter, under the walls of Montpellier;
that place having been succored during the preceding day by a gallant effort of Chatillon, who shewed
himself truly worthy of the great name he bore.
La Noue galloped forward into the space between

the two armies, at the risk of being shot; and the news which he brought soon put a stop to hostilities on both parts.

Thus ended the short war of 1577, by a treaty, which, though it curtailed several of the immunities granted to the Protestant party by the convention known as the Peace of Monsieur, yet gave more important securities for the maintenance of tranquillity than had ever yet been granted; but the weakness of the French monarch, as well as his treachery, the contempt in which he was held by both parties, as well as his irrepressible animosity towards the Protestants, rendered it unstable and doubtful even from the beginning. Henry III. boasted that the peace was his; and undoubtedly no one desired it more ardently than he did; for ere the war had continued many weeks, he felt bitterly the gross error he had committed in giving it his sanction at first. The open direction of the affairs of the League assumed by the Duke of Guise, after the death of La Tremouille, soon shewed the effeminate King of France, the danger of intrusting military power to the leaders of that faction; yet when he looked round his camp, he beheld nothing on every side but generals and soldiers imbued with the same spirit, subject to the same obligations, bound by the same vows; and he could not but feel that though the Protestant party might be a shoal in the way of the vessel of the state, it was much less to be dreaded than the whirlpool of the League. The total derangement of the finances of the realm; the impossibility of paying the debt due to the leaders of the German troops, who had been called into France by the Duke of Anjou, and who threatened daily to return and take part with the insurgents ;* the want of money to discharge the arrears due even to the Swiss guard, who had mutinied at Blois during the session of the States,† and the King's own indolence and love of pleasure, all made him thirst for peace and hurry on the conclusion of the treaty.

The principal points in which the edict of Poitiers and the peace of Bergerac differed from the treaty of 1576, were, the limitation of the mixed courts for trying the causes of Protestants and Roman Catholics to four of the Parliaments of the realm ;‡ the diminution of the number of Protestant counsellors in those courts ; and the exclusion of the public exercise of the Protestant religion from a circle of ten leagues round Paris.§ In compensation, however, eight towns were given as places of security for six years ; and these were especially placed in the hands of the Reformers,‖ whereas the places previously granted had been assigned to the confederate Protestants and Roman Catholics indifferently.

It has been remarked by Anquetil and others, that in this edict Henry III. speaks of the mas-

---

* A letter from the Chancellor Birague to the Duke of Montpensier, shews the terrible strait to which the court was reduced, and that the crown jewels had been pledged to Casimir for the payment of the debt. See Vie de Montpensier.

† Journal de Nevers.   ‡ Articles 21, 22, 23.

§ Article 10   ‖ Article 59.

sacres that commenced on St. Bartholomew's day, as
" the disorders and excesses of the 24th August,
and the following days, which happened to our great
regret and sorrow," implying that the King had now
for the first time used those terms, whereas, in the
edict of May 1576, he still more forcibly expresses
the same falsehood. But in the Edict of Poitiers he
did use language different from any that he had
ever employed before, towards those who might be
disposed to infringe its provisions, by which he intended undoubtedly to aim a blow at the League.
In the ratification of former treaties he had merely
commanded the insurgents to desist from levying
men, or committing any act contrary to the articles
agreed upon; but in the decree at present under consideration, he says, " And all leagues, associations,
and brotherhoods, formed or to be formed, upon any
pretext whatever, to the prejudice of this edict, shall
be broken and annulled, as we do break and annul
them, forbidding expressly all our subjects henceforth to make any subscriptions or levies of money,
fortifications, enrolments of men, meetings or assemblies without our permission, other than are authorized by this our present edict."

A number of secret articles were added to the
treaty for the security of the Protestants, amongst
which was one tending to guard the priests and
monks, who had abjured their vows, against any
persecution on that account, and insuring to their
children the succession of their personal property.

Having asserted that this act, so well calculated

to give tranquillity to France, was deprived of its natural result, in a great measure, by the contempt in which both parties held the King himself, it may be necessary to account for the scorn with which he was regarded, by giving some of the anecdotes of the time respecting his general conduct and demeanor. While the court was at Blois, during the session of the States, Henry was accustomed to shew himself to his court, in the pageants and spectacles of the day, dressed like a woman, with his bosom open, and displaying round his throat a necklace of pearls. In the course of the month of May, after the capture of La Charité, while his whole realm was convulsed with civil war, and his treasury completely empty, he gave a fête to his brother at Plessis les Tours, where the men were waited upon by the ladies of the court dressed in male attire, " half naked," says the historian ; " with their hair parted like a bride's." The entertainment was returned by the Queen-mother, in a grand festival at Chenonçeau, where she spent a hundred thousand francs, which she extracted from the richer members of the court.

The most horrible excesses also were not only tolerated by the King, but according to general suspicion were commanded by him. While at Poitiers, waiting for the final arrangement of the treaty of peace, René de Villequier, one of the most beloved of the King's minions, already infamous for the murder of Ligneroles, stabbed his wife and one of her maids, while the unfortunate lady was dressing, in

the royal palace, and at no great distance from the
monarch's apartment. Villequier was, however, pardoned without trial for this double murder; neither
reproach nor degradation followed; he retained all
his offices and the favor of Henry; and the general
opinion of the people of France remained that the
husband had assassinated the wife by order of his
sovereign, because she refused to prostitute herself
to the will of a vicious King.*

The state of society in which such things could
exist, is too dark and fearful to dwell upon; but we
must add some of the words used by one of the historians who records these facts, in speaking of the
court of Henry III. "Corruption," he says, "was
such in these times, that none but fools, buffoons,
courtezans, and minions possessed any credit with
the King."† But the further details of the vices
and crimes of that court, present facts too horrible
and disgusting to be admitted here; and I shall
only add, that murder was at this time but seldom
punished, except in those who had no influence at
court; and that, on more than one occasion, we find
the monarch himself, acting as mediator between an
assassin and the relations of his victim, in order, not
alone to shield him from the arm of the law, which
could always be done by the King's own authority,
but to guard him from vengeance, to which recourse
was generally had in the impotence of justice.‡

---

* De Thou. L'Etoile.   † L'Etoile.

‡ Such was the case when St. Sulpice was murdered at Blois
in December, 1576. See Journal du Duc de Nevers.

BOOK VI.

THE interval of peace which succeeded the short war of 1577, offers several incidents connected with the life of Henri Quatre, which are worthy of detail. That Prince, we have every reason to believe, entertained but little sincere regard for his wife, whose conduct was as licentious as his own ; yet we find, that even while in arms against her brother, he demanded loudly that she should be sent to join. him. Marguerite was by no means inclined to abandon the pleasures of Paris and the freedom which her separation from her husband allowed, to dwell with a Prince whom she had never loved, in the remote court of Bearn. As the negotiations for peace advanced, however, and she saw the probability of her mother being soon obliged to yield to his applications, she affected an illness which required the waters of Spa as its remedy, and set out in the end of July or the beginning of August for the baths.

She was met at Namur by Don Juan of Austria, who took advantage of a visit which she made in his company to the citadel, to render himself master of the town ; and there is reason to suppose that she entered into negotiations with the Spanish Prince, for the purpose of keeping up the civil war in France, lest she should be deprived of the fair pretext it afforded for remaining separate from her husband.

The treaty of Bergerac, however, put an end to her schemes; and the approach of winter drove her back to Paris, where she entered into all the intrigues of the court, taking part with her brother the Duke of Anjou in opposition to the King, towards whom that Prince's enmity had been revived in full force, in consequence of the insolence of the weak monarch's minions, and their incessant quarrels with Bussy and his other favorites.

It is not improbable that the open contempt which Marguerite shewed for the wishes of Henry III.,* and the part she now took in the second escape of the Duke of Anjou from the Louvre, induced the King and the Queen-mother to resolve upon acceding to the demand of Henry of Navarre, for the restitution of his wife. Accordingly, after an unsuccessful journey made by Catherine de Medicis to Angers, for the purpose of bringing back her youngest son to the court, she set out, in the autumn of 1578, upon a tour through the southern provinces of France, accompanied by the unwilling Queen of Navarre. The apparent object of Catherine was to place the wife once more in the arms of her husband; but many other motives actuated her in quitting, for the long period which her progress occupied, the court of Henry III.

* To avoid being present at the marriage of St. Luc, which was celebrated with the greatest splendor by order of the King, she accompanied the Duke of Anjou on a party of pleasure to Vincennes.

The treaty of Bergerac was no where exactly executed, and instead of union, tranquillity, and order being restored, the southern parts of France were almost in a state of anarchy, while daily proceedings in opposition to the edict of Poitiers, were committed by the Roman Catholic governors of towns and provinces, which threatened to re-plunge the kingdom in the horrors of civil war. It would be endless to dwell upon all the acts of aggression and retaliation which are recorded by the historians of the time; but it is necessary to notice the fact that but a few months after the proclamation of peace, the King's officers openly infringed it in many instances; and it is the more necessary to notice this circumstance, as the Roman Catholic writers* have, in general, omitted all mention of the violation of the treaty before the Protestants resumed hostilities.

In regard to one of these acts of aggression, how-ever, I must enter into some detail, as it was the first open infraction of peace by a person in autho-

* Especially Anquetil. We find numerous letters from Henry IV. at this time, complaining bitterly of the conduct of the opposite party, and appealing to all his own acts in proof of his strict adherence to the treaty. From two of these, one to M. Forget, and one to Damville, where he had no motive for concealing the truth, it appears that the pension stipulated, was never paid to him, that an impost on a blue dye which had been granted him, was diverted to other purposes, and that the Catholics had surprised St. Anastase, attacked Briateste, undertaken enterprises against Perigueux, La Reole and Mas de Verdun, besides murdering the Baron de Fougères and playing at football with his head in the streets of Lodeve.

rity that I find mentioned. As Lieutenant of the King in Guienne, Henry of Navarre had hitherto held his court in the town of Agen, where he was much loved and respected by the inhabitants. He was surrounded, however, by a body of gay and light-hearted young noblemen, over whom he found it difficult to exercise any control: it is probable also, that the censure implied by the good Bishop of Rodez, is well founded, and that a youthful and inexperienced Prince did not do all that he might have done, to restrain them from follies and excesses. These gentlemen one evening, at a ball given in Agen, thought fit to blow out the lights, and a scene of some scandal ensued. The consequence was fatal to the popularity of the King of Navarre in the town, and the inhabitants took the earliest opportunity of calling Biron within their walls, who first made himself master of Villeneuve, and then seized upon Agen.*

It was shortly after this event,† that Catherine de Medicis arrived at Bordeaux, and thence journeyed forward with Marguerite to Nerac, on the road to which place the King of Navarre met the royal party, at the head of five hundred gentlemen. The two Queens were each accompanied by a train of beautiful, but licentious girls,

* Perefix. Numerous armed bands of Papists and Protestants wandered through the country long after peace was proclaimed; and their enterprises had, more than once, called the King of Navarre into the field to repress them with an equal hand: but Biron was a royal officer, and acted undoubtedly under orders from the court of France.　　† Aubigné.

those of Catherine long inured to serve their politic mistress by every sort of intrigue, and those of Marguerite equally skilful and equally disposed to unhesitating docility. The train of Catherine had acquired the name of the flying squadron of the Queen, and she had taken care to bring with her the two ladies whose attractions had been previously employed with success against the young King of Navarre. Marguerite, completely devoted to her brother, the Duke of Anjou, was prepared to turn the arms which her mother used in negotiating with the Huguenots, against Catherine herself; and though perhaps she might not believe it possible, nor find it agreeable to exercise her own charms, for the purpose of bending her husband to her purposes, she was well inclined to leave that task to others, while she employed her powers upon the confidential friends and advisers of the Queen-mother.

Henry of Navarre met Catherine with every expression of respect, and received his fair wife with the utmost kindness, which was certainly not diminished when he found that, far from seeking to promote the designs of the court of France in opposition to his interests, she was perfectly ready to join her efforts to his in support of the Protestant claims. Thus, in the midst of amusements, mirth, gallantry, and intrigue, commenced a series of negotiations, which though from time to time interrupted by hostile efforts for the attainment of particular advantages, ended in producing a new

treaty of twenty-seven clauses,* explanatory of the
edict of Poitiers, but far more favorable to the Huguenots. By these articles it was agreed that the Protestants should enjoy the privilege of building con-
venticles in the places where their religion was tolerated, and of raising money for the support of their
ministers, while the number of places of security
granted to them was extended to fourteen.

In the course of these negotiations, one or two
curious incidents occurred, which may serve to
shew the manners and spirit of the times. The
Queen-mother, politic and unscrupulous as she was,
saw herself completely foiled and mastered by the
firm prudence of the King of Navarre, aided by the
talents and skill of her daughter. Henry called to
his conferences with Catherine, a body of deputies
from the Protestants of France ;† and, it would appear, that all his exhortations would not have
prevailed in maintaining a steady resistance against
the arts of the Queen-mother, and the repugnance
of many of the Huguenots to a renewal of the
war, had he not received assistance from a quarter
where he least expected to find it. Catherine had
brought with her Monsieur de Pibrac, a man
celebrated in his own times for a sort of eloquence
which seems turgid and pedantic in our eyes, but
was then considered most persuasive ; and the
whole fire of his oratory was employed, in conjunc-
tion with the blandishments of the Queen's ladies, to

---

* Signed at Nerac, 28th February 1579.   † Aubigné.

work upon the Huguenot deputies, in order to mitigate their demands. But while Marguerite engaged
her maids to captivate the other counsellors of her
mother, she applied her own powers to charm and
dazzle Pibrac himself ; and so skilfully did she
conduct her proceedings, that he became a mere tool
in her hands.*   A few plain straightforward words,
too, from one of the Protestant deputies, named La
Meausse, completely silenced his laborious eloquence ; and though Catherine herself endeavored
in private to bring the latter over to her views, his
rude good sense set her artifices at defiance.

The court of France was accompanied, in its
journey to Nerac, by the Cardinal of Bourbon, uncle
of Henry of Navarre, a good, weak, bigoted Prince,
whom the party of the League already looked
to, as the Catholic successor to the throne, in
case of the death of Henry III. and the Duke of
Anjou without posterity. Although the right of
the King of Navarre under such circumstances, was
clear and undeniable, the Queen-mother did not
scruple to point out to her son-in-law the probability
of an attempt being made to place his uncle on the
throne ;† and intimations of a similar kind reached
him also from various quarters. The Cardinal
himself thought fit to remonstrate with his nephew
on his attachment to the doctrines of Calvin ;
but Henry, who was famous for the readiness
of his repartee, replied, laughing, "They tell me,
my uncle, that some people wish to make you King.

* Perefix.   † Aubigné, liv. iv. chap. 3.

Bid them make you Pope. It would suit you much better, and then you would be greater than all the kings together."*

Jest and intrigue, negotiation and stratagem, peace in the hall, and combats in the field, formed the changing scene at the court while residing in Nerac, Auch, and Lisle Jourdain; and the manner in which all these several pursuits were mingled together, is remarkably evinced by the capture of la Reole, one of the towns of security given to the Huguenots. As a reward for a long life of service and attachment to the Protestant cause, the government of that place had been bestowed upon an old officer, named Ussac. He was advanced in years, enfeebled by wounds, and dreadfully disfigured by injuries in the face and head; he was esteemed as wise, calm, and prudent, as he was brave and stern; but, nevertheless, one of the ladies of the Queen-mother contrived to inspire him with a violent passion, which so shook his judgment, that he assumed all the airs of a young lover, and was not without hope of proving a successful suitor. The lady, afterwards Countess of Chateau-Villain, only laughed at his tenderness; and Henry of Navarre had the imprudence to join in the mockery of the court, not knowing that the most irritable of all passions is an old man's love. The unhappy Ussac was filled with rage and indignation; and, forgetting all the principles of honor which had been his boast through life, he quitted the Protestant religion, and called the Count de

* L'Etoile.

Duras to take possession of la Reole.*   The news
of this act of treachery reached Henry of Navarre
while dancing in a ball given by the court at Auch ;
and without further consideration, he whispered to
the Viscount de Turenne, Sully, and one or two
others, to escape unperceived from the room, gather
together what men they could, and join him at a
rendezvous in the country. Care was taken to
prevent their absence from being noticed ; and
meeting at the appointed spot, with their arms concealed as usual under the habiliments of the chase,
the young King and his companions marched on
during the whole night towards the object of their
enterprise. By day-break they arrived at the gates of
Fleurance, which had just been opened ; and finding
the town, as they expected, unprepared for resistance, they made themselves masters of it without
difficulty.†   The castle, however, held out ; but it
was speedily forced to surrender, though not without
some bloodshed.‡

When the news of this enterprise reached Catherine, on the following day, she wisely made a jest
of the whole matter, saying, "I see well that this
is in revenge for la Reole,§ and that Henry of Navarre is determined to give me cabbage for cabbage ;
but mine is the fullest."

A general peace nominally existed throughout the
whole kingdom ; but, as a partisan warfare was

* Perefix. Aubigné.   † Sully.   ‡ Aubigné.
§ Lettres Missives de Henry roi de Navarre, note, tom. i. p. 203.

actually carried on in the very neighbourhood of
the two courts, it was agreed that a truce should
be established for a certain distance round the cities
in which they held their residence. When the royal
parties removed to Coutras, some doubt arose as to
whether the small town of St. Emilion was within
the stated limits; but the citizens of that place,
having seized and plundered some Protestant
merchants, the Queen-mother declared the goods
taken, to be lawful booty. No sooner had she done
so, than Henry sent a party to sleep at St. Foi, beyond
the circle of the truce, whence they marched upon
St. Emilion, blew up part of a tower in the walls
and obtained possession of the place. Catherine
was now angry, and pronounced the act, a manifest
violation of the treaty; but Henry at once brought
back the case of the Protestant merchants to her
memory, and nothing more was said.

Such proceedings were of daily occurrence at the
courts of the Queen-mother and her son-in-law,
during the whole time of her stay in Guienne; and
gallantries, hostilities, negotiations, and intrigues,
were only further diversified by a bear-hunt, given
to Catherine by the King of Navarre, in the mountains of Foix. This sport, however, proved too rude
even for her taste, though she was passionately fond
of robust exercise. Several persons were killed, and
the entertainment was not repeated.

Catherine was induced during her stay to grant
the Protestants conditions, undoubtedly more advan-

tageous than she had at first proposed ; but, nevertheless, she succeeded in some of her objects, as
they are described by one who was present.
" She came hither," says Aubigné, " in appearance
to pacify ; but in fact it was, by every exquisite
contrivance, to draw her son-in-law to the court ;
and, failing with him, some of his principal followers ; or, at all events, to sow the seeds of
notable divisions amongst them, to endeavor to
make them give up their hold of the places of
security before the time, and in any case to discover
the state of the Protestant party."

Several of Henry's Roman Catholic officers, she
did contrive to debauch ; but the most mischievous
object of her arts, and that in which she best succeeded, was, the stirring up of dissensions between
the principal leaders of the Protestants.   The Viscount de Turenne, and the Prince de Condé had
previously been upon bad terms ; but the good
offices of Catherine, now rekindled a fire which was
almost extinguished, and the irritation of the Prince
became so great, that he challenged Turenne to
single combat.   The Viscount replied in terms full
of respect for the rank of his adversary, without
shewing any unwillingness to meet him in the field ;
and though we do not know, whether the duel did,
or did not actually take place,* no injury resulted to
either.   But, in another quarrel, which was mixed

* Aubigné implies that it did not take place, and Sully says
that it did. Both were then at the court.

up with this affair, more serious consequences ensued. An old dispute existed between Turenne, and John de Durefort de Rosan, who, urged on by the Queen-mother and her ladies, called the Viscount to the field, in the month of March, 1579. Turenne gave him the rendezvous he desired, in a field near the bridge of Agen, where the combat took place, between the two principals, and, as usual in those days, between the two seconds likewise. De Rosan was accompanied by his brother, the Marquis de Duras, and Turenne by John de Gontaut de Biron, Baron de Salignac. At first, the advantage seemed to be on the side of Turenne, who brought his adversary to his knee, but permitted him to rise, while Salignac allowed Duras to change his sword. In the midst of the fight, however, a number of armed men, supposed to have been servants of Duras, and of the Queen-mother, issued forth from under one of the arches of the bridge, where they had concealed themselves, and attacking Turenne, left him apparently dead, with seventeen wounds on his person.

The two brothers Durefort fled immediately ; but, to the surprise of all, Turenne recovered from the effects of the injuries he had received. He afterwards published a manifesto, complaining loudly of the murderous attack made upon him ; but, when the Queen-mother, finding her name implicated, gave orders for apprehending Duras and Rosan and bringing them to trial, he generously interceded for them, and contented himself with referring his case to Marshal Damville, who decided, that, after such treatment, Turenne was no longer bound to seek vengeance, according to what are called the rules of honor, *but might employ whatever means were most convenient;* another strong proof of the licence, which not only existed in men's actions, but with which their very thoughts were deeply imbued.

No sooner had Catherine quitted Guienne, to pursue her progress through Languedoc and Provence, than new infractions of the treaty so lately signed at Nerac commenced; and, whether with the connivance or by the negligence of Henry III., or at the instigation of the Queen-mother, I cannot discover, the officers of the crown in Guienne, without even seeking a decent pretext, violated all the stipulations in favor of the Protestants, and pursued a course which could only tend to a speedy renewal of the war. The letters of the young King of Navarre at this time, whether addressed to Henry III., to Catherine de Medicis, or to Marshal Damville (now become Duke of Montmorenci,) breathe constant complaints of the seizure of some towns, the razing of the fortifications of others, the pillage of protestant houses and castles, the murder of Huguenot noblemen and citizens, the leagues amongst the Catholic nobility who bound themselves by oath to destroy all the Calvinists they could find, the arrest, imprisonment, and trial of his partisans, on account of acts committed in the late war for which an amnesty had been obtained, and of the contemptuous rejection of all his applications for the payment of the sums promised to enable him to maintain his state and dignity. At the same time, his correspondence with his officers and friends, shews, in the clearest and most indubitable manner, his anxious desire to prevent any infraction of the treaty on the part of the Protestants, and to restore tranquillity to the land.

The Queen-mother had left the province, without giving ear to the complaints which the Huguenots had advanced; and a meeting of deputies, from the various reformed communities was summoned, to take into consideration the actual state of affairs. As Henry was on his way to attend this assembly, and also to open the States of Bearn,* he was seized with an attack of fever at Eause, which confined him to his bed for seventeen days; but no sooner was he sufficiently well to travel, than he hurried on, and met the general assembly of the Protestant deputies at Montauban, where it was decided that he should rather have recourse to war, than give up the towns of security, till the edict of Poitiers was fully executed. He then caused a number of crowns of gold to be cut in two, which he distributed amongst the persons who had attended the meeting, with an understanding, that the moment each received the other part of the piece he possessed, he was to take arms for the defence of the Protestant religion.

Nevertheless, hostilities, on a great scale, were not so soon recommenced as might have been ex-

* Lettres Missives, tom. i. p. 233.

pected.   The little court of Navarre remained at
peace, and occupied itself with pleasures.   Henry
wisely overlooked the misconduct of his wife, and
Marguerite, with the same facility, forgave the
gallantries of her husband.   Neither jealousy nor
religious differences were suffered to interrupt the
harmony of Pau and Nerac, and wit, sport, and
amusement, filled up the idle hours.

At length Henry III. was unfortunately tempted
to make an effort to disturb the tranquillity of his
brother-in-law in regard to his wife's conduct.
The Duke of Anjou, as we have before seen, had
made his escape from Paris, by the aid of the
Queen of Navarre, on the 14th February, 1578;
and the partiality which she evinced for her younger
brother, on this and other occasions, excited the
malignant jealousy of the elder.   From Paris the
Duke had fled to Angers, and from Angers had
proceeded to Mons, where he promised his assistance to the insurgents of the Low Countries,
and received from them various honorable titles,
which he had not the wisdom to merit.   Early in
the spring of the following year, however, he returned to Paris,* and cast himself upon the affection and generosity of the King, who received him
with the kindness which such an act of confidence
deserved, and promised him his support, both in
carrying on a war against Spain in her northern
dependencies, and in obtaining the hand of the
Queen of England.   But Henry's promises were

* 16th March, 1579.

rendered unavailing, by his indolent nature, and vacillating character. There was no real frankness nor generosity in his disposition, and he soon became jealous, and doubtful of his brother; shewed himself unwilling to take any step towards the proposed war in Flanders; hesitated, procrastinated, and deceived, till the wild and violent Duke of Anjou saw no way of driving him to fulfil the engagements he had made, but by instigating the Huguenots to renew the civil war.

For this, pretexts were not wanting; the aggressions of the Catholics were incessant; few of the obligations of the edict of Poitiers, and the explanatory treaty of Nerac had been fulfilled; the hereditary property of Henry of Navarre had been seized;* and daily applications, in a threatening tone, were made to the Protestant leaders, to give up the places of security, long before the time appointed. The Duke of Anjou, knowing the irritation which existed amongst the Huguenots, took advantage of the attachment of his sister, to employ all her art in urging on the King of Navarre and his friends, to open war; and Marguerite, devoted to her brother, scrupled not for a moment to obey his injunctions. On her husband, she employed the skill of her fair attendants, who spread forth all their allurements to captivate his heart, and filled his ears with arguments and inducements, favorable to the course in

* Letter from Henry to the Duke of Montpensier, 12th May, 1580.

which they sought to lead him. To the other
Protestant chiefs, the young Queen shewed herself
no niggard of her own favors, and went so far
with the Viscount de Turenne, that tidings of their
intimacy reached Paris, and were communicated by
Henry III. to his brother-in-law, with the view of
spreading dissensions in the Protestant party.

The King of Navarre instantly notified the charge
to the persons accused; but Marguerite, if she
did not succeed in persuading him of her innocence, effectually opened his eyes to the purposes of
her brother, the King of France, and redoubled her
efforts, to urge on the Huguenots into a resumption
of hostilities; till at length, by the artifices of
Mademoiselle de la Fosseuse, and one or two of her
companions, Henry himself was won to consent to
take arms once more.*   The machinery by which a
renewal of the civil strife was brought about caused
this war to be called " the war of the lovers."

The day fixed for the simultaneous arming of
Gascony, Picardy, Languedoc, Poitou, Anjou, Dauphiné, and all the other districts in which the Protestant party was powerful, was the 10th of April,
1580, and messengers were sent into the various
provinces to warn the leaders, and give them the
signal agreed upon. While making preparations
for carrying his purpose effectually into execution,
however, Henry of Navarre narrowly escaped falling
into the hands of his enemies. Having absented
himself from his court for a short time in the month

* Aubigné. Mem. de la Reine Marguerite.

of February, 1580, an ambuscade was laid in the neighbourhood of Mazeres, for the purpose of taking him alive, or killing him; but Marguerite, having received intimation of the fact, sent off messengers in haste to inform her husband of his danger. Henry, who was accompanied by very few attendants, immediately altered his course, and passing the Garonne by a ford, took refuge in Nerac; so that the stratagem, which, it is supposed, was devised by the League, in order to deprive the Protestants of their principal commander, was entirely frustrated.*

Some short time before the actual recommencement of the war, the small town of Figeac had been surprised by the Roman Catholics; and, in retaliation, the first act of hostility in which Henry took part himself, was an attack upon the town of Cahors, into the particulars of which we must enter, on account of the characteristic daring, and perseverance, which the future King of France displayed on the occasion.

Cahors is a considerable place, defended by water on three sides, and was at that time strongly fortified according to the state of military science in those days. The garrison, commanded by the gallant

* L'Etoile. Duchat. There are also allusions to this attempt, in several of Henry of Navarre's letters to Henry III. The latter demanded that his brother-in-law should give him the names of those who had furnished him with intelligence of the design against him, but Henry of Navarre refused to comply. Throughout the whole month of February, 1580, Henry was preparing for war.

De Vesseins, was composed of two thousand men, besides the citizens ; and both governor and soldiers were upon their guard against attack. Nevertheless, in the end of May, the King of Navarre, though at that period he had not been able to collect more than fifteen hundred men, determined to make an attempt to surprise the city. He accordingly began his march from Montauban, and advancing rapidly, reached the neighbourhood of Cahors at midnight on the 27th May. His approach had not been perceived ; and halting in a small wood of walnut trees, he gave his men a little repose during a violent thunder-storm, and then disposed them for the attack.* Two determined men, furnished with petards, a machine then just invented,† supported by ten picked soldiers, preceded the rest of the forces. These were followed by a mixed body of horse and foot, commanded by the King in person, and ten or twelve hundred arquebusiers brought up the rear. The petards, it would seem, effected less than had been anticipated against the gates of the city ; but the apertures they produced were enlarged by axes, though not to any great extent, some of the first who entered being obliged to creep upon their hands and knees. The noise of the petards, however, soon called the garrison to the defence of the gate, and a tremendous fight ensued ; the King leading on and encouraging his men

* Aubigné.   Journal de Faurin.   Letter of Henry to Madame de Batz.   Ditto, to M. de Scorbiac.

† Aubigné.

in the midst of a hot fire of small arms, and a shower of masses of stone, tiles, and logs of wood, from the tops of the houses. Vesseins was killed in his shirt at the beginning; and the King of Navarre forced his way forward, always in the thickest of the fire, wounded, though not seriously, and fatigued with a long march through a sultry summer's night. Body after body of the garrison were defeated; but still new forces appeared; the tocsin was rung; the citizens rose in arms; the small number of assailants became every instant more apparent; and even when Henry had pushed on to the market place, he found himself exposed to a heavy fire from a park of artillery which had been planted in the square.

Nothing, however, could daunt him, and the fight was carried on within the town of Cahors for four days; during the whole of which time the attacking party could obtain but a few minutes of repose, leaning against the houses and shops, without daring to quit their arms for a moment. At length, the news arrived, that a reinforcement was marching to the relief of the inhabitants; and Henry's officers besought him earnestly to abandon an attempt that seemed quite hopeless. The King, however, replied with a cheerful countenance: " It is written above there, what will become of me on this occasion. Remember, however, that my only retreat out of this town, without having won it, will be the retreat of my life out of this body. My honor is too much compromised to do otherwise ; and therefore let no one speak to me of any thing but dying or conquering."

In the mean time the expected reinforcement had arrived; but before they could force an entrance into the place, which was partly in possession of the Huguenots, Monsieur de Chouppes, at the head of the forces of Turenne, came to the aid of the King of Navarre, some of whose troops were in the act of abandoning the town. A crowd of these fugitives encountered Chouppes at the gates, and told him that all was lost; but that gallant officer, giving them nothing but reproaches in reply, rushed on into Cahors. Still, however, the defence was protracted; the streets were fortified with barricades; each public building became a citadel; and from the town-house to the college, from the college to the monasteries, the inhabitants and garrison were driven, till at length the last of their barricades was carried by Henry in person; and struck with panic they fled, leaving the city to the mercy of the conqueror.*

After having provided for the security of Cahors, Henry returned to Montauban, gathered his forces together, and hastened to disperse the levies which Biron was making in the county of Armagnac. "Night and day," says Aubigné, "he was on horseback;" and giving the enemy no repose, he forced Biron to shut himself up in Marmande. Henry,

* Sully. Aubigné. The first named of these authors was present.

then, in order to watch his movements, advanced to
Tonneins, where constant skirmishes took place without any important result. The King of Navarre
then determined to draw the enemy into an ambuscade; and having concealed himself with three
hundred horse in a small wood, he sent forward one
of his officers, named Lusignan, with a small body
of cavalry and a hundred arquebusiers. The foot
soldiers were ordered to lie down at a little distance
from the town, while Lusignan and his party advanced to the gates, daring the troops of Biron to
come forth. A hundred men-at-arms were soon in
the field to attack them; and, according to the orders
they had received, the Huguenot gentlemen retreated
towards their arquebusiers. Unfortunately, one old
soldier, hearing the enemy call upon him by name
to halt and fight, could not restrain himself, but
turned, and charging the person who defied him,
cast him dead to the ground. His own horse being
killed, his companions, though only twenty-five in
number, hastened to his aid, and a combat ensued,
during which, one of the grooms of the Protestant
gentlemen engaged, giving way to fear, fled at full
speed to the King, and told him that the party of
Lusignan, horse and foot, had been slaughtered to
a man.

Henry, we are assured by Sully, who was one of
those engaged, at once determined to advance, in
order to avenge his friends; but his officers dissuaded him; and, though with great regret, he

retired towards Tonneins.   He was much mortified, however, at having taken this step, when he found that the enemy, as soon as they saw the arquebusiers, who rose and rushed to the support of the Protestant horse, had retreated to Marmande; and the reproaches of Lusignan, who angrily declared the King had abandoned him, did not tend to mitigate the distress of a gallant and chivalrous monarch, at having been persuaded, by a false report of the enemies numbers and success, to relinquish an enterprise in which he had so far engaged.*

The hopes of the Huguenot party depended not alone upon the secresy with which their first efforts were conducted, but upon the union and mutual co-operation of the leaders.   Henry, however, had soon reason to find that those absolute requisites for conducting with vigor and certainty the operations of a great party, could not be obtained by a Prince whose military and political reputation was yet to be acquired.

Every leader, however small his force, however insignificant his position, thought himself qualified to undertake any enterprise upon the enemy, without the knowledge or consent of his chief; no one perceived the necessity of preconcerted or combined operations; every one made war upon the enemy apart, and strove to gain individual advantages, instead of submitting to a well organised plan.   Each

* I prefer the account of Sully to that of Aubigné, who was not present.

too was jealous of the other, and the transcendant abilities of the King of Navarre, had not yet become so apparent as to command the first place in esteem, as well as in rank, and to shelter him from the competition of inferior genius.* By different bodies of Huguenot forces, who found greater amusement and profit in pursuing separate enterprises, than in obeying the reasonable commands of their officers, more than forty towns were attacked in different parts of France, generally without the approbation, and very often against the express commands of the King of Navarre ; but only three of these attempts succeeded. The capture of Montaigue was the first; the citizens and garrison having been surprised by a small party of gentlemen of Poitou, who accidentally made prisoners four or five of the soldiery of the town, whose amusement during the peace had been plundering travellers on the highway by night. These brigands were forced by their captors to return with them to the castle, and give the word at the gates, which were immediately opened by the garrison, and seized by the Protestants.†

In the meantime the divisions which had mani-

---

* We find Henry complaining angrily in a letter to the Viscount de Gourdon, dated 3rd August 1680, of the disobedience shewn to his commands in the town of Cahors, as soon as he had left the place, and especially of the excesses of the Protestants in demolishing the Catholic churches and monasteries, and pillaging the inhabitants. The Viscount himself is not spared.

† Aubigné.

fested themselves amongst the Huguenots, bore their usual fruit during the spring of 1580. The Prince de Condé, casting off all connexion with Henry, sometimes remained inactive, negotiating with the Queen-mother on his own part, sometimes undertaking enterprises for the promotion of his personal views. It would seem that the King of Navarre, at this time, shewed no very eager desire to call foreigners to aid in the civil war; but Condé kept up a correspondence with John Casimir, the son of the Elector Palatine; and in order to give him security for the payment of his forces, he endeavored to seize upon several towns in Languedoc and Dauphiné.* Sully declares that his object was to form for himself an independent sovereignty; but, whatever might be his ultimate views, Henry of Navarre felt himself called upon to oppose his intrigues in the south, and for that purpose detached the Viscount de Turenne, with a considerable body of troops, to quiet the disputes in Languedoc, and make head against the Prince.

Frustrated in that quarter, Condé, after a short period of inaction, traversed the whole of France, and by a stratagem, made himself master of La Fere, in Picardy. No sooner, however, did intelligence of that event reach the court of France, than the proximity of the captured town to the capital, roused even the indolent monarch who occupied the throne, and the immediate siege of La Fere was determined.

* Sully. Aubigné.

Marshal Matignon was put at the head of the troops, all the principal noblemen of the court hastened to the army, and even the minions, casting off the sloth in which they lived, took arms at the King's command, and bore their gold and embroidery to the walls of La Fere.* Provisions were abundant in the camp, the weather was beautiful, merriment and indulgence reigned as much in the army as in the capital, and the attack upon this small town, which was prosecuted at first with but little energy, acquired the name of the Velvet siege.† The minions, however, displayed no want of manly virtues in the field, but exposing themselves, even rashly to all kinds of danger, were every one either wounded or killed.

Before the siege commenced, the Prince de Condé, finding that none of the other towns of Picardy joined him, as he had been led to expect they would, had left La Fere, in order to seek aid in Germany, after having put the town in a good state of defence. But Matignon carried on the operations against the place with skill and determination, though somewhat slowly; and although its position was excellent, the want of sufficient artillery and the failure of provisions, forced it to surrender, after having undergone a siege of two months.

* L'Etoile. Aubigne.

† Lettres Missives du roi de Navarre. It was supposed that Matignon's almost parental care for the minions of the King, somewhat interfered with his activity.

While these events were taking place in the north, the army of the King of Navarre, diminished by the absence of Turenne and his forces, was unable to keep the field against Biron; and mortified at the want of success which had attended the renewal of the war, Henry willingly listened to the first overtures for peace. The Duke of Anjou, who had aided more than any other person to instigate the Protestants to resume hostilities, as soon as he saw that the object of alarming the indolence of his brother was accomplished, offered himself as a mediator, on the condition of receiving aid in his attempt to deliver the revolted Flemings from the yoke of Spain. Henry III. gladly accepted his proposal; and the Duke, after concluding in haste a treaty with the deputies from the Low Countries, hurried into the south, and met the Protestant leaders and representatives at Fleix, on the Dordogne.* The terms were speedily settled; the edict of Poitiers, and the treaty of Nerac, formed the basis of the arrangement; it was agreed that Biron should be removed from Guienne; and a few unimportant concessions, made to the Protestants, saved the military credit of the insurgents, and afforded matter for the declamations of the League. The treaty was afterwards accepted by the Prince de Condé, and France once more fell

* The castle of the Marquis de Trans, where Henry of Navarre remained, from the 2nd to the 16th November, and probably a day or two more.

back into a state of agitated inactivity, which did not deserve the name of peace.

Before I close this account of the seventh civil war, it may be necessary to notice two or three events which occurred in France, though not closely connected with the history of Henry of Navarre. On the soft and criminal life of Henry III. I have already commented, and have pointed out the contempt which it called forth in his people. That contempt soon proceeded to outrage; and his minions became the objects of universal detestation. The friends and companions of the Duke of Anjou, though not without suspicion of the same monstrous vices which were attributed to the favorites of the King, led the way in heaping insults and defiances upon the heads of Quelus, Maugiron, St. Mégrin, and others. Paris was filled with tumults and duels. In a combat of three against three, Quelus* and Maugiron were killed by d'Entragues and his seconds, one of whom was also slain. The King shewed the most immoderate grief at the death of his favorites, gave them a public funeral, and erected upon their graves superb monuments of marble, bearing the statues of the dead minions. St. Mégrin soon followed his two companions to the tomb; but his fate was to fall by the hand of an assassin. He had long kept up, it would seem, an illicit connection with the beautiful Duchess of Guise, which did not remain concealed from the eyes

* Quelus survived in great agony during thirty-three days.

of her family. Her husband, however, was content to rest in apparent ignorance; and Bassompierre, having been instructed to inform the Duke of the fact, after hesitating long, as to how he should communicate such painful intelligence, put the case to Guise as that of a third person, asking his advice as a friend, upon the task which he had undertaken. The Duke, it appears, understood his meaning at once, but replied, after an eulogium upon the virtue of the Duchess, that if he were in a situation himself to be deceived by his wife, and any indiscreet friend, instead of taking upon himself to avenge him in silence, were bold enough to tell him his disgrace, he would punish him on the spot for his daring folly. Bassompierre was too wise to say more, and notified the reply he had received to the Duke of Mayenne, and the Cardinal de Guise, who determined to follow the hint given to their agent, and to avenge their brother as secretly as possible. On the twenty-first of July following, as St. Mégrin was leaving the Louvre, about eleven at night, he was attacked by a large party of armed men, who left him apparently dead upon the pavement, bleeding from more than thirty wounds. He expired the following morning ; the same honors were shewn to his corpse, as had been bestowed upon those of Quelus and Maugiron ; and to his memory also a statue was erected, so that it became a common saying on the lips of any one who had a quarrel with one of the King's minions, " I will have him sculptured in marble."

No inquiry was instituted into the particulars

of this assassination; for some of the attendants
of the murdered man, had recognised the beard
and *shoulder of mutton* hand of the Duke of
Mayenne amongst the assailants, and it became
evident to the King, that the murderers were too
powerful for his enfeebled arm to reach. When
the tidings of this event were brought to the King
of Navarre, with the addition that the act had been
committed by order of Guise, Henry exclaimed
aloud, that the Duke was quite right, that every
court gallant who dared to approach a Princess
with such purposes, ought to meet with such a fate.

But the favorites of the Duke of Anjou were not
destined to escape altogether without punishment,
while those of the King were slaughtered; and the
famous Bussy d'Amboise, one of the bravest but
the most sanguinary and quarrelsome of the court,
was betrayed by the King himself to the Count de
Montsoreau, with whose wife he was carrying on
an intrigue. A letter from Bussy, boasting of his
conquest, was placed by Henry in the hands of the
Count, who forced his wife to make an appointment
with her lover, at which he was assassinated by the
husband and the servants of the house, defending
himself to the last, with the same fearless courage
he had displayed through life.

The Duke of Anjou himself did not regret a
man whose pride was equal to his valor; and
shewed no resentment for an act of treachery in which
he is suspected of having had a share.*

* L'Etoile.

That Prince was now filled with the hopes of both
making himself Sovereign of the Low Countries and
obtaining the hand of Elizabeth, Queen of England.
In each case a prospect of success was opened to him,
which was specious though delusive. As the marriage with the English Sovereign was never concluded, and as the negotiations on the subject but
little affected the life of Henry of Navarre, I shall
not enter into any of the details. The affairs of the
Low Countries are more important, and, as they
were frequently interwoven with those of France,
some notice must be taken of the state of the insurgents in Flanders and Brabant, at the period when
the Provinces, after having struggled during some
years for liberty of conscience, without pretending
to independence, determined to cast off their allegiance to the King of Spain, and proclaim themselves a separate state.

But little union existed between the southern and
the northern parts of the Low Countries ; and before
the commencement of the year 1580 the want of funds
for carrying on the war, the excesses of the
soldiers, and the fear that Philip, as soon as he had
accomplished his designs against Portugal, would
direct the whole forces of his empire to the subju-
gation of the Calvinists in his northern territories,
had spread hesitation and discontent amongst the
people. The Prince of Orange, however, by his arguments and authority, stilled the clamor which had been
raised against him and others, who had opposed all

submission to the crown of Spain. In his public manifestoes, and his addresses to the States, he pointed out several of the errors which had been committed in the proceedings of the insurgents ; he proposed judicious measures for remedying such mistakes, and preventing their recurrence ; and, above all, he shewed the utter hopelessness of any reconciliation with Philip upon reasonable terms, and urged the necessity of taking the decided step of renouncing their allegiance to the tyrant who oppressed them, and electing another Prince, willing and able to give them assistance in the difficulties which surrounded them. Some resistance was offered by the Roman Catholic deputies in the States ; but it was ultimately resolved, that the proposed course should be followed, and that a foreign Prince should be called to their aid, with an offer of the sovereignty of the Low Countries, on the same terms as those under which it had been enjoyed by the house of Burgundy.

The States hesitated for some time between the Queen of England and the Duke of Anjou ; but at length they decided in favor of the latter ; and we are informed that the Prince of Orange as-- sured them, such a choice would be pleasing to the Queen herself.* A curious letter, however, exists from Elizabeth to her ambassador in Paris, in which she protests in the strongest terms against the elevation of the Duke to the sovereignty of

* De Meterens, liv. x. fol. 184.

the Provinces, and points out that if he accepted it, but little hope could be entertained of her bestowing her hand upon that Prince.* There can be no doubt, that on this, as on most other occasions, Elizabeth, who was possessed of consummate duplicity, was attempting to deceive both parties ; and certainly no judgment can be formed of what were her real intentions from the expressions which she thought fit to make use of to either.

The Duke of Anjou, notwithstanding her remonstrance, signed a treaty, as I have before mentioned, with the deputies of the United Provinces at Plessis les Tours, and having pacified the Huguenots in the conferences at Fleix, employed himself successfully in enlisting a number of the distinguished leaders of that party, under the banner which he was about to display. Amongst the most celebrated of those who joined him on this occasion, were the Viscount de Turenne and Maximilian de Bethune, afterwards Duke of Sully. A number of inferior officers and soldiers were likewise enrolled, and the Duke's preparations were rapidly completed, for leading a considerable force to the deliverance of Cambray, then besieged by the Prince of Parma.

The whole of Europe looked on with anxious expectation ; but the clear-sighted King of Navarre alone seems justly to have appreciated the character of the Prince, whom the people of the Low Countries had chosen for their sovereign, and to

* Letter of Queen Elizabeth to Sir Edward Stafford.

have foreseen the result of his enterprise.* In
taking leave of Sully, when about to set out, he said,
speaking of the Duke of Anjou, " He will deceive
me much if he fulfils the hopes conceived of him;
he has so little courage, a heart so double and
malicious, a body so ill formed, so little grace in his
demeanor, so little skill in every sort of exercise,
that I cannot persuade myself he will ever do anything that is great."

Henry also tried to dissuade the Viscount de
Turenne from accompanying the Duke, and exacted
both from him and Sully a promise, that they would
rejoin him, as soon as a renewal of the attempts
to suppress the Protestant religion, which he saw
that the court was determined to make, compelled
him again to have recourse to arms.

The Flemings, in the mean time, sent frequent
messages to the Duke of Anjou, beseeching him to
hasten to their aid; and at length, having collected
a large force, that Prince began his march towards the town of Cambray, which with its territory
had always been held as a fief of the Empire, and
had remained, in general, neuter in the contentions

* Nevertheless, at first, Henry held out to the Duke of Anjou
and several others, the expectation of aiding personally in the
war in Flanders. There are letters of his still in existence, directing his principal adherents to prepare to accompany him to
the Low Countries. These were written, it is true, before Sully,
Turenne, and the Duke set out from Guienne; and the only in-
ference we can draw from the facts, is, that Henry learned to
appreciate the character of the Duke more justly than he had
previously done, during his residence in the south of France.

which had lately desolated the neighbouring provinces.*   Finding itself menaced by the Prince of
Parma, however, Cambray had, some time before,
called several French officers to its aid, and had taken
a decided part against the Spaniards.   The facilities
which the possession of that city would afford to an
enemy, entering Brabant from the side of France,
decided the conduct of the Italian Prince as soon as
he found that the Duke of Anjou had accepted the
sovereignty offered to him by the States; and early
in 1581 he advanced against Cambray, with all the
forces he could draw together, and established a
strict blockade, which speedily reduced the inhabitants to a state of famine.

We have a curious account of the marriage feast
of one of the principal citizens, during the siege,
on which occasion the dinner began with a salad
without salt or oil, after which appeared, a piece of
boiled ass, and some hashed horse.   The second
course consisted of two ribs of a horse roasted at one
end, two roast cats at the other, and a cat pasty in
the centre.

From such delicacies the appearance of the Duke
of Anjou, with twelve thousand foot and four thousand horse, delivered the inhabitants of Cambray,
in the middle of August, 1581 ; but before the city
was relieved, the Viscount de Turenne, with several
other noblemen, were taken in a foolish attempt to
force their way through the enemy.   The Prince of
Parma presented himself on the morning of the

* De Meterens.

seventeenth in battle array; but his position was
too strong to be attacked without much previous
preparation; and the Duke of Anjou, with more
prudence than might have been expected, declined
the combat offered.   Parma, unable to contend with
the force brought against him, under the walls of
a hostile fortress, evacuated his entrenchments the
same night, and retreated, but in such good order,
as to present not the slightest advantage to his
enemy.   The Duke was received in the town with
every mark of gratitude and honor, and thence proceeded to the attack of Cateau-Cambresis, which
was taken by assault.*   He then returned to
Cambray, in order to commit one of those acts of
treachery which are not only infamous in a commander, but reflect a part of the disgrace upon the
nation to which he belongs; and, taking advantage
of the hospitality and confidence of Charles de
Gaure, Lord of Inchy, the governor, he shamefully
made himself master of the citadel, while receiving
a splendid entertainment from that officer.

Having perpetrated this crime, the French Prince,
notwithstanding all the entreaties of the United Provinces, to advance and give them aid, retired to France,
excusing himself upon the pretence of having great
difficulty in keeping his volunteer troops any longer
in the field.   He promised, however, to return with
larger and better organized forces, and then passed

---

* De Meterens says that it capitulated; but Sully was present
on the occasion, and himself took part in the storming of the
town.

over into England, to pursue those schemes for
obtaining the hand of the Queen of England, which,
as that politic and insincere Princess arranged her
proceedings, only served to render him ridiculous
in the eyes of Europe.*

After spending three months in England, the
Duke, strongly urged by deputies from the States,
returned to the Low Countries, accompanied by a
number of English noblemen; and, hurrying on to
Antwerp, where the highest honors awaited him, he
there received the ducal coronet and mantle, as Sovereign of Brabant.† He had not long returned to the
Netherlands, however, before an attempt to assassinate the Prince of Orange, which, for a time, was
supposed to have been undertaken at his suggestion,
created suspicions of a desire, on his part, to throw
off the obligations by which he had bound himself to
the people. The papers found on the body of the
murderer, and the confession of some of his accomplices, shewed that the criminal was a Spaniard
employed by Philip ; but the fears which the inhabitants of Antwerp very generally entertained in
regard to the designs of their new sovereign, were
shortly after confirmed in a striking manner.

Having no sufficient force to make head against

---

* It is impossible to conceive that Elizabeth entertained, as
Watson seems to believe she did, a temporary passion for a
prince the most ungraceful in person, the most unprepossessing
in manners, and the most deformed in mind that ever solicited
her hand.

† Nevers. Sully.

the Prince of Parma, the Duke earnestly implored his brother to send him reinforcements; and Henry III., after much hesitation, despatched a small body of men, amounting to eight thousand, under the command of Montpensier and Biron. But no sooner had these troops reached the Low Countries, than the Duke of Anjou determined to employ them in seizing upon Antwerp, Dendermonde, Dixmude, and Dunkirk. Antwerp was the chief object of the enterprise, and the attempt upon that place was reserved for the Duke himself. It was the only case in which the treachery was not successful; for various circumstances alarmed the citizens of that important place, and they held themselves upon their guard. The conduct of the French Prince first excited suspicion. We find from Sully, that, at this time, he treated his Protestant followers with contempt and want of confidence : one after another was excluded from his councils, and even Montpensier and Biron, whose honor was not to be doubted, were kept at a distance from his secret consultations.

At length, on the day appointed for the execution of the scheme, his troops in the neighbourhood of Antwerp having been prepared to act according to his wishes, the Duke endeavored to persuade the Prince of Orange to accompany him to the French camp, under the walls, in order to witness a general review of the forces. William, however, excused himself, and warned some of the Protestant officers in private, to absent themselves as little as possible from his own

dwelling; foreseeing that, in case of the outbreak of
any plot, they might be sacrificed, either to the
bigotry of the Roman Catholic soldiers, or to the
indignation of the citizens.* There can be no
doubt that Anjou's design, in asking the company
of the Prince, was to take him prisoner, or to
assassinate him ; but frustrated in this point, he set
out himself, accompanied by three hundred horse,
who, in passing the gate of Ripdorf, made themselves masters of it, and of all the outworks by which
it was defended. The French troops, from without
the walls, instantly rushed in, slaughtering all who
resisted, and shouting, as usual with a storming
party in those days, " Town gained! Town gained!
Slay, slay! Long live the mass!"

But their exultation was premature. In their
haste they neglected to secure the portcullis and
drawbridge; a party of the guard, who had been
driven into the guard-house, cut off their retreat;
the citizens, who had entertained many suspicions,
and taken some precautions, poured forth in thousands to the defence of their rights; the garrison
issued from the citadel to attack the treacherous
assailants; and, hemmed in amongst narrow streets,
under the fire of a furious and indignant population,
without a sufficient supply of ammunition, and deprived of all assistance from the rest of their forces,
the French were slaughtered in crowds; so that,
in the end, the gate was absolutely blocked up by
the dead and wounded. The arrival of the Prince

* Sully.

of Orange, alone put an end to the massacre.* Fifteen hundred Frenchmen were slain, and two thousand made prisoners, amongst whom were an immense number of persons of high rank, who had not scrupled to take part in one of the basest acts of treachery ever perpetrated. After this event the Duke lingered some time in Flanders, hated and distrusted, but still endured, partly from political, partly from generous motives; till at length, ill, disappointed, scorned and disgraced, he retired to his native country.

On his return from Flanders, Anjou was coldly received by his brother; and, retiring to Chateau Thierry, soon after expired, of the same disease which had terminated the life of Charles IX. His death was, as usual, attributed to poison; but the malady which afflicted him had been common in England and other countries, as a sort of epidemic, known by the name of " the sweat," in which the blood occasionally oozed forth from the pores of the skin;† and there is no reason to suppose that any measures were taken to bring his life to a premature conclusion.

During the space of nearly four years, which elapsed between the termination of the "lovers' war" and the death of the Duke of Anjou, Henry of

---

* Anquetil has the daring folly to assert, that the man who committed this act, and a thousand others of the same kind which I have not thought fit to insert in this work, was " plein de bonne foi, de candeur et de generosité."

† De Thou, liv. 78.

Navarre had remained in Guienne, enjoying a period of partial tranquillity, though his domestic life was troubled by his own errors, and those of his wife. Without trusting to such testimony as the "Divorce satyrique," there is ample evidence to shew that the Queen of Navarre, at this time, abandoned herself entirely to her libidinous temperament, forgetting even common decency. Henry was willing to be blind; but Marguerite's conduct would not suffer him to remain ignorant of her excesses; and we find, that at Cadillac, in the year 1580, she was detected in adultery with Monsieur de Chanvallon. What passed between her and her husband on this occasion, we do not know; but it would seem that Henry did not resent her conduct with any great acerbity: for he spoke of her with kindness in several letters during that and the following year, and accompanied her to St. Maixent in the spring of 1582.

At that small town the King and Queen of Navarre were met by Catherine de Medicis, who came with the apparent purpose of hearing the complaints of the Protestants in regard to the incessant violation of the treaty of Nerac, and of devising with her son-in-law some means of enforcing the provisions of that convention. Whatever were the promises which she now made, Henry seems to have been satisfied with them; and Marguerite, on the termination of the conferences, returned with her mother to the court of France.

There, however, she was coldly received by her
brother Henry; and as she met with daily insults
from the minions and the King himself, while her
husband required her return, she at length set out
for Guienne. But Henry III., determined to add
another affront to those which he had already
inflicted upon her, caused her train to be stopped
at a short distance from the gates, and her own
litter to be searched, upon the pretence of making
sure that no men were concealed therein. His
guards also arrested two of the ladies who accompanied her and several of her male attendants, who
were brought before him, and examined touching
the conduct of his sister, but more particularly as
to the supposed birth of a son, which she was said
to have had by Chanvallon during her stay at Paris.
The French monarch also wrote to Henry of Navarre, charging his own sister with gross immorality; but recollecting the consequences which
might ensue from such an accusation, he speedily
retracted it, and sent his minister Bellievre to en-
join the King of Navarre to receive his wife once
more. In the King's autograph letter upon the
latter occasion, he exceeded all the bounds of
decency and propriety; for after attributing his
first charge against Marguerite to a fit of passion, he went on to point out that every lady was
subject to scandal, and that even Jean D'Albret
herself had not escaped calumny. Henry of Navarre laughed aloud on reading the letter, and

turning to Bellievre, replied by a somewhat coarse, but very bitter jest. He subsequently sent his own squire Aubigné, and also Du Plessis Mornay, to demand satisfaction for the insult which had been offered to his Queen;* and a long negotiation ensued, in which Monsieur de Clervant also took a part. Innumerable subjects of dispute, were suffered to mingle with the course of the transaction; and Henry of Navarre shewed a strong disinclination to receive his wife again, requiring as a preliminary, that the royal troops should be removed from several of the fortresses in the vicinity of Nerac, into which they had been introduced contrary to the stipulations of the last treaty. So strong, however, was the desire of Henry III. to see his sister once more reconciled to her husband, that he acceded to many of his brother-in-law's demands; and in February or March, 1584,† the latter once more met his licentious wife; but their re-union

* Du Plessis Mornay. Aubigné. L'Etoile. Duchat. The statements of Anquetil are, as usual, far removed from the truth.

† Many French historians have asserted that Henry never received his wife after her return from the court of France and the accusations which her brother brought against her; but this is shewn to be incorrect by a letter from the King of Navarre to Henry III., in which he says, "Monseigneur, suivant le commandement qu'il a pleu à Vostre Majesté me faire, et le desir que j'ay d'y obeir et satisfaire, je suis venu en ce lieu pour y recevoir ma femme, qui y est des le treizieme de ce mois, &c." This letter is without date; but Monsieur Berger de Xivrey fixes it towards the end of February, 1584.

was not of long duration, though the events which
produced their speedy separation are very obscure,
and will probably never be made perfectly clear.
We find the Princess at Perigueux before the end of
the same year; but early in 1585 she returned to
Agen, where she prepared for acts of which I shall
have to speak hereafter, and which cast even a
darker shade upon her character than the vices and
follies which had stained her previous life.

Henry of Navarre himself, as is but too well
known, was by no means free from reproach on the
score of immorality, and at this time the principal
object of his passion was the Countess de Guiche,
widow of the Count de Grammont,* who had lost
his life before the walls of La Fere.   This lady
seems to have loved him with a deep and devoted
attachment; and, though undoubtedly criminal in
her intercourse with the King, she shewed, on many
occasions, qualities of mind and heart, which render her want of other virtues but the more lamentable.   Her advice and assistance were often highly
serviceable to her royal lover; and she is said, at
one time, to have raised a powerful army for his
support, at her own expense.

In the society of the Countess de Guiche, Henry
did not forget that attention to the affairs of France,
which his peculiar position rendered absolutely necessary to his own safety and that of the Protestant

---

* She was known at the time by the name of la belle Coris-
sandre.

party; and he foresaw, with that clear perception of
the designs of his enemies, which was one of his
greatest safeguards through life, that though the
League seemed well nigh extinct, the fire which
smouldered in its ashes, might, ere long, be blown
into a consuming flame, which would light up the
civil war with more fierceness than ever.   To watch
the conduct of his secret enemies at the court of
France, some sure and confidential agent was required; and for that post he chose the young Baron
de Rosny, afterwards Duke of Sully, in whose caution
and fidelity he could fully rely, and who had already,
in obedience to his commands, fulfilled a mission
of importance, which I must notice more particularly ere I proceed, as it shews, in a remarkable
manner, the candor and good faith with which the
future monarch of France acted towards the reigning sovereign.

So highly exasperated had the King of Spain become with the conduct of Henry III., in permitting
and aiding his brother to wage war against the
Spanish forces in the Low Countries, at a period
when the French monarch affected to maintain a
close alliance with his neighbour of the Peninsula, that, moved partly by anger and partly by
the desire of renewing those dissensions in the neighbouring kingdom, which had hitherto prevented the
French from taking an active part in the wars of the
Netherlands, Philip sent messengers to the King
of Navarre, offering his friendship and powerful as-

sistance, if he would once more raise his standard against the King of France.* Another cause indeed might also have some influence in leading Philip to seek an alliance with Henry of Navarre. That Prince's aid had been sought by Antonio, the exiled Pretender to the crown of Portugal; and Henry had so far listened to the overtures of the latter, as to make a perilous journey in order to confer with one of the ministers of the Portuguese Prince,† passing through the inimical town of Bordeaux, disguised as a servant of his own attendants.

To deprive the Prior of Crato of the powerful succor which Henry, with his Protestant forces, might have afforded; to renew a civil war in the heart of France, which would recall both Huguenots and Papists from the Netherlands; and to punish the French monarch for his insincerity, were objects which might all be obtained by an alliance with the King of Navarre. But Henry, who was then at the house of the Countess de Guiche, not only returned no answer to the message of Philip, but despatched Sully to the court of France, to communicate to his brother-in-law the offers which had been made by the King of Spain. The only effect of this generous confidence, was to cause the weak monarch, who then reigned in France, to renew his intercourse with Philip, to withhold any further aid to the United Provinces; and to intimate to

* Sully.   † Aubigné.

the King of Spain, that Henry of Navarre had immediately made him aware of his suggestions.

Sully returned from the court of France, some
time before the death of the Duke of Anjou, and
he was now, as I have said above, sent back to watch
the proceedings of the League, and to give his
master intimation of their designs.   A good excuse
for his presence in Paris was afforded by the station
which his two nephews held about the person of
Henry III.; but he found them, on his arrival, in
disgrace for reasons, which he significantly tells us,
it may be well to cover with silence.*   It would
appear that Sully did not make any very important
discoveries, at least he does not himself mention any,
and seems, by his own account, to have applied
himself as zealously, to increase his fortune by horse-
dealing, as to his master's affairs.   He was recalled
into Guienne in the end of 1584; the death of the
Duke of Anjou having suddenly revived all the energies of the League, and an immediate renewal of the
war becoming more than probable.

During the interval of peace between 1580 and
1585, several attempts were made to assassinate the
King of Navarre ; one of which was by a Frenchman, called by some historians Michau,† and by
others, Gavaret.‡   This person, watching his opportunity, joined the object of his treacherous de-

* Sully.   Confession de Sancy.   † Le Grain.

‡ Aubigné.   Various circumstances would seem to shew that
the same individual is spoken of.

sign when Henry was riding, in the year 1582, between Montauban and Gontaut, with few, if any, attendants. The assassin was mounted on a remarkably fine horse, which had been given him to facilitate his escape after the deed was done; but some intimation of his purpose had been conveyed to the King, who, pretending to admire his charger, made him dismount, that he might try the animal, and then springing into the saddle, seized the loaded pistols which were at the saddle bow. "I am told," he exclaimed, "that you seek to kill me: —I could now, if I pleased, put you to death instead;"—and he immediately discharged the two weapons in the air, without taking any farther vengeance upon the assassin.* Another attempt of the same kind was made by a gigantic Spaniard, named Loro; but his scheme was frustrated by the King's attendants. He was afterwards put to death, having confessed his crime and made many desperate efforts to escape. The means of poison were also employed, but failed; and the culprit, on this occasion, after having made a second effort to destroy the King, was put to the torture.† The names of the instigators, in this and the two former instances,

* Gavaret or Gabaret, as Henry himself writes his name, immediately went over to the party of the League, and made several other attempts upon the King's life. In May 1582, we find a letter from Henry to M. de Meslon, in which he expresses regret that Gabaret had escaped; and it is, therefore, probable that orders had been given for his apprehension.

† Busbecq. Epist. 46.

were carefully concealed; and all that we can discover is that some French Prince was suspected,
but that Henry III. established his own innocence,
by the zeal and frankness which he displayed in
causing a minute investigation of the facts to be
instituted.*

There is indeed every reason to believe that he
continued, notwithstanding all the disputes which
had taken place between them, to feel a sincere
regard for the King of Navarre, and that he entertained an unfeigned desire to secure the throne
of France for that Prince, on the failure of the
house of Valois; all hope of his having children to
succeed to the crown being now at an end. No
sooner was it known that his brother the Duke of
Anjou, was in a state that left no hope of recovery,†
than he despatched the Duke of Epernon into
Guienne, to beseech Henry to join him in Paris
and abjure the Protestant faith. The motives of the
Duke's journey were concealed under the pretence
of visiting his mother; but the real object soon became known; and the agitation of the Princes of
Lorraine and other members of the League was
soon felt throughout France.‡ The Duke proceeded

* Busbecq.

† The Duke of Epernon set out on the 16th of May, and the
Duke of Anjou did not expire till the 10th June; see L'Etoile.
Many authors inaccurately place Epernon's journey after the
death of the Duke.

‡ Henry III. did not scruple on many occasions to express
his regard and respect for his cousin the King of Navarre, even

to Guienne, and after a short visit to his mother at the chateau of Caumont, joined the King of Navarre at Saverdun.* Several conferences now took place between Henry and the envoy of the King of France; and Epernon followed the Bearnois Prince to Pamiers, to Pau, and to Nerac, endeavoring but in vain to induce him to accede to the wishes of Henry III.

There cannot be any doubt, that the arguments addressed to Henry of Navarre were well worthy of consideration. Exhausted by disease and debauchery, given up to vice and indolence, it was little probable that the French monarch would long remain upon the busy stage of human life. His death would leave the crown of France an object of fierce contention, if Henry of Navarre, holding fast by the faith in which he had been educated, armed the religious prejudices of the great majority of the

before those to whom he knew it would cause the greatest pain. Thus we find it stated in one of the letters of Du Plessis Mornay, that in April 1584, in the presence of the Duke of Mayenne, Henry spoke of the approaching death of his brother, and added, " I acknowledge the King of Navarre my sole and only heir. He is a Prince, well brought up, of a good disposition. My inclination has always been to love him, and I know that he loves me. He is somewhat sharp and choleric, but his heart is good."

* The Life of the Duke of Epernon gives the place of meeting as above; and if so, their first conference must have taken place before the Duke of Anjou was actually dead, for Henry was never at Saverdun in May, June, or July, 1584, except on the 7th June.

nation against himself; and that crown would be dangerously hazarded by the lawful heir remaining shut up in a remote province, while a thousand eager hands were stretched out in the capital to seize the supreme power.

Many of the Bourbon prince's most sincere friends too, urged him strongly to follow the counsel and embrace the offers of the King; and, on one occasion, while a Protestant minister, marking his hesitation, was eagerly admonishing him to cast away all doubt where his faith was concerned, La Rochefoucault exclaimed, addressing the clergyman, " I should like to see them place before you, on one hand two or three Psalms, and on the other the crown of France. Which would you choose, minister?"

But various considerations, besides those connected with religion, were to be taken into account, in opposition to the views of the French monarch. Henry had to remember, that if he abandoned the strong party of which he was the head, and returned to the capital, he must appear as an inferior personage at the court of France, exposed to the machinations of many enemies, the caprices of a vicious and perfidious Prince, and the arts of an unscrupulous and deceitful woman. He must bend before minions, he must endure the will of a master, he must be constantly on his guard against poison, the pistol, and the sword. Every word must be watched, every movement must be careful; and perhaps, after all precautions had been taken, he might see the weakness, the passion, or prejudice of the King, place him in a more perilous situation than he could be cast into even by a renewal of the war. He chose, therefore, the bolder as well as the more sincere course; refused to yield his faith without conviction, and resolved to trust to his own sword for his own defence. He replied, however, with the utmost moderation and respect; protested his devotion to the King, and assured him that he would never take arms against him, except in the case of extreme necessity.

We find it asserted by an author, who had every opportunity of knowing the truth,* that the Duke of Epernon was charged, after using every persuasion to induce Henry to return to the court and conform to the Roman Catholic religion, to inform him that, although the King of France regretted his determination, he looked upon him still as his nearest relation and heir to the crown; that he would hold him justified in using every means to resist the League; that he besought him to provide for the security of the places which he held, believing them to be safer in his hands than in those of the opposite party; and that, although he could not openly favor his cause, while he remained attached to the Protestant religion, he would take no umbrage at any thing he might do for his own advantage.†

---

* Gerard, Vie du Duc d'Epernon.

† The assertion of Gerard is strongly confirmed by some of the letters of Henry IV. to M. de Bellievre, an envoy sent, as I

Thus terminated the conferences beween Henry of Navarre and the King's envoy; and each party prepared against the coming events, according to the spirit by which they were actuated: the League, having the Duke of Guise at its head, with all the fierce energy and decision which characterized its early movements; Henry III. with the same vacillation which he had incessantly displayed since the battle of Jarnac; and Henry of Navarre with that calm and tranquil firmness, which the consciousness of a good cause, high genius, and strong courage can only bestow.

have shewn, by Henry III. to his brother-in-law. One of those letters contains a remarkable postscript, from which we find that Bellievre and the King of Navarre were acting together confidentially, and taking measures for frustrating the designs of the Leaguers, even in cases where the latter were invested with authority by Henry III. himself.

BOOK VII.

From the history of France in those times, three persons stand forward in bold relief; Henry Duke of Guise, Henry King of Navarre, Henry of Valois: one by the force of talents and ambition; one by genius and circumstances; one by position alone. A multitude of minor characters crowd the scene, amongst whom the principal personages are, Catherine de Medicis, the Popes, the King of Spain, and the Cardinal de Bourbon.

The Duke of Guise now entered once more into the arena of civil strife with infinite advantages; supported by a numerous, brave, skilful, and ambitious family, by high courage, great military and political talents, vast possessions, a handsome person, immense corporeal powers, an active, determined, and unhesitating mind, manners eminently popular, a high reputation, consistency of conduct, the religious zeal of the powerful faction of the League, perfect unity of purpose between himself and his brothers, the interests of the King of Spain, and the sympathy of every bigot throughout the Roman Catholic states of Europe.

Henry III. on the contrary, inconsistent in his whole demeanor, contemned for his vices and his weakness, detested for his oppression and his insincerity, trusted by no party, loved by few, without the qualities that attach, that lead, or that command, had nothing in his favor but the royal authority which had become enfeebled in his hands ; courage without activity, skill without energy, art without perseverance, a large body of favorites whose safety was bound up with his own, all of them brave, many of them skilful, some of them resolute, the habitual veneration of a people, who were then proverbially loyal, and the cold support of the good and the wise, who abhorred the man, and despised the monarch, but reverenced the crown and loved their country.

For months and years, the faction of the League, and its leaders of the house of Guise, had laboured assiduously, to lower the sovereign in the opinion of the people, by every artful means that could be devised. All his actions were made the subject of comment, libel, and pasquinade, his secret vices were exposed, his follies magnified, his weakness held up to derision. The regular Clergy were enlisted against him, the dark and mighty order of the Jesuits was taught to employ the most subtle of its arts to poison the minds of the people against their King. The public ear was accustomed to hear the necessity of dethroning him openly canvassed ; and even his very table was not free from sarcasms at his person and his court.*

* One day the King having quitted Chenonceaux in haste, because the plague had appeared at that place, Ruscelay told him at table that he need not fear that malady, for his court was a worse pest, on which the other could have no power. L'Etoile.

Henry III. on his part, seemed to labor to give point to the accusations of his adversaries. His indolence, his vices, his vacillation, his luxury, his extravagance, might have been tolerated or forgotten, had not his activity in intrigue and treachery, his fits of superstitious repentance, and hypocritical devotion, his stern rigidity against those he hated, his sumptuary laws severely executed against all who had not his sanction for excess, his persecution of those whose peculations had been subservient to his own, and his exactions from his people to enrich his minions, formed a frightful contrast between the measure that he dealt to his subjects and his favorites, and raised the indignation of all classes, against conduct which was equally devoid of decency and equity, equally vicious and unjust. Scorn, however, is the most dangerous feeling that a monarch can generate in the hearts of his people. He may be hated and yet tolerated; his actions may be condemned, and yet his talents may command; he may oppress, and yet rule; but the sovereign must either be respected in his person, or by virtue of his authority, who would retain his crown or his life. If he be once despised he is lost, unless there be laws in the land which secure veneration for his office if not for himself, and in submitting to which, the throne itself is fortified by the attachment of the nation to institutions above the effects of personal depravity or weakness. Such was not the case in France at that time; the law did not make the monarchy, and consequently

did not secure it.   The monarch made the law, and
consequently founded his throne merely upon the
traditional obedience of his people.   He might
retain his power by force, he might retain it by love,
he might retain it by habit; but his authority, by
being placed above the control of law, was virtually
placed beyond its protection, and his personal
qualities always more or less affected the measure
of his subjects' submission; for, when in the common
form he pronounced, "the King wills it," it required
a powerful voice to make the words heard throughout
the whole of France.

No sooner were the eyes of the Duke of Anjou
closed, than the question of the succession to the
throne became agitated in all quarters, in public
and in private.   As we have seen, the King himself
had been roused from his indolent lethargy, by that
important consideration, even before his brother
was actually dead, and shewed more activity and
energy than he had displayed for years.   It would
appear too, that before the course which the proceedings of the League would take, was developed, he
divined several of the steps which the members of
that association would be induced to pursue ; and it
is more than probable that the Queen-mother, while
secretly urging him to violate the existing treaty of
peace with the Protestants, and to co-operate with
the house of Guise, discovered to her son many designs which were intended to be hidden from his eyes.

That Catherine, with the view of ultimately raising

the son of her daughter the Duchess of Lorraine, to the throne of France, took a very early part in the machinations of the family of Guise, is proved by many facts ; and in a letter still extant, from Henry of Navarre, to the Protestant Counsellors of the Chamber of Justice, at Lisle, dated 13th July, 1584, he states that he had, at that time, received certain intelligence of the Queen-mother having treated with Messieurs de Guise, having resolved upon the revocation of the edict of pacification, and having obtained the King's consent to such a course.*

It does not appear however, that Henry III. ever seriously entertained an intention of promoting the views of his mother and the Duke of Lorraine ; but, whatever were his feelings upon that head, it is clear he treated the pretensions of the other competitor for the throne that was to become vacant by his death, with utter contempt. As early as the beginning of September, 1584, he sounded the intentions of the old Cardinal de Bourbon, under cover of a jest. He spoke openly to that weak Prince of the probable

---

* Recueil des Lettres Missives de Henry IV. par M. Berger de Xivrey. I cannot refrain from calling attention to this collection, one of a great series, undertaken by the command of the French Government, and executed in a manner equally honorable to those entrusted with the task, and those who appointed them : nor can I help expressing deep regret, not altogether unmingled with shame, that in our own country, where such immense collections of historical sources have been rotting for centuries, in confusion and oblivion, no national efforts should have been made to render them really available to the historian or the statesman.

extinction of the line of Valois, and asked if, in that case, he did not judge that the kingdom must fall to him, the Cardinal, rather than to his nephew, the King of Navarre. After much pressing, the old man admitted that he thought it must, and that he should certainly contest it; upon which, the King, putting his hand upon his shoulder, told him, that the lower classes might give him the crown, but that those above them would wrest it from him; and he retired laughing.

An attempt to trace all the intrigues that now took place, through their various ramifications, would be a task equally tedious and vain. It appears, as I have shewn, that the Queen-mother was privy to the movements of the League, and hoped so to direct them, as ultimately to secure the crown to the son of her daughter, the Duchess of Lorraine;* that the name of the Cardinal de Bourbon, was only put forward to conceal the deeper views of the parties, and that the Duke of Guise, operating for his own interests, yielded in appearance to every suggestion, which increased the strength of a faction that he alone could direct, and concealing from all men his own purposes, offered himself as a creature in the hands of others, in full confidence of being able to use all the power he gained, for his personal objects. With these designs, he negotiated with the King of Spain, and obtained from him promises of assistance and support, and in the same course, it seems, that

* Mem. de Nevers, tom. i. p. 163.

he entered into even more criminal intrigues, amongst which, one had for its objects to seize upon the person of Henry III., in the chapel of the Capuchins, to imprison him, and employ his name to sanction whatever edicts the League might think fit to promulgate.*

In the meantime, the meetings of the Leaguers were numerous, and their efforts to obtain fresh signatures in all parts of the realm, incessant. Day after day numbers were added to the list, and more and more daring steps were taken towards the assumption of supreme power. Frequent assemblies were held in the college of Fortet, which obtained the name of, the Cradle of the League; and some members of the law, many of the clergy, and still more of the burgesses, crowded to these meetings, where the most treasonable propositions were entertained, and the most criminal acts devised.

From such assemblies, and from the little court which the Duke of Guise held around him, innumerable libels, tracts, treatises, and even pictures, issued forth to the world, imputing to the King the oppression of the Roman Catholic party in the realm; displaying in a false and odious light his negotiations with the King of Navarre, with the Queen of England, and with the Calvinists of the Low Countries; and representing every act of justice which had been performed upon the assassins and incendiaries who attacked the persons and dis-

* Mem. de Nevers, tom. i. p. 163.

turbed the peace of Protestant sovereigns, as the most horrible persecution of the Papists wherever the Reformed religion was predominant. By these means the fears were raised, and the passions excited of the Roman Catholic population, and multitudes of sincere and well meaning men were gained to the party of the League, who would have strongly resisted the selfish and ambitious views of its leaders, and its tendency to shake the best institutions of the country, had not the most consummate art been employed to conceal all that might shock or offend, and to put forth to every one, those objects alone, which were best calculated to move his feelings and secure his co-operation.

As Henry III. had taken steps to meet the machinations of his enemies, by negotiating with the King of Navarre before the death of his brother, the Duke of Guise saw the necessity on his side of providing for the future extension of his party; and as soon as the Duke of Anjou was declared beyond hope of recovery, he called a meeting in the town of Nancy, at which agents of the King of Spain attended, as well as a number of French nobles, and the Duke of Lorraine. With the particulars of this assembly's proceedings we are not fully acquainted; but it was determined that steps should be taken for the general diffusion of the League throughout Roman Catholic Europe, and that preparation should be secretly made for that recourse to arms, which, it was evident to all, must sooner or later be

had.* The Duke of Guise himself conducted his proceedings with the most consummate art; and I
cannot give a better picture of his conduct during
the end of the year 1584, than by translating the
words of a Roman Catholic writer, of high repute,
when speaking of the character of that extraordinary
man as it appeared at this time:—"The Duke of
Guise," says Le Laboureur, "was on his part so
covered in his thoughts, that his very brothers knew
nothing of them. He had a secret for each of
those who believed themselves to be his confidants;
and the promises which he made to the Pope, to
the King of Spain, to the Duke of Lorraine, and to
the Cardinal of Bourbon, were all different, so that
there was no one who knew what he meditated but
himself. And even the Queen-mother was taken
in, thinking that he acted in good faith for the
Duke of Lorraine, who lent his house for the assemblies, and received the honors as the future King, at
the same time that they were promised to the Cardinal of Bourbon, whom he took a pleasure in seeing
deceived. The Duke of Guise had always a secret
ready for the ear of any gentleman interested, who
came to pay his compliments, another for the
zealous citizen who hastened to see him, and who
returned to his family with his heart swelling with
the honor he had received, and which he did not
fail to exaggerate a hundred-fold, as well as for the

* As all writers agree upon the points above stated, it may be
unnecessary to burden the margin with authorities.

crowd of nobles and distinguished men who thronged the Hotel de Guise."

The daring proceedings of the League, however, and the movements of many of its inferior sections, could not be long concealed, notwithstanding all the arts of its great leader ; and Henry III., in the end of 1584, awoke to a sense of his full danger. In order to avert it, he had recourse to means, which, at a former period, might have been successful. An assembly of the King's chief counsellors was held at St. Germain, early in November ; and amongst other noblemen summoned was the Duke of Nevers, who, from the active part he had taken in the League, was at one time called the soul and council of the union.

Having informed the persons present, with his usual eloquence, of all the movements derogatory to his honor, and dangerous to his authority, which were taking place in every province of France, the King turned to Nevers ; and, after boldly touching upon his connection with the agitators, he professed the utmost reliance in the Duke's faith and honor, and asked his advice as to the best means of putting a stop to so lamentable a state of things. Nevers was moved to tears by this mark of confidence, and was never after a zealous partisan of the League. By his advice, and that of the rest of the council, Henry III. published, on the 11th of the month, a declaration against all leagues and associations entered into without his express consent,

forbidding the enrolment of men and the administration of unlawful oaths, on pain of prosecution for
high treason.* The Leaguers, however, had proceeded too far, and the King's authority had sunk
too low, for any of those who were engaged in the
conspiracy to be frightened by proclamations; and
not long after, the Duke of Guise, in a visit to the
Sorbonne, told the worthy doctors, who had hitherto
aided his proceedings, that if they were not strong
enough with the pen, they must contrive to be so
with the sword.†

In the end of December, another great meeting
of the leaders of the League took place in the house
of the Duke of Guise, at Joinville, where envoys
from the King of Spain, and several other Roman
Catholic Princes were present. The general course
of proceeding was now definitively arranged, and a
treaty was drawn up for the signature of the parties
assembled, by which they bound themselves to exclude a Protestant monarch from the throne, to
suppress every religion but the Roman Catholic in
the kingdom, to expel all who would not conform
to its doctrines, and to unite together in a bond
offensive and defensive for its maintenance in
France and the Low Countries. The envoys of
the King of Spain especially engaged their master
to the various Catholic Princes taking part in the

---

* The declaration is to be found at full in the Memoires de
Nevers, tom. i. p. 635.

† Journal de L'Etoile, ed. 1744.

proceedings, and promised a body of men, and a large monthly subsidy, for carrying out the measures determined upon.*   It was also arranged, that the decrees of the Council of Trent should be received in France, and that all alliance with infidels should be renounced.   The treaty was signed on the 31st of December, 1584; but it was agreed to keep it secret till sufficient preparations had been made for putting it into execution.   There can be little doubt that all the most important articles were dictated by the King of Spain, who had a means of control over the proud Duke of Guise, which that nobleman, however high his courage, did not dare to resist, as I shall ere long have occasion to shew. But it would appear, that the Duke was anxious to delay as long as possible the explosion of the plot, foreseeing that if the schemes of his confederates were too speedily developed, his own personal objects would certainly be endangered, though those of the King of Spain, which he clearly perceived, might be secured.

Philip's chief desire, indeed, was once more to plunge France into a sea of civil contentions, in order to divert her energies from any further interference in the affairs of the Low Countries; and events soon occurred, which increased his anxiety for such a result, and induced him to force forward the unwilling Duke of Guise to active aggression upon the royal authority.

* The sum was a hundred and fifty thousand francs per month.

William, Prince of Orange, the great stay and support of the insurgents in the Low Countries, had been assassinated at Delft on the tenth of July, 1584 ; and, after long deliberation,, the States sent ambassadors to the Court of France, beseeching Henry to take upon himself the protection of the United Provinces, and deliver them from the yoke of Spain. The deputies arrived at Senlis in the beginning of February, 1585, from which place they were conducted with great honor to Paris, where they continued their negotiations for some time. The French monarch hesitated long whether he should accept the glorious but perilous task they sought to put upon him ; and there is great reason to suppose that the ambassadors of the Queen of England, who about the same time arrived to invest him with the Order of the Garter, interceded zealously in favor of the oppressed people of the Low Countries.* Tidings of these negotiations were not long in reaching the ears of the King of Spain ; and, fearful lest Henry should ultimately accede to the wishes of the States, and that the fiery courage of the French, diverted from their internal dissensions, should be turned to the nobler object of giving freedom to the neighbouring people, Philip commanded his ambassador, Don Bernard Mendoza, to summon the Duke of Guise to perform his engagements, and put himself in arms at the head of the League.†

* The Queen of England, according to the account of L'Etoile, offered to pay one-third of the expenses of the war.

† Le Laboureur. Mem. de Nevers.

Tired of delay and evasion, and perhaps divining that the Duke was anxious to wait, till the death of the King and the circumstances of the heir presumptive, placed the crown of France nearer to the grasp of his own ambition, Philip directed his minister to threaten, if Guise did not immediately comply, to expose the whole of his intrigues, both in the past and the present, and to place in the hands of Henry III., not only the treaty he had lately signed, but the proofs of still more criminal intrigues, which had been found amongst the papers of Don John of Austria, after the murder of his secretary, Escovedo.*

* See Le Laboureur. It is certain that Henry III. was already aware that treasonable correspondence had been carried on by the Duke of Guise, with Philip II., and that he derived his information from the active and energetic King of Navarre. In one of the letters of the latter, published for the first time, I believe, by M. Berger de Xivrey, we find the King of Navarre using these remarkable words to the French monarch, who, it would appear, had conceived suspicions of his designs, from the fact of his having sent Monsieur de Segur on a mission to some of the Protestant Princes of Europe. " I have always thought, my Lord, that being born in my kingdom and sovereignty, and having a right and title by succession to my said kingdom, which is one of the most ancient, though I have lost it, or at least three parts thereof, for the service of your crown, I was, nevertheless, in no degree fallen from the right and power of keeping up friendship and alliance, as the other Kings and Princes of Christendom, for the benefit of my affairs, and for the union of the confessions of the religion which I profess. Many of your subjects who have no such quality are not reproved for so doing, or at least do not cease from treating with foreigners on whatever matter seems good to them."

The Duke, alarmed at this menace, no longer
hesitated, but immediately began his preparations
for war, and all was silent haste and activity in
Picardy and Champagne.   It became necessary,
however, that some person should be put forward to
claim the succession to the throne, whose title might
be so specious as not to rouse the Parliaments of
the kingdom to interfere, and array the influential
body of the law against the party of the League.
The Duke of Guise himself, utterly without claim,
did not dare to demand as a right, that sceptre
which he hoped ultimately to snatch in the character
of a successful soldier.   The salic law was directly
opposed to the Duke of Lorraine, and to the
daughter of the King of Spain.   Neither would it
have coincided with the views of Guise, to recognize the title of any aspirant, whose power, talents,
youth, or influence, would render his hold upon
authority, firm and permanent.   None of these objections, however, existed in the case of the old
Cardinal de Bourbon.   A doubt might be entertained, whether, in collateral branches of the royal
house, what is termed representation existed, and
whether a son succeeded to the dormant rights of
his father deceased; or whether, on the contrary, the
nearest male surviving of the original stock, did not
take of right, to the exclusion of the children of a
nearer male defunct.   This was the legal question
between Henry of Navarre, and his uncle, regarding
the succession to the throne of France.   Although

the title of the uncle was certainly but weak in law, as the Duke of Guise well knew, he might hope that the heretical faith of the nephew would induce the Parliament to make a precedent which in itself would tend to shake the fixed rule of succession, and be a step towards the transfer of the crown from the descendants of Capet to himself. Unless some such expectation was entertained by Guise, the recognition of the rights of the house of Bourbon at all, can only be considered as a measure of absolute necessity, forced upon him by the injunctions of Philip to commence the war, at a time when all the Duke's preparations for the execution of his ambitious purposes, were incomplete ; as this recognition was certainly a barrier to the advancement of any other claims. It has indeed been hinted by contemporary authors, that the Cardinal,* in truth, only pressed the recognition of his own title, in order to secure beyond doubt the succession of his house.

It must be remembered, however, in considering the motives of the Duke of Guise, that the concealment of his ultimate views, until his schemes were mature, was absolutely requisite to the success of his enterprise, that, if he had refused to admit the title of the Bourbons altogether, his designs would at once have become manifest to all, and that not only would the adherents of that family without exception have ranged themselves against him, but all

* Victor Cayet.

those who had joined the League from conscientious convictions, would have abandoned it on discovering that religion was but the pretext, and usurpation the object.

On all these considerations, he determined that he would put forward, as a veil for his deeper purposes, the name of the Cardinal de Bourbon, whose age and state of health promised a speedy release from worldly cares, and whose mental powers were as weak as could be desired. By the advice of Guise, the Cardinal retired to Gaillon, in the diocese of Rouen, and waited there for the opening of the formal proceedings of the League. The first step commanded by the great leader of the revolt, was a solemn deputation of the nobility of Picardy, to invite the old prelate to put himself at their head. By rapid journeys he was brought to Peronne, in the month of March, 1585, and on the last day of that month, he published a declaration or manifesto, prepared in his name by the confederates.* It would appear, that the original document did not absolutely name any of the Princes, who had taken part in the meetings of Nancy and Joinville ; but in order to give it more weight, a list was subsequently added specifying the foreign sovereigns, the states, the ecclesiastics, and the nobles, who had bound

---

* The proof that this document was not the production of the Cardinal himself, is found in the fact, that a copy was sent from Champagne to Provence, about a fortnight before it was published at Peronne.

themselves, or were assumed to have bound themselves, to aid by various means in the projects of the League. Amongst these appeared the Pope, though the supreme Pontiff had shewn no great cordiality towards the undertaking, the King of Spain, the Emperor, the Grand Master of Malta, the States of Venice, Genoa, and Lucca, and likewise the Grand Duke of Florence, who, there is every reason to believe, was opposed to the undertaking. The Dukes of Lorraine and Guise, were pointed out as Lieutenants-General of the League; and their names were followed by those of all the Princes of their house, and those of the Dukes of Nevers, Savoy, Ferara, Nemours, Cleves, Parma, and the Bishops of Mayence and Cologne.* Many of these names were undoubtedly put forward without authority; but it was a part of the policy of the Leaguers to deceive the King and the public, in regard to their real strength; and in the attempt to do so they were completely successful.

The manifesto itself is too long for insertion here; but the principal matters worthy of remark therein, are the fierce declamations against the Protestants; the attack upon the King of Navarre, who is designated a relapsed heretic, and is distinctly pointed out as excluded thereby from the succession to the throne; the charges indirectly made against him and the Protestants, of intending with the aid of foreign troops, to overthrow entirely the Roman Catholic religion; the vehement denunciation of the minions

* The manifesto and list are to be found in the Mem. de Nevers, tom. i. page 641.

of the King; the lamentations over the oppressions and exactions under which the people groaned; and the condemnation of the extortions which had been practised upon the church. All the evils specified the Leaguers proposed to correct and oppose with arms in their hands, but in the gentlest and kindest manner possible, without violating their allegiance to the King, or in any shape burdening the people.*

---

* The proceedings of the League had for many months been made known by rumors, and it is also clear that some manifestoes had been printed, by order of the Duke of Guise, without signature, but at what period they were published I do not discover. Early in the year 1585, the agents of the League were busy in every part of France, and it is not improbable that they circulated false reports, regarding the co-operation of Henry III. in the designs of the faction. We find, that Henry of Navarre, in a letter to Segur, dated by Monsieur de Xivrey 25th March, speaks of an edict having been published, revoking that of Pacification. Now we find no such edict, and even the declaration of Peronne, the publication of which might have given rise to the report, was not signed till the 31st of March. I am, however, inclined to believe that the learned and careful editor of the " Lettres Missives," has, in this instance, been deceived as to the date, by various circumstances referred to in that letter, which appears in manuscript to have been without date. Henry certainly refers to a meeting between himself and Montmorenci; and M. de Xivrey imagines that their first conference which took place at Castres, must be the meeting spoken of. Henry and Montmorenci, however, met again between the 5th and 11th of August, at St. Paul Cap de Joux, after the edict of revocation had issued, and as in the letter he speaks of the revocation of the edict, and also of his meeting with Montmorenci, I cannot but imagine that the date of the letter should be St. Paul, August.

While such proceedings were taking place at a short distance from the capital, an event occurred well calculated to awaken Henry III. to his danger, and to rouse him to active resistance.   On the 29th of March, a large boat was seized upon the Marne, as it was making its way to Chalons, though from what circumstances of suspicion it was detained, we do not know.   On board was discovered M. de la Rochette, one of the attendants of the Cardinal de Guise; and on examining the wine barrels with which the boat was laden, they were found to contain nothing but arms.   La Rochette was arrested and carried in haste to Paris; and the greatest consternation spread amongst the members of the League, lest their full designs should be exposed by the confession of their emissary.   The Duke of Guise and his brother the Cardinal, who were both at Rheims, wrote in haste to the Duke of Nevers, beseeching him to look to the affair, evidently in the hope of inducing him to interfere for the purpose of preventing La Rochette from being compelled to speak; and the Cardinal uses the significant words, " I beseech you most humbly to think of this, for he is not ignorant of any-thing, as you know ;"—clearly shewing that, amongst the principal leaders, much more criminal actions were already proposed than the mere taking of arms against their sovereign ; for that purpose was already announced to the Parliament of Aix, and was the very next day proclaimed at Peronne.* What these

* See letters from the Duke of Guise and from the Cardinal,

designs were, is displayed by a contemporary letter from the Jesuit, Claude Matthieu, in which he states that the Pope was opposed to the idea of putting the King to death, but that he approved of the plan of seizing upon his person, and obtaining possession of all the principal towns of France in his name.

Whether the Duke of Nevers did or did not exert his influence over the court, which was still great, for the deliverance of La Rochette, we do not know; but it is certain that the emissary of the League was not only set free, but that the arms, which he had been conveying to Chalons, were permitted to reach their destination. Such acts on the part of the King,—acts which it was scarcely possible to attribute to any depth of indolence or folly— naturally awakened the fears of the Huguenots. Two agents, who were maintained by the King of Navarre at the French court, named Clervant and Chassincourt, by his orders remonstrated warmly with the monarch, hinting that he was suspected of intelligence with the leaders of the League.*

in the collection of Nevers. L'Etoile, it would appear, places the arrest of La Rochette wrongly on the 12th March; or otherwise the Duke of Guise must have been kept in ignorance of the fact for a fortnight.

* The Leaguers themselves spread this report; and the King of Navarre, in one of his letters to Chassincourt, written in March or April, 1585, says, after speaking of the inactivity of the King in opposing the proceedings of the faction, and the passive assistance afforded to them by the royal officers, "Those of the League who see this, encourage themselves therewith, and find

Henry, in reply, called down the curse of God upon his head if he had any intercourse with them whatever; and in a letter which he, shortly after, wrote to the King of Navarre, he declared that he saw clearly, the proceedings of the League "tended to nothing but an enterprise against his person and his state." He besought his cousin, however, to remain quiet, and to forbear from taking arms, in order that people might judge easily who were the real disturbers of the public peace.*

arguments therein to raise the spirits of their adherents, making them believe, that it (*i. e.* the King's conduct) is a farce which is played, of which all the results will fall upon the Protestants."

* Cayet Chronologie Novenaire. Peirre Matthieu. It is evident that several letters were written on this subject by Henry III. to the King of Navarre; for the latter alludes, in his correspondence, to various injunctions and requests of the French monarch. One of these letters has been preserved by Don Vaissette, in his History of Languedoc, in which Henry III. writes as follows:—" My Brother, I give you notice, that notwithstanding all the resistance I could make, I have not been able to prevent the evil designs of the Duke of Guise. He is in arms; keep on your guard, and wait for nothing. I hear you have been at Castres to confer with my cousin, the Duke of Montmorenci, of which I am glad; in order that you may look to your affairs, I will send a gentleman to you at Montauban, who will inform you of my will,

"Your good Brother,

"HENRY."

It is stated that the King of Navarre received this letter on the 23rd of March; but I do not find that Guise was actually in arms at that time.

This advice might have been judicious had he followed it up by energetic measures, on his own part, against his rebellious subjects ; but, on the contrary, he contented himself with manifestoes, in answer to their accusations, and messages exhorting them to tranquillity, in opposition to actual rebellion, taking at the same time precautions for his own safety, which he now found was menaced.

The League, after the arrest of La Rochette, found that it was impossible to delay any longer without danger; and the first blow struck was the seizure of Chalons sur Marne, which the Duke of Guise determined to make the centre of his operations. Thither the old Cardinal de Bourbon was afterwards carried from Peronne in triumph, and received all the external honors of royalty.

Henry III. was now roused to some activity ; and the Duke of Montpensier, who had lately succeeded his father, was sent to Orleans with Marshal D'Aumont and a considerable force, to take that city out of the hands of the Count D'Entragues, who was known to be attached to the house of Guise. D'Entragues, however, ordered the guns of the place to fire upon the royal troops; and mortified and disappointed, Montpensier retired from before the walls. This was only one out of many instances in which the want of care and precaution, on the part of Henry, proved destructive to his best interests. The whole of Picardy was overrun by the Duke of Aumale at the head of a feeble body of horse ; no defence was made; town after town declared for the League, and opened its gates to the officers of the faction. Lyons was also taken; and Marseilles was surprised by one of the officers of the town, named Daries, and a captain Boniface. Thoul and Verdun were likewise seized by the agents of the League; and a number of other places in Anjou and Poitou fell into their hands without offering any resistance. An enterprise against the strong town of Metz, indeed, was frustrated; and the inhabitants of Marseilles, rising against the faction, hung Daries and his companion, and called in the officers of the King.

It was now sufficiently apparent that religion had but a small share in the motives of the Leaguers. As the historian, Matthieu, justly observes : " The League waged war against the Huguenots, in attacking the best towns the Catholics possessed in the kingdom. The Reformation is in Guienne, they hasten to drive-it out of Picardy. The Huguenots are at Rochelle, and the army of the League marches towards Paris; they are at Montpellier, and the Leaguers undertake to surprise Marseilles." That Henry III. saw their real objects, is clear from his letters to Henry of Navarre; and he had two courses, equally honorable, but not equally politic, before him; while a third, full of weakness, danger, and disgrace, was also pressed upon his attention. With the forces at his command, with a number of gallant gentlemen devoted to him, with the calmer, but not less powerful support of the lovers of public order, he might have placed himself

at the head of his troops, and, adhering to the
terms of his proclamation of November, have encountered the power of the insurgents in the field,
without permitting the Huguenots, who were still
perfectly tranquil, to take any part in the contest.
By such conduct he would have secured the confidence of the sincere Catholics, restored respect to
the royal authority, and removed one half of the
dangers of his position.

It is now ascertained that, during the four first
months of the revolt, the utmost force the Leaguers
could bring into the field, did not amount to more
than one thousand horse, and four thousand infantry; while the party was as deficient in money
as in men. There can be no doubt, that had the
King thought fit to act energetically at first, he
might have crushed the insurrection in the bud,
with the forces he could call around him without
delay. But if the exaggerated reports of the power
and numbers of the League, which were industriously circulated, and were pressed daily upon
his attention by Catherine de Medicis, who was
undoubtedly cognizant of the intrigues of the
faction,* alarmed him for the result of a contest
unsupported, he might have called to his assistance
the King of Navarre and his friends, amongst
whom were ranged a number of sincere Catholics;
and the necessity of the case would have justified
him in the eyes of all but his most bigoted subjects.
The third course, and the one which he chose, was

* L'Etoile. Perefix.

to negotiate with armed insurgents; who, whatever might be the faults or crimes of the King, had no reasonable pretext for their rebellion. The members of the League were suffering under no oppression; neither injustice nor tyranny had been exercised towards them; and all that they could reproach the monarch with, was his tolerance of their religious opponents.

Nevertheless, after long hesitation, after manifestoes in his own justification, after accusing them of rebellion, falsehood, treachery, and ingratitude, Henry thought fit to send his mother to treat with the chiefs of the faction. Manifold conferences took place, and it would appear from a letter of the Cardinal de Bourbon, that the Leaguers purposely made their demands as extravagant as possible, in the expectation of their being ultimately rejected;* while their activity in the field was undiminished, and Bourges, Dijon, Mezieres, and several other places, were added to those which they had already obtained.† Troops were marching also from various foreign countries for their support. German forces were hired to aid in their enterprise; and Pfifer engaged to bring a powerful body of Swiss Catholics to their assistance.‡

The forces of the League, every day increasing, now began to menace Paris itself; and the apprehensions of the King became extreme. Miron, his

---

* Mem. de Nevers.   † Davila.
‡ See letters of the Duke of Guise.

physician, known to be intimately connected with
the house of Guise, was sent to negotiate, and close
upon his steps trod Louis Davila, gentleman of
honor to the Queen-mother. Lansac also took
part in the conferences, and by his skill, seems to
have excited some degree of jealousy between the
old Cardinal de Bourbon and the house of Guise,
which contributed not a little to attain the object
of the Queen-mother. There is every reason to
believe that the assertion made by many contemporary writers regarding the views of this Princess,
was not without foundation, and that these negotiations were in fact but a trial of skill between
herself and the Duke of Guise; the design of
Catherine being to maintain the party of the
League, so far as to exclude Henry of Navarre
from the throne, yet to employ it merely as an
instrument for the aggrandizement of her grand-
children by the Duchess of Lorraine, without
suffering it to gain such an ascendancy as might
transfer the crown, on the death of Henry III.,
either to the Cardinal de Bourbon or the Duke of
Guise. Such purposes, as I have said, were very
generally attributed to her at the time ; and, if she
indeed entertained them, her policy was so far
successful that, after manifold discussions, she concluded a treaty, which bound both her son and the
opposite faction to oppress the Huguenots, and exclude the King of Navarre from the succession, so
long as he persisted in adhering to the tenets of

the Reformation, and which also checked the progress of the League against Henry himself, without
formally admitting the claims of the Cardinal.
She doubtless hoped so to complicate the intrigues
of the court and the faction, as to leave no course
open for the zealous Catholics of France but to
create, or recognize, a title in the Duke of Lorraine
or his son; but while she spun the spider-web of
intrigue thus finely, the merciless hand of fate was
preparing to sweep it all away.

The principal articles of the treaty, so disgraceful
to the King of France, were arranged in the end of
June, and on the 7th of July the document was
signed at Nemours by Catherine, the Cardinals de
Bourbon and Guise, and the Dukes of Guise and
Mayenne. The principal clauses consist of stipulations for the publication of a decree, by which the
ministers of the Reformed Church were ordered
to quit the realm within one month, and all others
who should adhere to the doctrines of Protes-
tantism within six months, while heretics were
declared incapable of holding any office in the
state. Other articles provided for the resumption
of the towns granted as security to the Huguenots;
for the recognition of all the late acts of the League,
as approved by the King, and done for his good
service; for the suppression of the mixed courts
in the Parliaments; for the surrender of nine important towns to the party of the League for five
years; for the maintenance by the State of a body

guard for the principal leaders of the faction; and for the payment of the foreign troops which they had raised. On the part of the confederates the only important promise made was one which they never intended to keep, namely, that they would abandon all leagues and associations, within and without the realm.

It may be necessary, before I proceed to speak of the events which rapidly followed the signature of the disgraceful treaty of Nemours, to trace the steps which had been taken by Henry of Navarre for the purpose of resisting the incessant efforts made by the Catholic party to encroach upon the treaty of Nerac, and thus reduce the Protestants by slow degrees to a state of weakness which would render them an easy prey on the breaking out of a fresh war.

Although the government of Guienne was nominally left in the hands of the King of Navarre, Marshal Matignon was sent into that province in 1581 as Lieutenant-General; and, according to the orders he received from the court, he continued to exercise therein, all the powers of Governor, except in such parts as were secured by the presence of Henry of Bourbon or his principal officers. He was a man of a milder and less enterprising character than Biron, whom he succeeded; and notwithstanding the painful nature of the relations which were now established between himself and his future sovereign, he maintained a certain degree of friendly intercourse with him, and seems to have entertained a sincere regard and admiration for that prince.

Nevertheless, under his eyes, and at least with his connivance, the war of encroachment which had commenced against the Protestants, was carried on with silent but unintermitting steps. The amnesty which had been granted by the King of France for all crimes committed during the late wars, proved only serviceable to the Papists; and multitudes of persons of the Reformed religion were arrested, tried, and executed, in direct violation of the stipulations of the treaty. To such a shameless excess was this course carried, that in one of his letters, the King of Navarre complains that more Protestants had perished, by the cord, during a short interval of peace, than during the preceding period of hostilities, by the sword.

It was in vain Henry remonstrated, it was in vain that he appealed to the King's edict; the parliaments paid no attention to the amnesty, where Calvinists were concerned, and Matignon made no vigorous effort to give it effect.

As another means of weakening the Protestant party, and keeping it in such a state that resistance would be each day rendered less practicable, the garrisons of the towns of security were left for months unpaid; the pension granted to the King of Navarre fell into arrear; the taxes which had been assigned to him for the maintenance of his station

in Guienne were diverted to other purposes ; and his
hereditary dominions were subjected to a regulation,
from which they had been previously free, by which
certain articles of first necessity entering that territory from France, were burdened with a severe ex-
port duty. At the same time no scruple was made
on the part of the Roman Catholics to seize upon
any places belonging to the Navarrese monarch or
his partisans, and especially upon the towns given
as security for the execution of the treaties of Bergerac and Nerac. We have seen that Villeneuve
and Agen had been taken by the forces of Biron,
and Perigueux had also fallen into the power of the
Papists. Tartas, a town belonging to the King of
Navarre himself, was held against him by the
enemy, and the same was the case with the important city of Mont de Marsan, though directly de-
pendent upon Bearn.

It would appear from several of the letters of
Henry of Bourbon, that many other places, to which
he had an indisputable right, were also retained ;
but it is not to be doubted, that various bands of
Protestants, or of those who had sided with them in
the late war, took advantage of the disturbed state
of the country, to hold any strong places which they
could seize, and that troops of partisans on both
sides, still carried on a war of pillage and robbery.
Nevertheless we find that on all occasions the King
of Navarre was ready to use, first authority, and
then force, to oblige those who affected to be attached

to his party, to evacuate the fortresses they illegally
held, and that he was always ready to punish severely those who infringed the provisions of the
treaty. On the part of the Roman Catholics his
remonstrances were unattended to, and the en-
couragement of impunity was afforded to the most
manifest infractions of the act of pacification. In
the case of Perigueux, indeed, after long negotiations, a small and almost indefensible town, or
rather village, named Pemyrol,* in the neighbourhood of Agen, was offered in exchange for that
most important city, with a sum of money to the
King himself. He at first refused both; but finding that nothing else could be obtained, accepted
Pemyrol, and spent the small portion of money that
was paid, in maintaining the garrisons in the places
of security, and providing against other expenses
imposed upon the Protestant party.

In regard to Mont de Marsan, the people of
which were actually his subjects, Matignon made
him daily promises of restoring him to his rights
therein, but still found some excuse for delaying the
execution of his engagement; and, while Henry was
proceeding, with a mixture of remonstrance and
force, to compel some of his Protestant partisans,
who had fortified themselves in the neighbourhood
of Bazas, to demolish the works they had thrown
up, to execute the terms of the treaty with the
utmost fidelity, and to dismantle several places which
had been strengthened during the war, the Catholics

* Or Puymirol, for I find it written both ways.

made themselves masters of St. Sardos and Auvillars. At length, the patience of Henry was exhausted; and he resolved to do himself justice in regard to Mont de Marsan with his own arm. It must be recollected that this was no ordinary case, that the town was a very important one, that it was a part of the inheritance of the King of Navarre, that its surrender, without any delay, had been promised by the treaties of Bergerac and Nerac, and that the commands of the King of France had been laid upon Matignon to restore Henry of Bourbon to his rights in the place.

Determined to force his way into the city, Henry set out from Nerac, on the 20th or 21st of November, 1583, accompanied by the Prince de Condé and their several guards. A body of six hundred arquebusiers had been collected in the Landes to give assistance in case of need; and a few noblemen had been summoned to meet the King on his march, with their adherents; but the enterprise was conducted with so much skill and secrecy, that it did not become necessary to use the forces held in reserve. Henry and his companions passed the river during the night of the 21st—22nd of November, in small boats prepared for the purpose, armed with ladders to scale the walls. The escarpment, however, was very steep, and covered so thickly with bushes, that it was found necessary to send for bill-hooks to cut them away.* The approach of the assailants was, nevertheless, not discovered; and it

* Vie de Du Plessis Mornay.

was not till a ladder had been placed very near one of
the sentinels, and the troops of Navarre were actually on the walls, that a pistol shot gave intimation
to the garrison of an enemy being at hand. An
attempt at resistance was then made; but it was
overcome with so little difficulty, that only one
person was killed in the affray; and, at eight o'clock
on the following morning, the shops in the town
were open, all the people at their work, and not a
trace of hostile feeling remaining on any part.
Henry, with his usual lenity, inflicted no punishment upon his rebellious subjects; but it soon appeared from the proceedings of Matignon, that the
delay which had taken place in reinstating the King
of Navarre in his own town, had been instigated
by those who had pledged themselves to restore it.
Loud accusations were made against Henry, for
the resumption of his rights, even though guaranteed to him by treaty; Matignon, immediately
took possession of Bazas and Condom; and the
Protestant inhabitants of the former were subjected
to every sort of injustice and severity. At the
same time, means were taken to misrepresent the
actions of the King of Navarre, at the court of
France; and even his punishment of some refractory
Protestants, for deeds of violence committed against
the other party, was made a charge against him.

Towards the end of 1583, and the beginning of
1584, it became evident to Henry of Navarre, that
the various encroachments of the Catholics, the

opposition of Matignon and other royal officers to
the execution of the treaty of Nerac, the retention
of his own pension, and of the pay of the garrisons
and guards allowed him, even when the money was
in the hands of the collectors, were not acts of
individual malice, but parts of an organized system
for reducing himself and the Protestant church of
France to a state, in which resistance to further
aggression would be impossible; and, in his letters
to his most intimate friends and counsellors, we
find continually, such expressions as, " Our very
innocence and obedience ruin us," " How am I
recompensed for my obedience to the commands of
the King."

The movements of the League also, long before
the manifesto of Peronne, shewed him clearly that
a time would come, when Henry III. must either
yield to the influence of his ambitious vassals of the
house of Lorraine, or call upon all his more faithful
and obedient subjects to support the throne; and
Henry of Navarre saw that it would be necessary to
make preparation for an appeal to arms in either case.
As soon as he became convinced that such must be
his course, in justice to himself, to his fellow Protestants, to the state, and to Henry III., he displayed
all his wonderful energy and activity, in order to be
ready for whatever part might be forced upon him,
without shewing the slightest disobedience to the
commands of the King, without giving any countenance to turbulence and disorder. Relations of

the most intimate character had arisen between him and the Duke of Montmorenci,* governor of Languedoc, from their joint efforts to restore tranquillity in the provinces committed to their care; and with him Henry now took every means to cement an alliance which was equally necessary to the safety of each. Although the Protestants of Dauphiné were divided amongst themselves, and personal enmities and jealousies raged in their ranks to a frightful extent, the great influence of Lesdeguieres, his vast military talents, and the dignified elevation and resolution of his character, promised, in case of renewed hostilities, to give him complete command of that province; and Henry lost no opportunity of marking his sense of that great commander's merits, and supporting his authority. Thus the materials for a formidable resistance to the iniquitous projects of the League were prepared in the south of France, over a space extending from sea to sea, and from the Alps to the Pyrenees.

With the Swiss Cantons, with the Protestant Princes of Germany, and with the Queen of England, Henry, by means of ambassadors and secret agents, kept up a constant communication. He laid before them his doubts and difficulties; and, while he took particular care to shew his allies that he was anxiously desirous to preserve peace, and perfectly contented with the degree of toleration

* Formerly known as Damville, but who had by this time succeeded his brother.

awarded to the French Protestants, by the treaty of
Nerac, he prepared them to support him, if the
malice of his enemies and the virulence of the
opponents of their faith, should compel him unwillingly to draw the sword.   His views even took a
wider range; and, intimately convinced that the
persecuting spirit of the schismatic church of Rome,
which had already been so disastrously active
against all who ventured to throw off its yoke,
required some more powerful barrier than the
divided efforts of small bodies of Protestants, scattered through various countries, he conceived a
scheme for uniting all the Reformed Princes and
States in one general League, for the defence of
their religion against the assaults of their enemies.
To propose this confederacy, and induce other sovereigns to combine with him for that great purpose,
was the chief object of the first embassy of M. de
Segur to the courts of England and Germany.
Numerous letters, all tending to the same object,
are to be found in Henry's correspondence during
the year 1583, and, although his negotiations were
not crowned with full success, yet they secured for
him the sympathy and respect of those with whom
they were carried on.

Money, however, was still the ingredient wanting
in all his schemes of preparation, and this he was
never able to obtain to such an amount, as to render
the commencement of a war aught but highly dangerous to himself and the Protestant party in France.

Measures the most unjust,* were taken in France, as I have already shewn, to keep him in a state of comparative poverty, and the long wars which had preceded this important epoch, had exhausted the means of the Huguenot nobility, and left most of them in great penury, if not in debt. At one time, indeed, an opportunity of obtaining pecuniary resources seemed to open before Henry, and he skilfully endeavored to take advantage of it, without a breach of that good faith which he so carefully preserved.

In the month of May, 1583, a Spanish gentleman named Undiano, was employed to commence a negotiation, through his brother-in law the Viscount d'Eschaus, one of the vassals of the Navarrese monarch, with a view to engage that Prince in a treaty with Philip II. The object of the King of Spain, was to induce Henry of Bourbon to take arms against Henry III. of France; and to tempt him to such a course, he offered to pay at once three hundred thousand crowns, and to supply one hundred thousand each month, for the expenses of the war. But, in his eagerness to stir up fresh hostilities between the opposite parties in France, Philip had miscalculated the probity of the man he sought to seduce. Henry rejected his proposals firmly; but in order to prepare for the events he

* The pension, which was left unpaid, had been granted to the Sovereigns of Navarre by the French monarchs, as compensation for the loss of territory they had sustained by their adhesion to the cause of France in her wars with Spain.

saw approaching, he authorized De Mornay and St. Genies to borrow, in his name, five hundred thousand crowns from the King of Spain, offering to pledge his whole property for that sum. Philip was not inclined to lend the amount required, without those political stipulations, to which Henry would not listen, and the negotiation was consequently broken off.

Somewhat later in the year, the Spanish monarch again sought to treat upon the same subject, but in vain; and Henry remained anxiously watching the progress of events, endeavoring, to the best of his ability, to suppress the spirit of civil strife which still reigned in Guienne and Languedoc, and warning the King of France from time to time, both of the infractions of the edict, which were committed daily by the more vehement Papists and encouraged by the royal officers, and of the secret machinations of those who used religion as a pretence, but whose real designs threatened the person of the monarch, and the fundamental principles of the monarchy. Week after week, and day after day, we find his remonstrances addressed to Henry III. upon the seizure of towns and fortresses; the persecution of the Protestants wherever the Roman Catholics had the ascendancy, the pillage of the country by bodies of armed men, the murder of unoffending citizens, and the execution of soldiers and gentlemen for acts which had been consigned to oblivion by the edicts of amnesty. But, at the same time, it is clear from the whole correspondence of that period, that the weak monarch of France was surrounded by persons who sought to poison his ear against the heir to his throne, and to misrepresent all the actions of his brother-in-law; and, in one letter to Bellievre, Henry of Navarre complains in terms of bitter indignation of the attention paid to their reports by the French sovereign, and appeals to that statesman's own observations while in Guienne, for a complete refutation of the calumnies circulated against him.

At length, towards the close of 1584, and in the beginning of 1585, the danger became imminent, not only to Henry of Navarre, but to the King of France, from the open and daring machinations of the League; and the Bourbon Prince seems to have forgotten the causes of complaint which existed against Henry III. in his anxiety to open that monarch's eyes to the real designs of the house of Guise, and save him from the snare laid for him. He exhorted him to employ the services of his nearest kinsman against those who were equally the enemies of both, and offered to hasten to his assistance the moment he was called: but Henry, as usual, hesitated; and, in the meanwhile, measures were taken against the King of Navarre, as against an enemy, even in his own government of Guienne. Troops were raised; cannon were cast; soldiers were called out; and as, day by day, the proceedings of the League assumed a more open and daring character, the situation of the Navarrese Prince be-

came more embarrassing.   Resolved to remain tranquil to the last, and not to unsheath the sword till
compelled to do so, he still endeavored to soothe his
fellow Protestants, and to prevent a desultory and
partial resumption of hostilities ; but he felt himself
justified in adopting fresh means to guard against
surprise ; and the known weakness of the King of
France, as well as the demonstrations of his officers,
seemed to call upon him imperatively to strengthen
his own position, even while he waited patiently for
the result of Henry's hesitation.   His correspondence
with the Queen of England and the German Princes
became more active ; he gave orders for repairing
the fortifications of all the cities he held ; a large
quantity of gunpowder was manufactured ; no
soldiers were allowed to quit the principality of
Bearn without express permission ; the King's own
guard, and that of Condé, as well as the company
of Turenne, were called out, in order to form
the nucleus of a future army ; the inhabitants of
all Protestant towns were warned to keep upon their
guard ; and in a meeting which took place at
Castres between Henry and Montmorenci, in the
middle of March, they bound themselves to support
each other against the authors of the League.

Still the position of the King of Navarre was very
difficult and embarrassing ; frequent letters passed
between himself and the French Monarch ; and
while the Bourbon Prince reiterated his warnings,
and besought his brother-in-law to employ his arm

against their mutual enemy, or at least to suffer him to take means for crushing the League in his own government, Henry III., while approving of his conference with Montmorenci, and bidding him be prepared, commanded him to refrain from all energetic measures, withheld both authority to act, and money to pay his troops, and assured him that he himself would oppose the League to his satisfaction.

At the same time, the zealous Roman Catholics of Guienne and Languedoc were not inactive; innumerable attempts were made upon different fortresses; regiments were raised for the service of the faction under the very eyes of Matignon; and it is not improbable that he too remained passive, in consequence of distinct orders from the court to that effect. Catherine de Medicis was also known to be negotiating with the rebels; and a rumor spread generally throughout the south of France, that it was the intention of herself and her son to revoke the edict of pacification, and unite with the house of Guise in waging war against the Protestants.*

Of the truth of this report, Henry of Navarre, whatever were his suspicions, was not yet personally cognizant, the whole particulars of the negotiation

---

* Lettres Missives du Roi de Navarre, from which, together with some letters preserved by Dom Vaissette, and the Life and Memoirs of Du Plessis Mornay, the Hist. Gen. d'Aubigné, and the Memoires de la Ligue, the principal statements regarding this period of Henry's life are derived.

having been concealed from him ; and we find, that
on the 17th of May, he addressed a powerful and
eloquent remonstrance to his brother-in-law, in one
part of which he recapitulates the various daring
acts of the Leaguers in Guienne, and states the
culpable negligence of the royal officers in re-
pressing them, while he points out that he had,
notwithstanding, labored successfully to keep the
menaced and injured party in perfect tranquillity,
in consequence of the King's directions ; "pre-
ferring," he adds, " obedience to your commands,
to that which was, perhaps, absolutely necessary to
your service." He then mentions the reports that
had reached him, and adds that he had assured his
friends they were not to be believed ; " for it is not
probable that your Majesty would be inclined to
satisfy foreigners at the expense of Princes so nearly
allied to you, nor purchase peace from those who
trouble your kingdom, by the detriment of those who
desire nothing but to pass their lives in obedience
to your edicts."

Nevertheless, Henry of Navarre could not be
without suspicions and apprehensions ; and a suggestion which, at this time, reached him from the
court, whether directly or indirectly we do not
know, was certainly not calculated to diminish his
alarm. The course which was offered for his consideration was as follows :—The Protestants were
required to amalgamate their troops with the royal
forces, and to place them under the command of

Roman Catholic officers ; and it was held out as an inducement, that the King would thus be able to combat the power of the League, while no jealousy of the Huguenot party would be excited in France, as the names under which the companies were enrolled would all be those of Papists.

Notwithstanding nearly thirty years' experience of the fraud and violence which the court of France thought itself justified in employing against the Protestant subjects of the realm, there were many of the friends of Henry who were willing to adopt the plan proposed ; and at a meeting of the principal Huguenot noblemen held at Guitres, near Coutras, towards the end of May, twenty gentlemen of great influence were found to favor the suggestion, while at their head appeared the brave and skilful, but turbulent and intriguing Viscount de Turenne. The business of the assembly was opened by Henry himself, in a speech too characteristic to be omitted. " If I could have believed, my friends," he said, " that the present state of affairs only menaced myself, and that ruin of my fortune, the diminution of my influence, and the loss of all that is dearest to me, except my honor, might have obtained for you peace and security, you should have heard no tidings of me ; and with the counsel and assistance of my own adherents, I would, at the expense of my life, have made head against the enemy. But the question being the ruin or preservation of all the Reformed churches, and thereby of the glory of God,

I have thought it a duty to deliberate with you upon that which affects you all. The matter which first presents itself for our inquiry is, whether we ought to stand with our arms crossed during the contest of our enemies, and send all our soldiery into the army of the King, without name or authority—which is an opinion on the lips and in the hearts of many—or whether we ought separately to succor the King in arms, and take the opportunities which may present themselves to strengthen ourselves. This is the question on which I beg every one here assembled to give his judgment without passion."

The first twenty voices were all, as I have said, more or less in favor of the plan suggested by the court; but at length an inferior officer,* speaking in his turn, exposed the danger and folly of such a course in plain but convincing language, and Henry, giving way to his natural impetuosity, exclaimed aloud, " I am with him." These words, joined with the solid reasoning of the last speaker, which was supported by Du Plessis Mornay and the Prince de Condé, decided the assembly, and the plan was rejected.

The assembly of Guitres was followed immediately† by a manifesto on the part of the King of

* Aubigne and the Marshal de la Force, both claim the honor of the speech which turned the feelings of the assembly of Guitres. I have dated the meeting at Guitres, from the invaluable itinerary published by M. Berger de Xivrey.　　† 10th June.

Navarre, the particulars of which must be dwelt upon at large, premising, for the better understanding of the young monarch's reply to the accusations of his enemies, that the League had published another appeal to the people of France and the Catholics of Europe, subsequent to that which had issued from Peronne on the 31st March, and had insinuated that Henry of Bourbon was eagerly looking for the death of Henry III., in order to grasp the crown of France.

In his famous declaration, which breathes in every line the high and chivalrous spirit with which he was animated, Henry began by refuting the charges brought against him on the score of religion, pointing out that he had been educated from infancy in the tenets of the Reformed church, and that he could not be expected to quit them, unless a free and legitimate council should shew him that he was in error, and that until such a council was held he should repel the name of heretic, adding that though, hitherto, efforts had been made to destroy him, none had been made to instruct him. He then refuted the accusation of having relapsed into heresy from the Roman Catholic faith, pointing out that his attendance upon the mass, after the massacre of St. Bartholomew's day, was compulsory, and against his will, and that the moment he had recovered his liberty he had boldly avowed the religion he had always adhered to at heart. He proceeded to declare, that in all the civil wars he had never had any thing in

view but the service of God and of the King; as a
proof of which he shewed that, no sooner had liberty
of conscience been secured, than he laid down his
arms, dismissed his troops, and sent back the foreign
allies who had come to his support.   He next proclaimed that he was anything but an enemy to the
Roman Catholics; dared his accusers to prove
that he had persecuted them, and appealed to his
conduct towards those of Bearn, who were left
in the peaceable exercise of their religion, while his
principal officers and friends were members of that
church, and his life and fortune were continually
trusted in their hands.   The concordat of Magde-
bourg, which the League declaimed against, he
treated as a mere chimera, and shewed that in many
particulars their assertions regarding it were evident falsehoods.   He then went on to notice the
charge, that he retained the towns granted as a security, after they had been demanded by the King;
pointing out that the dangers which they were intended to guard against were more menacing than
ever, but offering to resign them before the time fixed,
if the Leaguers would lay down their arms and restore
the places they had seized.   He then touched upon
that part of the League's manifestoes which declared him incapable of succeeding to the crown,
acknowledging that this was the point of the greatest
importance, but yet the point on which he had
thought the least, having contented himself with the
hope, that God would give the King of France a

long life and numerous posterity for the good of his kingdom, and to the discomfiture of all those who thought fit to represent the Monarch and his Queen as barren, in the flower of their age, and to build, as it were, their evil designs upon Henry's tomb. He repelled the charge of desiring the death of the King, and in plain terms declared that all who had called him a perturber of the public peace, or an enemy of the Catholics, had grossly and maliciously lied. The document concluded by an entreaty to the King, to spare the effusion of Christian blood, and to permit him to descend from his station so far as to decide the quarrel that agitated France, in combat with the Duke of Guise, man to man, two to two, or ten to ten, in order that the people might be no longer oppressed by these contentions. He, moreover, we find, offered, if the Duke of Guise doubted the security of any part of France, for the combat proposed, to quit the realm with him, and void their dispute in any country where it might be honorably decided.*

To this defiance Guise replied, that he had no enmity to the King of Navarre, and that his cause, being that of religion and the state, could not be submitted to the chances of a duel. Henry, however, caused a copy of his declaration to be presented not only to the King, but to all the parliaments of France and all the principal sovereigns of

* Davila, Pierre Matthieu, Cayet, Aubigné, Mem. de Messire P. de Mornay.

Europe. Nor was the effect less than he expected, for the sympathy of many, even of the Roman Catholics, was enlisted in his favor, and the Protestants who had long been divided in their councils, and had shewn themselves unwilling to submit to any one chief, turned their eyes thenceforth to him as their leader, and yielded to his guidance with more unanimity than they had displayed since the death of Coligni.

Nevertheless, neither Henry's declaration, nor the knowledge of his truth and loyalty, made any impression upon the weak King of France. No measures were taken for stopping the progress of the League; nor was the King of Navarre authorized to resist its efforts, even in Guienne.

Encouraged by the rumors of a negotiation between the court and the house of Guise, and by daily information of the direction which that negotiation was taking, the faction grew more and more insolent and enterprising in the south of France; and at the same time the position of Henry of Bourbon became more embarrassing than ever, from the fact of his wife putting herself at the head of his enemies, in the province under his government, fortifying herself in the town of Agen, and gathering together soldiers under the Viscount de Duras, thus offering a common centre for all the operations of the League in the Agenois. Issuing from that town, bands of armed men carried on a desultory system of warfare on the neighbouring

Protestants, made themselves masters of several small towns and castles, and undertook various enterprises of greater importance, in which they were frustrated by the activity of the King of Navarre and his adherents.   There is much reason to believe, also, from many of that monarch's letters, that Marguerite or her adherents, not content with open resistance to his authority, aimed secretly at his life.

Still Henry was commanded to remain tranquil; still the King of France assured him by letters under his own hand,* that in any treaty with the League, his interests should be attended to ; and all that he was permitted to do, was, to make preparation for the worst.   In that course he displayed all the energy which might have been expected ; and gathering the Protestant chiefs around him, keeping up a constant communication with England and Germany, maintaining a frank and cordial communication with Montmorenci, fortifying his towns, increasing the number of his troops, laying in stores of ammunition and arms, warning every leader and every community to be ready at a moment's notice, he guarded against surprise; while he maintained tranquillity in his own party, and resisted all the solicitations of those who urged him to strike the first blow.

No man ever shewed greater moderation, or a more sincere desire of peace ; and it is, indeed,

* Lettres Missives, tom. ii. p. 93.

marvellous how one so impetuous in his character, restrained himself and his followers under circumstances the most irritating. It is evident from all his letters, that during the months of April, May, and June, the struggle with himself was as severe as any that he ever endured with his enemies in the open field; and in one epistle to Segur, on the 28th of June, he alludes to this internal contest, exclaiming, "Our patience lasts as long as it may: God grant that it may continue."

On the 15th of that month he received news of the capture of the town of Bourg by the Leaguers, although, on the 8th, he had given full intimation to Marshal Matignon of their designs upon that place, and had earnestly besought him to frustrate the attempt.

Another party of the Leaguers, under Monsieur de Lansac, had taken possession of a point at the confluence of the Dordogne and the Garonne, and known as the Bec d'Ambez, where they had built a fort, commanding the course of the Gironde; but in this instance Matignon, perceiving that the trade of Bordeaux and other towns in his own hands, was menaced, displayed a degree of activity, which principally served to shew how easily he might have prevented the capture of Bourg, had he thought fit to make the attempt. The fort at the Bec d'Ambez was taken by storm, after a vigorous resistance; and amongst the prisoners was found the infamous Gavaret, or Gabaret, who had so frequently attempted to assassinate the King of Navarre. Henry

immediately demanded that he should be brought
to trial and punished for his crimes; but Matignon,
well aware of what was taking place at the court,
did not think fit to adopt such a course at once; and
succeeding events screened the assassin from the
arm of justice.   The King of Navarre had advanced in person to Tonneins, to support Matignon
in case of need, and had ordered a reinforcement to
be sent from Montsegur; but no sooner did he
hear of the Marshal's success than he retired to
Nerac, in order to give no occasion for suspicion or
offence.   He had scarcely arrived at the latter place,
however, when a rumor reached him of the conclusion of a treaty between Henry III. and the rebels of
the League; and seeing that no time was to be lost,
the King of Navarre hastened all his preparations,
in order to resume hostilities the moment the intelligence was confirmed.

Such was the haste required to avoid being taken
by surprise, and the rapidity with which event succeeded event, that, in writing to Segur, on the
eighth of July, he says, "Excuse me if I do not
write with my own hand; for I have so much business that I have not leisure to blow my nose;"
and Segur, in a memoir addressed to the Queen
of England, declared, "that the affairs of Christendom were in such a state, that whereas, formerly,
events ran by years and months, they were now to
be counted by hours and minutes."

Elizabeth herself was deeply interested in the

welfare of the King of Navarre ; and the negotiation which had been opened by his ambassador in London, was carried on by an envoy from the English queen, who arrived in Guienne on the second or third of June. The precise particulars of this transaction I do not discover ; but it is evident that promises of support, in money, men, and ships, were made by Elizabeth ; and though there is some reason to believe that she did not perform all that she had led Henry to expect, yet she rendered him most important assistance, not only by furnishing him with the means of carrying out the war, but by sending the famous Lord Willoughby to advocate his cause with the German Princes.*

Still the King of Navarre refrained from every act of hostility ; for Henry III. to the very last, reiterated his assurances that he would look upon that Prince's interests as his own, and neither agree to, nor grant, anything contrary to the edict of peace, which he declared to be irrevocable. Even after vague information of the signature of the treaty of Nemours reached Henry of Navarre, he seems to have doubted that Henry and his Parliament would confirm it, and to have hesitated to take arms. No official communication of the fact had been made to him up to the beginning of August; but some time before that period positive intelligence must have arrived at Bergerac, of the forced registration of the edict confirming this treaty, by the parliament

* Letters of the reign of Elizabeth.

of Paris, notwithstanding the strong opposition of that body : and the Protestants of France now found that the King, terrified by the menaces of the League, and misled by the counsels of his mother, had sanctioned all the proceedings of his enemies ; had revoked the edict under which the Huguenots enjoyed a certain degree of toleration and security ; had given numerous strong towns into the hands of the house of Guise ; had placed the forces of the state at their disposal ; had violated his word as a gentleman, his oath as a Christian and his duty as a king ; and had granted to fear, all that had been required by his rebellious nobles with the very view of making their demands so extravagant, as to preclude the possibility of accommodation.

Such concessions on the part of the King might well surprise the whole of Europe ; and it may not be amiss to shew how the conduct of the League, in exacting such conditions from the sovereign, was regarded by one of its wisest and most conscientious members. " You will pardon me," says the Duke of Nevers, in a letter to the Cardinal de Bourbon, "if I say that you have gone beyond that upon which we were agreed, and that the Duke of Guise has not adhered to the measures that were arranged with us. You ought not to go to work with the King as if he were a declared enemy ; yet you push things with him to the last extremity ; you impose upon him insulting conditions, and not remembering

that we are all his subjects, you speak as if you were
a sovereign."

Again he goes on, " The edict that he has carried
to the Parliament has frightened me, when I read
an act by which he sanctions the assumption of
arms, the seizure of the public money, the taking of
prisoners, and other acts of hostility. He wills afterwards that the past should be forgotten, and imposes
oblivion upon all men. Believe me, that in this, he
does not speak as he thinks ; and that this oblivion,
commanded to others, is a notice to himself to remember it all his life, and to make you repent it on
the first occasion."

After exhorting the Cardinal, in eloquent terms,
to return to his duty, to restrain the Duke of Guise,
and to labor with all his energies to efface from
Henry's mind the memory of the past, he ends with
the following warning : — " Sovereigns are born too
jealous of their authority to suffer its partition ; and
all those who have sought to frighten their masters
have perished before they did them any harm."*

The opinion of the Sovereign Pontiff was not
less strongly pronounced.   " The Pope has just said
to me," says Nevers, in another letter, " that there
never was formed a conspiracy more pernicious to
religion and the state than that of the League. He
praises God, that it appears smothered by the good-
ness of the King, and by the approbation which he
seems to have granted to all that has passed ; but, he

* Mem. de Nevers, tom. i. p. 670.

says, if this pardon and reconciliation be not sincere, we shall see, in a short time, the unhappy consequences which they will have. ‘The King of France will soon be obliged,’ he added, with tears in his eyes, ‘ to treat the Catholics as his greatest enemies; he will be compelled to draw forces from Germany, England, and other Protestant countries, in order to become the strongest in his own state; he will have to enter into a disgraceful accommodation with the King of Navarre and the Prince de Condé, and to inundate all France with Lutherans and Calvinists. See,’ continued the Pope, ‘ what good results will have proceeded from your association, and your fine raising of the buckler.’ ”*

If such was the effect produced upon the minds of Roman Catholic Princes, it may be well supposed that the surprise of Henry of Navarre and his friends was not less.   Whatever he might have feared from the knavery, wickedness, and indolence of the King, the terms of the edict, which he received towards the end of July, 1585, went far beyond his expectations; and he himself related to the historian Matthieu, that, while reading the document, the mustache, which leaned upon his hand, became white in the space of a few minutes, so terrible was the effect upon his mind. Henry, however, was pre-eminently a man of action; and he now hesitated no longer to take arms in his own defence.   In a few days, messengers were hurrying over the whole country; some

* Idem. p. 672.

carrying letters of reproach and remonstrance to the King, and to the Parliament; others summoning his friends and adherents to take counsel for meeting the impending danger; others notifying the state of the Huguenots of France to the Protestant Princes of Europe.*

At the assembly of Guitres, no less than sixty Protestant deputies were present; but, in order to decide upon the means of carrying on the war, a smaller meeting of the nobles opposed to the League, including several distinguished Catholics, as well as Huguenots, and an envoy from the Elector Palatine, was held at St. Paul,† at which also appeared the Prince de Condé and Marshal Montmorenci. There, a new protestation against the proceedings of the League was signed, by which the nobles assembled, reminded the people of France, that the King had solemnly declared that all who took arms, without his express command and commission, should be considered guilty of high treason, arguing thence, that as the League had done so, not only contrary to his permission, but actually against his person, they had fallen under this censure, and therefore, that those who opposed them in the field, were but rendering good service to the King. Much division of opinion, however, unfortunately existed amongst the Protestant Princes and nobles assembled at St. Paul; and a rash and extraordinary proposition was made, it would appear, by the Viscount de Turenne, having for its object to

* Davila.　　　　　　† Davila.

unite the Protestants of France into a sort of republic, under the protection of the Elector Palatine
and the guidance of five or six lieutenants appointed
by that Prince.*

This scheme, as may be imagined, was most obnoxious to the King of Navarre, and he consequently
opposed it strenuously ; but, had it not been for the
assistance and support of Montmorenci, it is supposed, his resistance to an arrangement which reduced him to the rank of a mere agent for a foreign
sovereign, would not have been successful. The
plan, however, was rejected ; and all eyes turned,
once more, to the Bearnois Prince, as the great
hope of the Protestant party. Nor had the Huguenots any reason to regret their confidence in him ;
for, from the moment war was determined upon, a
new spirit seemed to animate Henry of Navarre.

Shackled and embarrassed by the promises and
exhortations of Henry III. he had appeared, to many
of his followers, to be acting a hesitating and irresolute part, so long as the King of France affected to
regard the Leaguers as his personal enemies ; and
all his letters shew that he felt painfully the difficulties of his situation. But the moment that war
became inevitable, even the painful necessity seemed
a comparative relief. His spirit rose, the vast resources of his genius displayed themselves ; and, as
the first stroke of the war, in returning from the
meeting at St. Paul, accompanied by his ordinary

* Sully.

guard, he defeated three companies of the League, suffering only eight persons to escape.

The activity which Henry of Navarre displayed, the justice of his cause, the evident ambition of the house of Guise, and the consolidation of the party opposed to the League, by a community of danger, as well as a community of interest, together with a thousand of those minor intrigues, which, in all moments of turbulence and civil contention, induce men to attach themselves to others with whom they have many points of difference, soon remedied all the evils which had been brought about by the unwillingness that the King of Navarre had shewn to take arms, even while the League was organizing its forces, and marching with a steady pace towards the attainment of its objects.

Montmorenci cooperated zealously in his views, as soon as his decision was made ; the new Duke of Montpensier was won over to the same course ; the Count de Soissons and the Prince de Conti joined the confederates; and a long list of illustrious names is added by the historian of Henry IV. which it is unnecessary to give in this place. Five Princes of the blood were arrayed against the weakness of Henry III. and the vigor of the house of Lorraine ; and the Protestant sovereigns of England and of several German states, were ready to counterbalance the weight of Spain and Rome. At the same time, a considerable number of the French nobles, who were forced to take part in the proceedings of the League, did so against their will. The

minions of the King were all inimical to the family
of Lorraine; the Duke of Nevers had openly
detached himself from their faction.   Marshal
Matignon leaned strongly towards the race of Bourbon; and the Cardinal de Bourbon was at once
doubted and despised by the League, equally a tool
and a burden.   The young Tremouille, Duc de
Thouars, shortly after the commencement of the war,
embraced the Protestant faith, and brought with
him a great accession of strength in Poitou.   Lesdeguieres, whose valor had raised him to the highest
rank amongst the commanders of the day, was master
of Dauphiné, and held the Duke of Savoy in
check; Languedoc was secured by the adhesion
of Montmorenci; and a thousand isolated points,
throughout all France, contained men of energy and
decision, ready to seize the first favorable opportunity
of opposing in arms the progress of a faction whose
designs were every day becoming more apparent,
and whose pretexts were gradually discovered to be
weak and unsubstantiated.

The sudden development of such great resources
surprised and alarmed the leaders of the League;
and they pressed the King of France eagerly to
hasten his operations against the Huguenots, even
before the time allowed them for conversion was
expired.   The unwillingness shewn by Henry III.
to recommence the persecution, soon caused suspicions and libels to be busily spread against
him; and the memorable words which he had addressed to the Cardinal de Bourbon in going to the

Parliament to register the edict of Nemours, exasperated the more furious members of the faction almost to madness. " My uncle," he said, " against my conscience, but very willingly, I published the edicts of pacification, because they tended to solace my subjects. I now go to publish the revocation of those edicts, according to my conscience, but very much against my will, because upon this publication hangs the ruin of my state and my people."* But it is evident, that in binding the League to tranquillity, while he gave the Protestants six months to quit the realm, to conform, or to arm and prepare for resistance, Henry had in view the raising up of a great party to oppose the house of Guise ; and but little doubt can be entertained of his having secretly notified to Henry of Navarre, that whatever he did for his own security would meet with approbation. Even the governors of particular towns were instructed to give them up to the Huguenots, though the weakness and perfidy of the King, on some occasions, rendered their obedience fatal to themselves.†

The rapid preparations of the King of Navarre, however, and two or three successful enterprises made by the Protestants, shewed the Leaguers that this was no time for delay ; and they stirred up the people of Paris to demand loudly the renewal

* L'Etoile.

† This was the case with Du Halot, who introduced a party of Huguenots into Angers, and was afterwards broken on the wheel, protesting to the last that he had the King's orders for what he had done.

of the war, for the recovery of the towns granted as security to the Protestants. Many, even of the Catholics, had already remarked with bitter indignation, that the League, one of whose chief pretexts was to relieve the people from the excessive burdens under which they groaned, had totally forgotten that object in the treaty of Nemours. Not a word was now said of deliverance from exaction; and as the measures which they sought to force upon Henry, were calculated to increase all the expenses of the state, the King determined to turn their own acts against themselves, and to shew his subjects that their factions compelled him to load them with taxation, while he made the Leaguers themselves smart for the proceedings to which they drove him to have recourse. He assembled in the Louvre a number of those who had taken a principal share in opposing his pacific schemes,* and in a tone of bitter irony informed them, that being quite ready to fulfil their wishes, he had determined to carry on the much desired war with vigor, and therefore that he was about to bring three armies into the field; one to protect his person; one to oppose the entrance of the German auxiliaries of the King of Navarre on the frontier; one to attack that Prince in Guienne. He then pointed out that those who had counselled hostilities should support them, especially as it was against his own will that they were undertaken. He notified to the first president that he should expect not to hear a word of remonstrance

* Davila.

from the Parliament regarding the retention of their salaries, for the prosecution of an enterprise which they had so strenuously advocated. To the Prevôt des Marchands, he stated, that the annuities on the Hotel de Ville would be applied to the same purpose. The Cardinal de Guise was informed that though the clergy would be spared for the first month, they must furnish the rest of the expenses of a war which they had declared to be holy and religious; and Henry added, that he would wait for no authority from the Pope, but, justified by their own words, would confiscate the revenues of the clergy, for the righteous purpose which they had so often urged upon him. Every one sought to remonstrate; but the King stopped them sternly, telling them that they should have believed him in time, and preserved peace, rather than decided upon war in a shop or in a choir.*

This vigorous conduct might have produced some effect, if corresponding energy had been shewn in other matters, and if Henry's incredible profusion to his favorites, had not refuted the plea of necessity in regard to his exactions. The Leaguers, however, felt that they might be in some degree affected in popular opinion by his proceedings, and that the burden of the war might soon render the people eager for its termination, unless some new move was made in the game they were playing; and therefore, while they ceased not to pour forth libels upon the head of the King, they labored at the Court of

* Davila.

Rome to obtain a bull of excommunication against the Protestant Princes of the House of Bourbon. As we have seen, Sixtus had openly expressed his disapprobation of the League and its objects; but, regarding the King of Navarre as a relapsed heretic, the very fear of seeing the faction force Henry III. into an union with his cousin, made him anxious to interpose every barrier against such a result, so that he was easily induced to take the step required. On the 9th of September, the bull was fulminated against the King of Navarre and the Prince de Condé; and the Pope thereby declared them both to be relapsed heretics, the instigators and protectors of heresy, and as such under the censure of the laws and the canons, deprived of lands and dignities, and incapable of succeeding to any sovereignty, especially in France. Moreover, their vassals and subjects were absolved of all oaths towards them, and were expressly forbidden to render them any obedience.

The bull appeared in Paris towards the end of the month; but the result was not such as the Pope and the League expected. The power affected by the Pontiff, stimulated the Gallican church to resistance; and the Parliament solemnly protested against the bull, and condemned the tone as well as the matter; one of the counsellors declaring, that the only way to treat it, was to commit it to the flames in the presence of the assembled Church.* A number of treatises were also published against it, both by Protes-

* L'Etoile. Duchat.

tants and Roman Catholics; amongst which the most
celebrated were the *Brutum fulmen* of Hotman, a
distinguished jurisconsult, and the *Moyens d'abus et
de nullité* of Pierre de Belloy, Advocate-general of
Toulouse.

Henry of Navarre himself did not remain quies-
cent under the injury ; he complained loudly to the
King of the insolence of the Pope, pointing out
the danger of suffering such a bull to be published
in the kingdom ; and not content with its suppression in France, which was immediately ordered by
Henry III., he drew up the following protest :—
" Henry, by the grace of God, King of Navarre,
Sovereign of Bearn, first Peer and Prince of France,
opposes the declaration and excommunication of
Sixtus V. calling himself Pope of Rome ; maintains
that it is false, and appeals against it as abusive to
the court of the Peers of France, of whom he has
the honor of being the first; and, as touching the
crime of heresy, of which he is accused by the said
declaration, he says and sustains that Sixtus V.
calling himself Pope, has, saving his Holiness, falsely
and maliciously lied, and that he himself is heretic,
which he will prove in any full and free council, law-
fully assembled ; to which, if he do not consent and
submit, as he is bound by the canons, he, the King
of Navarre, holds him and declares him to be An-
tichrist and heretic, and in that quality declares
against him a perpetual and irreconcilable war.
He protests also nullity and recourse against him

and his successors, for the reparation of the injury offered to him and the whole family of France, as the present act and the necessity of the case require : and, as in times past, the Princes and Kings, his predecessors, have well known how to chastise the temerity of such gallants as the pretended Pope Sixtus, when they have forgotten their duty, and passed the bounds of their vocation, confounding temporal with spiritual things, the said King of Navarre, who is in nothing their inferior, hopes that God will give him grace to avenge the injury done to his King, to his house, to his blood, and to all the Parliaments of France, imploring for this purpose the aid and support of all truly Christian Princes, Kings, towns, and communities affected by this act. Also he prays all the allies and confederates of this crown of France, to join him in opposing the tyranny and usurpation of the Pope, and the leagued conspirators in France, enemies of God, the State, and the King, and of the general peace of all Christendom."

Under this bold document was written, " In as much protests Henry de Bourbon, Prince de Condé;" and adherents of the two Princes were found resolute enough, to fix their protest to the gates of the Vatican itself. The Pope, though at first irritated, was not too bigoted, we are assured, to admire the vigorous determination of the King of Navarre, and to lament publicly, his separation from the Church of Rome ; declaring, that to him and Elizabeth of England alone, of all the monarchs of

Europe, would he have communicated the important projects which he meditated, had they not been heretics.*

Before the publication of the bull, a curious attempt had been made to convert the King of Navarre, by a commission consisting of theologians and lawyers. They were preceded by the Abbé d'Elbene, one of the counsellors and confidants of the Queen-mother, sent by that wily woman to assure Henry of Navarre of her good-will and affection, at the very moment that she was conspiring with his enemies to effect his ruin. Henry, however, understood her character well; and he replied with perfect courtesy, but sarcastic bitterness. " I feel sure," he said, in the letter which he charged her envoy to carry back, " that, as you have taken great pains to treat and make peace with the strangers, who had risen in arms against the King to the prejudice of the public peace and repose, and of the state and royal family of France, so you will not be less careful of the children of the house. For although, Madam, I am not worthy that you should take this trouble for me, I believe that I am more worthy than those for whom you have taken it."

The Abbé d'Elbene returned with this somewhat severe reply, and he was almost immediately suc-

* Perefix. Anquetil passes altogether over the opposition of the Parliament to the Papal Bull, and says that Henry did not attempt to stop the publication of it in France; though both facts are as clearly established as any others in the range of history.

ceeded by M. de Lenoncourt, Bishop of Auxerre, accompanied by Bruslart, Marquis of Sillery, who had been educated as a lawyer, Monsieur de Poigni, and two Doctors of the Sorbonne. Their object was to induce the King of Navarre to abandon the Protestant faith, or at least to abstain from the exercise of the Reformed religion during six months, and also to give up the towns of security. Henry replied with his usual straightforward candor that, he could not with honor or a safe conscience abandon a religion from fear, which he had adopted from conviction, but that he was willing to receive instruction, and to submit to a free council ; that he saw no use of suspending the outward exercise of that religion for a time ; and that it was too much to expect that the Protestants would give up the places they held, at the very moment when their enemies were actively arming for their destruction.*

With this answer the theologians and lawyers were obliged to return ; but on their journey from Paris to Nerac, they had been closely followed by a royal army, commanded by the Duke of Mayenne, which caused the witty Duchess d'Usez to remark, that the Bourbon Prince must certainly be already con-demned, and near his hour of death, as they first sent him the priest, and then the executioners. The Parisian world seemed indeed at this time to think his situation hopeless ; but Henry speedily taught his enemies, that the energetic resistance of

* De Thou.

brave men in a just cause, is always to be feared, however small may be the means apparently at their command.

A few weeks after the assembly of Protestant deputies had been held in the neighbourhood of Coutras, the war, called that of the three Henries, was begun; but those few weeks were employed by the incessant activity of the King of Navarre, to the greatest advantage. His proceedings are thus described by Davila: " As in body and mind, he was indefatigable, he enlisted armed men from every quarter, he fortified the places he held, he supplied them with provisons, he furnished them as far as he could with ammunition and artillery, obtained supplies of money, strove to gain the nobility, disciplined his soldiers, and never reposing, had an eye constantly upon every means that he judged necessary for supporting the attack of so great a power." The forces collected were numerous; and money flowed in both from the zeal of his own followers, and the sympathy of foreign nations; but as soon as he had gathered his troops together, Henry divided his army; and, while Condé, Rohan, La Rochefoucault, Clermont d'Amboise, St. Gelais Lansac, with a number of inferior noblemen, hastened towards Poitou, to ensure that important province, and oppose the advance of the Roman Catholics upon Rochelle, Henry of Navarre remained to make head against the enemy in Guienne, and to maintain the advantageous position of the Protestants and their Catholic allies in the south of France.

For this purpose he retained with him in Guienne but a small body of veteran troops, lightly armed, accustomed to incessant fatigue, and totally without baggage'; while at any time, by draughts from the neighbouring garrisons, he could increase his numbers, and yet scour the country with a rapidity, which, when the time of action arrived, surprised and confounded the Duke of Mayenne, whose slow and cautious proceedings contrasted strangely with the daring activity of his opponent.

The first important actions of the war took place in Poitou, almost immediately after the publication of the edict of July. The Duke de Mercœur, one of the most vehement and eager of the Leaguers, no sooner learned that armies were collecting, to recommence hostilities against the Protestants, than, hurrying from Britanny, of which province he had lately obtained the government, at the head of a small force, supposed to have numbered between two thousand three hundred* and four thousand five hundred men,† he entered Poitou from the side of Nantes, having sent forward several small parties to support the Roman Catholics, who had already taken arms in the neighbourhood of Niort.

The head quarters of the Prince de Condé were at this time at St. Jean d'Angeli, and his levies

* Davila says 1500 foot, and 800 horse.

† Aubigné 4000 foot, and 5 to 600 horse. Discours du premier passage, &c. 2000 horse and foot.

were by no means complete. Various skirmishes, however, had already occurred, the success of which had given the Huguenots confidence in their own strength ; and Condé did not hesitate to take the field, and advance to meet the enemy. Mercœur was at this time in the neighbourhood of Fontenoy, and seized with surprise and some degree of apprehension at the approach of a considerable force, when he had expected to find no enemy to oppose him, he retired upon that city. But the governor, either ignorant of the engagements between the King and the League, or privately instructed by Henry III. to favor the Protestants, refused to give him admission, and the army of the Duke, hotly pursued by Condé, was forced to seek shelter in the suburbs. A skirmish took place under the walls, without any remarkable advantage on either part ; but, during the succeeding night, Mercœur retreated secretly, losing a great portion of his baggage before he regained the town of Nantes.*

The espousals of Condé, with the beautiful Charlotte Catherine de La Trimouille, which were celebrated immediately after this event, secured the full co-operation of her brother with the Protestants, and obtained for them possession of the strong town of Taillebourg, famous in the wars between France and England, which formed part of the dowry of the bride. Without pausing, however, to taste the first sweets of that union, which ultimately

* Aubigné. Davila. Discours.

proved so disastrous, Condé pursued his advantage over the enemy, hunted down numerous parties of Leaguers, who were gathering themselves together in various parts of Poitou, forced the Count de Brissac to cross the Loire in haste, took Soubize and Fouras, and marching rapidly upon Brouage laid siege to that important place, with the aid of money, vessels, and men, from Rochelle, after having made himself master of several towns which might have harassed the operations of the Protestant army, had they been left in the hands of the Catholics.

After some fierce skirmishes beyond the walls, the garrison of Brouage was driven into the place, and the city was invested, as well as the weakness of Condé's force would permit. Provisions and ammunition were known to be scarce in the town, the garrison was feeble, and some of the best Catholic officers who held command in the neighbourhood had been wounded, killed, or taken in preliminary operations. Every thing promised success to the Protestant arms, though the resistance of the besieged was likely to be resolute. But while the affairs of the Huguenot army before Brouage were in this prosperous state, a sudden rumor reached the Prince's ears, towards the end of September, that du Halot, captain of the castle of Angers, had called into the place Rochemort, a partisan of the King of Navarre, and was besieged by the inhabitants of the town and a party of Leaguers and royalists. At first he paid little attention to the tale ; but three days after, despatches arrived from Clermont d'Amboise giving him further intelligence.* He now learned that Rochemort was actually in possession of the citadel, but that du Halot having attempted, while the inhabitants were in a state of consternation at the sudden surprise of the castle, to gain the town itself, had been arrested by the citizens. No doubt can be entertained that the conduct of this unfortunate officer was authorized by Henry III., but the King did not venture to acknowledge the commission, and du Halot was broken on the wheel for his imprudent obedience.†

Condé found, however, that the small party who who were closely besieged in the castle still held out ; that Clermont d'Amboise was levying men in haste to relieve them ; and that while Brissac, with a small body of Leaguers, was attempting to compel them to surrender, Bouchage, one of the King's officers, was also in the town with a superior force, the conduct of which might be decided by his appearance before the place. Under these circumstances, with the rash and somewhat headstrong valor which characterizes all his proceedings, he determined to leave his infantry before Brouage, and with his cavalry, and a large body of horse arquebusiers, to cross the Loire and advance upon Angers. The danger of such a course was im-

---

* Discours du premier passage du Duc de Mercœur, a contemporary account by a Protestant.　　　† L'Etoile.

mense ; the risk of defeat great ; and the probability of losing Brouage, which was now almost
within his grasp, still greater. The armies of the
League under Mayenne, La Chatre, and Biron, were
advancing slowly. Bellegarde and Matignon, each
at the head of considerable forces, were at no great
distance from the besieged city ; the Duke of Joyeuse,
with a large body of troops, was marching through
Normandy ; and the Prince, before he could secure
Angers and return to Brouage, had to pass and repass
the Loire at a most difficult point, in the face of several
strong parties of the enemy. But nothing could dissuade him from the attempt ;[*] and after having made
hasty arrangements for the prosecution of the siege
of Brouage during his absence, he began his march
on the 8th October, with between seven and eight
hundred men at arms, and from a thousand to twelve
hundred horse arquebusiers. The passage of the
Loire was effected a few days after, between Saumur
and Angers, with great difficulty and much dis-
couragement on the part of the soldiers, intelligence
having been received that the Duke of Joyeuse,
with a superior force, was advancing rapidly upon
the latter city. Beaufort, however, opened its gates
to the Prince, who was there joined by Clermont
d'Amboise with above a thousand men ; but on the
march from that place to Angers, tidings reached
him of the citadel having surrendered to Bouchage.

Persisting to his ruin, Condé would not believe

* Discours, &c.

that such was the fact; and an attack was made upon
the town, by an army without artillery, and greatly
inferior in number to the regular troops within.
These rash efforts were prosecuted during two
whole days, after which the Prince retreated to
Beaufort, knowing well that forces were hurrying
from all sides to attack him. Yet at Beaufort he
spent the whole day of the 24th October in perfect
inactivity, although the dangerous passage of the
Loire was before him, and even one hour might cut
off the only chance of safety. M. de Laval, indeed,
had been sent forward with a small corps to secure
the river, and had succeeded in crossing, and taking
up a position at St. Maur; but, on the morning of the following day, the Duke of Joyeuse, who
had hastened to Saumur, caused several gun-boats to
descend the stream and guard the passage, so that the
army of the Prince was now divided, without a hope
of being able to reunite. At the same time the
Roman Catholic troops from Angers followed in
haste; the Duke of Mayenne had passed the Loire
at Orleans, and was marching down its course;
Biron and others with a large force were at Bonne-
val in Beausse, and La Chatre was sweeping the
other bank of the Loire with his army.

Nevertheless the Prince still shewed a firm face,
and made surprising efforts to make his way through
the toils in which he was entangled, endeavoring to
reach the higher Loire, and pass in the direction
of Beaugency. But the soldiery could not be

encouraged to the attempt, and desertion began
upon such a scale that even the nobles gave up all
hope, and separated themselves from their leader.
The Duc de Rohan left him at St. Ernoul, and
effecting a passage for himself and his followers,
reached Rochelle in safety. For a short time after
quitting St. Ernoul, the Prince maintained his confidence; but having received certain information that
he was surrounded on every side, he at length gave
orders for the general dispersion of his forces, and
made his escape with the Duke of Trimouille
and a few attendants. He succeeded in reaching the
sea coast of Britanny, where hiring a vessel, he made
his way to England, whence he returned soon after
to Rochelle, as I shall have occasion to shew in
another place. The rest of his troops in small
parties fled over the country, and one by one, with
much less loss than might have been expected, re-
crossed the Loire, and gained a place of safety.

The news of these disasters, even before they were
complete, and the advance of Marshal Matignon
towards Brouage, struck the Protestant army which
had been left under the walls of that place, with so
much terror, that the siege was raised in confusion;
and the royalist officer, St. Luc, with an inferior force,
pursued the Huguenots towards Soubize, slaughtering a considerable number, and making many prisoners. The plague, which ravaged that part of the
country, added to the consternation caused by other
misfortunes; and the Huguenot army of Poitou melted

rapidly away; so that before the end of the year not a regiment was seen in the field to oppose the progress of the League, on the banks of the Loire and the Charente.*

We have seen that the Duke of Joyeuse, who had married the sister of the Queen-consort, took an active part against the Prince de Condé; and I must now pause for a moment to remark that the army under his command had originally been raised by the King, to check the progress of the League, before the signature of the treaty of Nemours.†
Henry had given the Protestants every assurance that this force would act in their defence; and the events which took place in all parts of France during the end of 1585, clearly shew: first, that the King had issued general directions to his officers to oppose the proceedings of the League, which caused great confusion and embarrassment after he allied himself to that faction; and, secondly, that he never sincerely co-operated with the Leaguers, recalling his former commands with no great zeal or activity, and wherever he could, taking possession of towns and strong places, to the exclusion of the confederates.‡ Du Halot certainly fell a sacrifice to this double policy, and no sooner had the citadel of Angers surrendered than it was seized by the King's troops; while

* Aubigné. † Sully.

‡ Henry IV., in one of his letters to the German princes, says, in speaking of the King of France, "I know that his wishes and his sighs combat for me against the Leaguers, though I see his arm employed with them against me."

Brissac, the governor, who was a violent partisan of the house of Guise, was refused admittance, and shortly after deprived of his government.*

In Guienne but little was done on either side during the autumn of the year 1585. Marshal Matignon, with secret orders from the court to spare the Huguenot party as much as possible, acted feebly, and undertook no enterprise of importance, while the King of Navarre was sufficiently strong to frustrate the efforts of the partisans of the League. Towards the end of the year, however, the remonstrances of the confederates, and the thinly covered threats which they uttered, induced the indolent monarch of France to publish a new edict against the Protestants, and to take more vigorous measures for their destruction. The time allowed them to renounce their religion or quit the realm, was abridged to fifteen days, and orders were sent to Matignon to act more energetically in Guienne.

In answer to the edict, Henry of Navarre immediately put forth a declaration, commanding the provinces in which he had established himself to pay no attention to it ; and he added a general order to his officers to seize and sell all the property of those who held with the opposite party.† This bold step, however, produced but little effect upon the

---

* Discours, &c.

† It is stated by Anquetil that Henry caused all the property of the Catholics to be seized and sold ; but this was not the case, for he was supported by many persons of that religion, who were exempted from confiscation.

finances of the Prince; and in the mean while the
host of Mayenne, comprising some of the best troops
in France, advanced slowly towards Guienne.

Shortly after the commencement of the war, four
armies had threatened the Protestants in the south
and west of France, commanded by Matignon,
Biron, Joyeuse, and Mayenne; but that of Joyeuse
had been nearly destroyed by the ravages of the
plague before the end of 1585, and the Duke himself, leaving a small body of forces under the command of Lavardin, to form the nucleus of another
more important corps, returned to Paris in search
of money and reinforcements.

The end of that year, and the beginning of 1586,
were marked on the part of the King of Navarre, by
numerous proclamations and addresses to the people
of France, said to have been drawn up by Du Plessis
Mornay; in which the pretences, objects, and conduct of the Leaguers were displayed with a firm hand,
and in their true colours; but the house of Guise,
though they occasionally replied, trusted more to
the force of arms than to discussion for success, and
vehemently urged the French monarch forward, in
the course which he so unwillingly pursued.

It was not, indeed, without apprehension that
they trusted themselves in such near communication
with the King; and the Duke of Guise himself is
said to have admitted that, conscious of his own
unpardonable offences, and aware of the treacherous
character of his sovereign, he trembled when he
first found himself unsupported in the presence of

Henry III., and surrounded by his guards. The
King, however, contented himself with taking mild,
but artful, means to frustrate the designs of the
Leaguers, appointing the rapid and energetic Duke
to command the army which was to wait, in tedious
expectation, on the frontier, for the approach of the
German Protestants, while to his brother of Mayenne, slow, cold, and calculating, though brave and
determined, was assigned the command of the forces
destined to act against the quick and impetuous,
but skilful King of Navarre.

Mayenne did not quit Poitiers till the month
of November, 1585, nor did he reach St. Jean
d'Angeli till December.   Thence, taking a few
small and unimportant towns by the way, he
approached the Garonne, and decided upon attempting to shut in Henry of Navarre between that
river and the Pyrenees, while Matignon on the one
side, and he on the other, besieged the different
fortresses of the Province, and reduced the King to
narrower and narrower limits.   But the royalist
commander, and the general for the League, by
no means acted in concert; and the first effort
of Matignon, in 1586, was signally unsuccessful.
In order to deliver the inhabitants of Bordeaux
from the excursions of the garrison of Castres, a
small town on the Garonne,* he advanced against

---

* It must be remarked, that Castres on the Agout is not the
town here referred to, as it has strangely enough, but not unfre-
quently, been confounded with that place.

the place in the month of February, with a force of between four and five thousand men. Henry, however, aware of the importance of the place, marched to its relief with an army not exceeding two thousand men ; and at his approach Matignon instantly raised the siege and decamped. The King of Navarre, to mark that he had actually relieved the town, entered at the head of a small party, dined within the walls on the 20th February, and then immediately retired, as if in contempt of the enemy.*

Notwithstanding this success, the advance of Mayenne, reduced Henry to a strait of some difficulty, and spread consternation amongst his friends, several of whom advised him to retire into Languedoc, while others urged him to pass into England and endeavor to obtain succor from that country. It was admitted by all that he must quit Guienne; but the monarch seems to have been much less alarmed at the approach and probable junction of two superior forces of the enemy, than his followers ; and, in a letter to Monsieur de St. Genies, he calms that officer's apprehensions regarding his proceedings, by explaining to him his plans.

It is always fortunate for science when the views of eminent men, expressed before hand, in regard to any course of action they are about to adopt, can be recovered after the result has taken place; for persons of limited mind and irresolute character are too often apt to attribute the great advantages ob-

* Aubigné. Pierre Matthieu, Sully. Cayet.

tained by superior intellect and conduct to mere
accident ; whereas, in almost every case of long continued success we find, on examination, that it was
gained by just combinations, and foreseen, as far as
anything can be foreseen under the overruling will
of God.

The letters of Henry IV., like the despatches of
the Duke of Wellington, shew all the results calculated before the events took place ; and it is especially satisfactory in the present instance to be able
to prove this fact, as the conduct of the King of
Navarre, in remaining with a small force in Guienne, satisfying himself with harassing and im-
peding the enemy, and then leaving his opponents
to attack his fortresses without any further effort
for their deliverance, has been attributed too frequently to anything but calculation. In his letter
to M. de St. Genies, however, before Mayenne had
set his foot in Guienne, and three months before he
himself quitted that province, the King says, " Do
not fear that I will risk anything. Such is by no
means my intention. My design is only to check their
(the enemies') fury for a time, in order to give our
fortresses a better opportunity of ruining them."

After seeing with his own eyes that all was prepared for this purpose, Henry at length determined
to get into the rear of Mayenne, in order to keep
up his communication with Poitou ; while Turenne
remained with a small force in Gascony to make head
against the League, and Lesdeguieres and Damville,

secured Dauphiné and Languedoc. He shewed none
of the haste of apprehension, however ; observing,
" The Duke of Mayenne is not so terrible a person
as to stop one from walking about Guienne for some
time to come." Accordingly, having to provide for
the defence of the country, he visited Pau, and several
other places,* and then returned to Montauban,
where he learnt that, the armies of Mayenne and
Matignon having effected their junction on the
Garonne, those two generals entertained the intention of sweeping the course of that river of all the
Huguenot forces collected in the different towns on
its banks.

His situation now became critical ; the passage
of the Garonne was narrowly watched ; and so certain did Mayenne feel of being able to capture the
great Huguenot commander, that he wrote to Paris,
announcing to the King that Henry of Navarre
could not escape from the net he had laid for
him. That Prince, however, determined to make an
attempt to cross the river, at all risks ; and I shall
give the account of the plan he followed, in order
to effect that purpose, in the words of Sully, who
was with him.† " He set out from Nerac," says

---

* Aubigné states that he was led to Pau by new amours ; but
Sully, who was with him, declares that his journey thither was
indispensable.

† Henry, in all his letters, speaks of the proceedings of Mayenne and Matignon with the greatest contempt, even while he
was most energetically and carefully exerting himself to frustrate
them. To Segur he writes, " Our enemies, whatever expense
they go to, whatever men they risk, have not done us much harm

that statesman, "followed by two hundred horse, with whom he marched towards Castel-jaloux ; but instead of going on to that place, he separated his force half way between it and Nerac, retained only those who were best mounted, to the number of twenty, with an equal number of his guards, and assigned all the rest a rendezvous at St. Foy (on the

as yet, and will do us less hereafter, I am sure." To Casimir he says, "Thank God, our enemies have gained nothing against us ; we, on the contrary, much against them in various encounters, where it has been very evident that God and their consciences fought for us and against them." To Queen Elizabeth he writes, "You have heard, Madam, the great noise of their arms. Up to the present moment they have not dared to attack any strong place ; and I can say with truth, in all the places where they have fought they have been beaten." Even when surrounded by the enemy, he speaks in the same tone of confidence and gaiety ; and when writing to Monsieur de Batz, to join him for the purpose of forcing his way through the posts of Mayenne, the terms he uses are as follows :—"Monsieur de Batz, They have surrounded me like a beast of the chase, and think that they will take me by the net. For my part I intend to pass through them or over them. I have chosen my good men, and one of them is my Mower (*i. e.* de Batz himself, whom he called by this name on account of his deeds of arms at Eausse). Great Devil, I will keep from my cousin, the secret of thy petticoat at Auch ; but do not let my Mower fail me in such a good enterprise, and do not go to amuse yourself in the straw, when I expect you in the field." And on the day following he writes to the same brave soldier, "My Mower, put wings to your best beast. I have told Montespan to break the wind of his. Why ? Thou shalt know at Nerac. Hurry, run, come, fly ; such is the order of your master, and the prayer of your friend."

Dordogne). Then turning short, he took a road in the midst of the woods and heaths, which he knew by having been often there in hunting, and arrived at Caumont, where he slept three hours. We passed the river after sunset, and marched all night through enemies' quarters, even up to the very trenches of Marmande. After which, making another turn by Sauvetat, we reached St. Foy two hours before day, where all the rest of his people, who had been separated into little parties, arrived likewise without the least loss, even of baggage."*

At St. Foy, or in its neighbourhood, the King of Navarre remained six weeks, either engaged in watching the operations of the enemy, and providing the towns in which he had garrisons with means of defence in case of attack, or amusing himself with hunting,† notwithstanding the proximity of Mayenne. While the Duke and Matignon proceeded to attack and capture Montignac Le Comte, and St. Bazeille, making such slow progress that it would have cost ten years of similar operations, according to the calculations of persons on the spot, to deprive the Huguenots of the places they possessed in Guienne alone, the King of Navarre strengthened the garrisons and fortifications of Montsegur, Castillon, St. Foy, and Monflanquin, in the rear of the Roman Catholic army ;‡ and then, fully persuaded that disease, weariness, and dissension would, without his presence, effect the dispersion

* Sully, liv. 2.　　† Pierre Matthieu.　　‡ Sully.

of Mayenne's forces,[*] he turned his steps towards Poitou, where many important events had occurred since the raising of the siege of Brouage.

Early in January, 1586, the Prince de Condé, with a small body of followers, suddenly appeared at Rochelle, in vessels lent to him by the Queen of England, and in a very short time found himself once more at the head of a considerable force. A number of Protestant noblemen, from different parts of the country, hastened to his standard, the scattered fragments of his army were gathered together, and the war on that side recommenced by the capture of Tors, Dampierre, and Royan. A brief interval of inactivity succeeded in March, during which the marriage of the Prince was consummated with Charlotte de la Trimouille, who had now formally embraced the Protestant religion. Soubize was recaptured shortly after; and Mornac, Aunay, Mondevis, Sansay, and Chizay, were taken by the Huguenots. But a victory more prejudicial than a defeat, from the number of distinguished men who fell in the contest, was achieved in the neighbourhood of Sainctes. Two brothers of the house of

[*] Discours de la Guerre, &c. Lettres Missives. The fall of St. Bazeille, after a very weak and inefficient defence, greatly enraged the King of Navarre, who ordered the governor, M. des Pueilles, to be immediately arrested, on his presenting himself before him at Bergerac and endeavoring to justify his conduct. Henry calculated, however, that the army of Mayenne had lost, by sickness or the sword, between five and six thousand men from December 1585 to May 1586.

Laval were mortally wounded; Laval himself, the eldest son of the famous D'Andelot, died eight days after; and another brother, having expired some short time before, four gallant gentlemen of one family, were lost to the Protestant cause in the space of one month.

The town of Brouage, however, remained the most galling thorn in the side of Rochelle; its harbor was considered the second in France, and its ships scoured the sea at the mouth of the Gironde, and swept away the commerce of the neighbouring city. To remedy the inconveniences which the Protestants suffered from the retention of this place by the Roman Catholics, Condé, though hopeless of reducing it by siege, decided upon making an attempt to block up the harbor by sinking a number of loaded vessels across its mouth; and preparations were accordingly made at Rochelle for that purpose.

St. Luc, the governor of Brouage, was not long in discovering the designs of the enemy, and all the vessels at his command were soon at sea to frustrate them. Numerous skirmishes took place amongst the islands with which that part of the French coast is thickly studded; and several weeks elapsed in this naval warfare, so that intelligence of the proposed operation reached the King of Navarre at St. Foy or Bergerac. At the same time he received information, that the army of Marshal Biron, which had been detained for a considerable time upon the Loire by causes not very apparent, was now marching rapidly towards the Charente, to counterbalance the predominance which the Huguenots had recovered in that quarter. These tidings at once determined the conduct of Henry of Navarre, in whom the thirst for military glory had now become paramount. Other objects too, of a more justifiable kind than the mere acquisition of renown, were to be gained by his presence at Rochelle ; for though the courage and skill of Condé could not be doubted, his prudence and his wisdom were not to be trusted ; and the want of discipline which he permitted in his troops, as well as the small consideration which he shewed for the peasantry, excited a degree of irritation in the minds of the people highly detrimental to the Protestant cause.

The King of Navarre accordingly set out from Bergerac* in the middle of May, and passing by Rochefoucault and Lusignan, arrived at Rochelle on the 1st of June. He immediately proceeded to join the fleet engaged in blocking up the port of Brouage, and, according to the account of Aubigné, exposed himself rashly to the fire of the enemy.† St. Luc had erected a fort to protect the harbor, and from it was poured an incessant shower of shot upon the Huguenot forces ; but, nevertheless, his gallies were worsted in the skirmishes at sea, and his efforts on shore proved impotent to prevent the enemy from sinking so many vessels at the entrance of the port, as to render it nearly useless for the purposes of

* Sully. Discours de la Guerre, &c.
† Aubigné, tom. iii. liv. 1, chap. iv.

commerce, and totally unfit for ships of war. He afterwards made skilful attempts to remedy the evil by floating up the barks which had been sunk ; but before he could effect that object, except in one or two instances, the sand had accumuláted round the wrecks to such a height that a bar was formed which no exertion could remove.

While the operations were going forward against Brouage, Marshal Biron, the most famous artillery officer in France, was marching towards Marans, a small town strongly defended by water and marshes, at a short distance from Rochelle. He made himself master of several insignificant places on his way; but as soon as his intention of laying siege to Marans was ascertained,* the King of Navarre hastened with several bodies of veteran troops to provide for the defence of that important fortress. The activity and energy he displayed, restored confidence to the inhabitants ; the citadel was strengthened, and amply supplied with ammunition and provisions. A strong garrison was thrown into the place, new outworks were erected, and cannon were brought from Rochelle ; so that when, on the 10th of July, the forces of Biron appeared before Marans, it was in a fit state to offer the most vigorous resistance. In the very first operations, that general himself lost two fingers by a musket shot; and although he made great efforts during several days to open a breach by means of forts

* Henry was aware of Biron's intention before he reached Rochelle.

erected in the neighbouring marshes, not the slightest effect was produced upon the walls of Marans; and we find that only one man of the whole garrison was killed before the siege was raised, after having been carried on from the 10th of July to the 5th of August.*

The determination of the King of Navarre to defend Marans to the last, had been strongly opposed by all the oldest and most experienced officers in Rochelle, though its position near the mouth of the Sevre, its proximity to Rochelle on the opposite side to Brouage, and the command which it at that time assured to the party possessing it of the Pertuis Breton, rendered it of infinite importance to the Protestants. Every one had judged that it was indefensible, except Henry, whose wisdom in taking the resolution, and skill in carrying it into execution, were remarkably shewn by the result.

The raising of the siege of Marans, however, was not altogether brought about by the resistance of the garrison, though there can be no doubt that it might have held out for months; but events, which I have now to relate, afforded Biron a fair excuse for withdrawing from an undertaking in which he must have foreseen great difficulties, and retiring for a time from hostilities which he was known to disapprove.

The mind of the weak King of France had vacil-

* Discours de la Guerre; a most useful collection of statements and papers on the Protestant side, gathered together by an eyewitness of many of the events discussed.

lated ever since the signature of the treaty of Nemours, between his hatred of the League, and his
apprehension of its power. Bound by that treaty
to afford it support, he did so with reluctance and
insincerity. His officers, beyond doubt by his direction, thwarted the objects of the house of Guise,
and gave but little assistance to the generals of the
confederacy; and, while the demands of the faction,
for exertion against the Huguenots every day increased, his inclination to break off all connection
with the League, and call the King of Navarre to
his aid, became more and more strong. He entertained no apprehension of the progress of the
Protestants, only acting in opposition to that party
so far as to keep up the appearance of fulfilling
his engagements with the League; and he saw
with pleasure the slow progress of Mayenne in
Guienne, and his army wasting itself away in the
siege of unimportant places, till its commander,
falling into ill health, was obliged for a time to resign his post to Matignon, who well understood the
King's wishes.* At the same time, Lesdiguieres
in Dauphiné supported vigorously the Huguenot
cause, and made himself master of various towns
and castles, with a force and reputation daily increasing.

The absence of all brilliant success upon the
part of the League, and the state of inactivity
to which he had reduced the Duke of Guise,
Henry clearly perceived must in time sink the

* Aubigné.

faction low in the opinion of the people; and it
cannot be doubted, that he also entertained the design of rendering the war altogether odious to the
nation, by the enormous load of taxation which was
necessary to keep so many armies on foot.   With a
malicious pleasure, too, he contrived to make the
burden rest most heavily upon the shoulders of the
ecclesiastics, who had been the chief instruments in
the hands of the house of Guise for stirring up the
people against the Protestants ; but in so doing he
only increased their animosity towards himself,
without detaching them from the party to which
they were bound by prejudice and bigotry.*   They
made vigorous efforts to resist the will of the
monarch, but in vain ; for the Pope, by no means
satisfied with the stout adherence of the French
clergy to the rights of the Gallican Church, was
well disposed to see them mortified, and yielded
with but little unwillingness to the King's repeated
applications for permission to sell ecclesiastical property in order to carry on the war.

Had Henry III. been as successful in other respects, he might possibly have been content to see the
force of the League exhausted, and its popularity
diminished by long protracted, burdensome, and un-
profitable hostilities against the Protestants.   But
various causes arose in the course of 1586 to make
him long for peace on any terms.   The courts of
law resisted his attempts to load them with new
impositions, and gained their point; and, during a

* Davila. L'Etoile.

visit of the Duke of Guise to Paris, in the spring
of 1586, Henry beheld the popularity of that Prince
augment as his own decreased, while manifold indications proved to him that the very foundations of
his power were giving way, and that his authority,
if not his crown itself, would be wrested from him,
unless he could obtain the sincere support of one of
the powerful parties in his dominions.   The famine,
too, which overspread the land, the utter destitution
of the lower classes, who ran though the fields
eating the unripe heads of corn for want of other
nourishment, the indignation of the people, which
the Guises adroitly turned from themselves against
the monarch, all shewed that a general insurrection
was to be apprehended, in which the throne itself
would, in all probability, be first assailed.   At the
same time, a vigorous and reasonable remonstrance
on the folly of the course he was pursuing, was addressed to him by the Queen of England ; some
passages of which must be here given to display
the view taken by the clear-sighted Elizabeth of the
conduct of the French monarch.

  " I am astonished," says that extraordinary
woman, after speaking of the treaty of Nemours,
" to see you betrayed in your very council, even
by those who are nearest to you in the world, and
yet that you are so blind as not to perceive it in the
least."   And, again : " Alas ! is the mantle of religion, with which they cover themselves, so double
that one cannot see, that it is only to reign, under
your name, but at their own will, that they assume

it? And I pray God that they may end there. I do not believe it; for one rarely sees Princes live who are so subjugated." And she goes on, after offers of assistance against the League, to say: "Ah! God forbid that a king should not sooner risk his own life in a battle, than submit to disgrace every day increasing. It were better to lose twenty thousand men than reign by the good pleasure of rebels." She adds, farther on: "Jesus! was there ever seen a Prince so taken in the snares of traitors, without having the courage or the counsel to answer them." And she continues: "For the love of God, sleep no more this too long sleep! Learn from me, your very faithful friend, that I will not fail to assist you, if you do not abandon yourself. I hear something of a pause for some days; employ this time to fortify yourself, not to ruin yourself; and take care not to grant their conditions, which will work your dishonor, and the loss of your state."

Such was the language of Elizabeth in addressing the King of France; and the effect produced thereby upon his mind, together with the dangerous position into which he had brought himself by his own indolence and weakness, and the insolent menaces of the house of Guise, must have been very great. Every day the faction displayed a spirit more and more daring; and scarcely an hour passed without intimation of some fresh design against his person or his life, reaching the ears of the French monarch.

These causes brought about the most anxious

desire in the mind of Henry, not only to conclude a peace with the King of Navarre, but to engage him in support of the royal authority against the incessant attacks of the League.   The danger of irritating the bigoted Papists was the only difficulty in the way, the sole means of obviating which seemed to be, in the eyes of the King, to induce Henry of Navarre to abjure the Protestant religion.

As early as the month of April, 1586, it is clear that the French monarch entertained the design of negotiating with the Protestants by the instrumentality of his artful and politic mother ; and a letter was written to the Duke of Nevers, beseeching him to come to Paris, in order to co-operate with Catherine de Medicis, in which epistle Henry gives way to all his rancor against the League, and seems to regard the Protestants more as friends than enemies.*

At the same time that he carried on these open overtures for peace, there can be no doubt that Henry had frequent private communications with his brother-in-law. We have an authentic statement of all that occurred upon one of these occasions, which is too important and too characteristic to be omitted here ; and I shall consequently give it as nearly as possible in the words of Sully himself.†

* Mem. de Nevers, tom. i. page 766.

† Sully, liv. 2.   It is a curious fact, that Henry IV. received his pension as King of Navarre during the war of the three Henries, and seems to have obtained payment with less difficulty than during the preceding peace.

" There were moments when Henry III.," says that
statesman, " ashamed of the disgraceful character
which the League made him play, greatly desired to
find some means of avenging himself upon them : but
he wished to do so without risking anything, and
therefore rejected always the idea, which sometimes
presented itself, of calling the King of Navarre to his
aid, and uniting himself with him. Deputies from the
four Catholic cantons of Switzerland having arrived
in Paris, to treat regarding the succor which had
been demanded some time before from that republic, the King, who was at that moment enraged
against the League, proposed, for the gratification
of his anger, to employ these Swiss, which, with the
troops that he had at his own disposal, and those
of the King of Navarre, would have formed a corps
capable of bringing the League to reason.   He
wrote to the King of Navarre to give him information of his new designs, and to ask him to send a
trustworthy person, with whom he might confer
upon all this affair, and particularly upon the em-
ployment of the Swiss.   A blank passport was
joined to the letter, which the King filled up with
my name, and caused me to set out without delay.   I
arrived at St. Maur, where the court then was, and
proceeded to the house of Villeroi, with whom I
dined and passed the rest of the day.   On the day
following he presented me to the King ; and I shall
never forget the absurd attitude and paraphernalia
in which I found this prince in his cabinet.   He

had a sword by his side, a hood upon his shoulders, a little bonnet upon his head, a basket full of small dogs hung round his neck by a large riband; and he held himself so still, that in speaking to us, he neither moved head, nor feet, nor hands. He began by pouring forth all his bile against the League, from whom, his rage made me suppose, he had received some new affront; and he treated his union with the King of Navarre as a point of which he felt all the importance. But a remnant of fear caused him always to add, that he looked upon it as impossible, so long as the King of Navarre should persist in refusing to change his religion. I, thereupon, took up the word, and replied to the King, that it was useless to propose that expedient to the King of Navarre, because, in following it, he would act against his conscience; that even, if he was capable of so doing, it would not have the effect his majesty hoped for, because the motive which agitated the League, was neither desire for the public good, nor the interests of religion; that the only thing which could happen in consequence of that precipitate action would be, that the King of Navarre would lose all the aid which he could hope for from the Protestants, without, thereby, detaching a single man from the League; but that, on the contrary, such an act of weakness would but increase the pride of their common enemies. The King replied, and I persisted in contending, that the King of Navarre, if he followed the course proposed, would bring him nothing but his own person ; whereas, by opening his arms to him in the state in which he was, without exacting the sacrifice of his religion, the King would strengthen his party by a very powerful body in the state. I used the same language to the Queen-mother ; and I perceived that both agreed as to the strength of my reasons, and that fear of the change which their union with a Prince of the Protestant religion might produce, was all that restrained them. I did not despair of bringing them to strike this great blow ; and from the manner, both gracious and frank, which their majesties displayed towards me, I had reason to flatter myself that I should succeed.

" I left them in this good train, and went to Paris to confer with the Swiss deputies. I had not so much trouble to bring them to my object ; it only cost me a little expense in good cheer, and above all in wine : in consequence of which they promised us, without restriction, a body of twenty thousand Swiss, of which number, four thousand alone were to remain in Dauphiné, and the other sixteen thousand to be employed for the service and at the will of the two Kings. The King assured me still, by MM. Lenoncourt, Poigny, and Brulart, that he had not changed his mind, and that he ardently desired the union. The King of Navarre did not wish it less strongly. In the despatches which I received from him almost every day, he exhorted me to put every thing in operation to bring it about, and even to sacrifice a portion of his interest for that object. On my return to St. Maur, and after having given the King an account of my journey, I brought forward the question of the use to which the sixteen thousand Swiss were to be put, and the route that they should take. The King required that he should be permitted to bring them into the neighbourhood of Paris, and even to employ them, in case of need, against the League. I felt all the inconvenience which might arise from this arrangement, and only gave up the point, after having received the express commands of the King of Navarre, who did not think fit for so small a matter to miss the agreement. It will be soon seen, that this point was not so frivolous as was imagined, and what occurred in consequence of this weak compliance."*

Sully then left an agent in Paris to watch the progress of the affair, and to take the first opportunity of proceeding to Germany in order to hasten the march of the troops, which the Protestant Princes

---

* With Sully was joined in this mission, M. de la Marsilliere, and they arrived at the court at the end of May. It may be necessary to state, that wherever I have quoted Sully in the text, I have used an edition in which that minister is made to speak in his own person. It is well known, of course, to the reader, that in the Œconomies royales, Sully caused his secretaries to address the Memoirs, which they compiled from his dictation or information, directly to himself; so as, in fact, to make them tell him his own history : a form too inconvenient to be adopted, when it is necessary to extract a long passage, such as the one above.

of that country had promised to the King of Navarre. Before entering vigorously into the interests of the Huguenots, the German sovereigns thought fit to send an embassy, at the head of which were several distinguished members of their own body, to remonstrate with Henry III. upon the revocation of his pacific edicts, and the persecution of the Calvinists of France.

The King, in order, it is supposed, to avoid meeting the ambassadors, set out for Lyons, before their arrival in Paris, giving directions that they should be splendidly treated during his absence, and promising to return in the month of October, to receive the messages from "his brothers in Germany." He assigned, as a pretext for this extraordinary want of courtesy, the necessity of organizing two armies between the Loire and Rhone, one to be commanded by his favorite the Duke of Epernon, the other by Joyeuse; and he, moreover, alleged that the baths of Bourbon were absolutely necessary to the recovery of his health. But the German Princes were not satisfied with the excuse, and the Counts of Montbeliard and Issemberg, retired in disgust, to hurry the levies, which had already been commenced for the support of the French Protestants at the instigation of Theodore Beza, and other agents of the King of Navarre. The rest of the ambassadors remained in Paris till the monarch's return; but the truths which they then spoke more plainly than is customary in the ordinary course of diplomacy, offended the monarch, who was often more vigorous in speech than in action; and his reply served but to exasperate still more the German envoys, who instantly set out for their own country to communicate the irritation which they felt to those who had sent them.

In the mean time the Queen-mother, having been joined by Nevers, who had separated himself from the League, and by Montpensier, who had co-operated for some time with the Protestants, advanced towards the scene of war, and sent messengers from Chenonceaux, where she paused on the way, to require a conference with the King of Navarre, and to propose a truce for that purpose.

After numerous communications on both parts, Henry agreed to meet Catherine, at Champigni, on condition that the army of Marshal Biron immediately retired behind the Loire, raising the siege of Marans, and passing by Tonnay Charente, without attacking that fortress. This demand was speedily granted, and Marans was in consequence delivered. But while the preliminary arrangements were under discussion, the fleet of Bordeaux suddenly appeared before Rochelle; and it was discovered that this movement, on the part of the Catholics, was made with the consent, if not with the approbation, of the Queen-mother.* Great doubts and apprehensions had been previously entertained by the friends of the Navarrese Prince, regarding the meeting with Catherine; and those fears seemed

* Lettre d'un Gentilhomme Français, &c.

now so strongly confirmed, that even Henry wavered
in his purpose, and announced to the Queen-mother
that he could not quit Rochelle while a strong
armament lay before the port. Jealousies and suspicions, however, existed on both parts. The
Queen forwarded passports for the agents whom the
King of Navarre sent to consult his friends in regard to the publication of a suspension of arms;
but at the same time, she, herself, proclaimed a truce
without waiting for his consent. In this act, he saw
one of Catherine's cunning contrivances to stop the
levy of German auxiliaries, and complained accordingly. Then an attack made by a body of Protestants
upon a corps of royalists, alarmed the Queen; and
the conference was again delayed. But at length
it was agreed that Henry should advance to Jarnac;
and, establishing his quarters there, should visit the
Queen at the chateau of St. Brie, a few miles distant
from that town.

The impediments which had occurred, caused
the meeting to be deferred till the 13th of December, when Henry, who had arrived at Jarnac
with a strong escort three days before, rode
over to the castle, and held the first of several interviews with the Queen. So many anecdotes are
told of these celebrated conferences in Poitou, that
I must only venture to give those which are best
authenticated, and which tend to display the character of the future monarch of France, without

dwelling upon all the turns and passages of a negotiation which produced no important result.

Catherine had, as usual, taken care to bring with
her from the capital, the most beautiful and docile
ladies of her court, knowing well the foibles of her
son-in-law, as well as those of his somewhat too
ardent and facile followers. On their first meeting, after a few brief observations, she asked
him, in a sharp tone, what it was he sought?
Henry gazed round the ring of loveliness, by which
the Queen was surrounded, and replied, with his
usual frank gaiety, "Nothing that you have here,
Madam."*

Some days after, when many angry words and
bitter reproaches had passed on both parts, the
Queen endeavored to alarm the young King's spirit
of independence, and boldly declared that he could
do nothing with the refractory Rochellois.

"I can do all that I wish, Madam," he replied,
"because I wish nothing but what I ought."

"You cannot even impose a tax," rejoined the
Duke of Nevers, who was present.

"True," answered the King, "we do not understand any thing of taxation, for we have no Italians
amongst us."†

* Perefix. Pierre Matthieu.

† Lettre d'un Gentilhomme Français. Aubigné. It must be
remembered that Nevers was descended from an Italian house, and
that the principal financiers of that day in France were foreigners.

These replies, indeed, were mere repartees; and they are only cited here to shew the mixture of good-humored jest and sarcastic rebuke, which Henry failed not to employ when severity was required; but another speech of his to the Queen-mother, on this occasion, evinces that, even at this period, he entertained that longing desire for the happiness of the people of France, that fixed purpose of consoling, restoring, and protecting them, which rendered him the most beloved, as well as the most respected, of all the monarchs that ever occupied the throne of that country.   In answer to one of Catherine's observations, regarding the condition to which the civil war had reduced the land, he exclaimed, " It would indeed be glorious for the state to be re-established by a man proscribed, and his country saved by an exile."

He steadily resisted all Catherine's efforts, however, to induce him to change his religion and abandon his friends ; and, indeed, he seems at this time to have been equally well armed against her arguments, and against the seductions of her women. Very often, during the conferences, the Queen-mother, abandoning the serious subjects under consideration, apparently gave way to jest and gaiety ; and on one occasion, affecting to be somewhat sportive, she tried to tickle the ribs of Henry of Navarre, with her fingers. The monarch, at once understanding her object, opened his pourpoint ; and, exposing his bare breast, to shew that he had no coat of mail below, he said, " I, Madam, have nothing concealed."

During the various interviews at St. Brie, the Protestants were full of suspicions of the Queen-mother and her designs, and some of Henry's officers, counting fully upon the readiness of the Catholics to take any advantage, devised a cunning scheme for leading them on to a breach of the truce, which would have afforded the young King a valid excuse for seizing upon the person of Catherine, and making her court prisoners. It would seem that the Papist garrison of Fontenoy were anxiously looking for the opportunity of recovering the small town of Vouvans, which had been taken by the Huguenots two months before ; and the governor of the latter place suggested that they might be led on to make the attempt even during the suspension of arms. This would have justified the Protestants, it was contended, in at once arresting the whole party at St. Brie ; but Henry, notwith-standing the urgent solicitation of most of those by whom he was surrounded, refused to give the slightest countenance to such a proceeding, and the project was consequently abandoned.*

The generous conduct of Henry did not meet with a suitable return, for barely was the truce at an end, when a party of the royal forces made an attack upon two regiments of Huguenot arque-

* Aubigné.

busiers, at Maillezais, and nearly cut them to
pieces.* Before that time, however, Catherine
having exhausted all her arts, having even offered,
we are assured, to obtain a divorce between Henry
and his wife, and to bestow upon him the hand of her
granddaughter, the beautiful Christine, daughter
of Claudine Duchess of Lorraine, if he would
renounce the Protestant faith, and having with
as little success made several other proposals, in
all of which the adoption of the Catholic religion
was an ingredient, broke off the conferences in
order to return to Paris, complaining bitterly of the
obstinacy of her son-in-law, and declaring that she
desired nothing but tranquillity.

" Madam," replied Henry, " I am not to blame
in this war. It is not I, who prevent you from
sleeping in your bed; it is you, who prevent me
from sleeping in mine. The trouble that you take,
nourishes and pleases you; tranquillity you look
upon as the greatest enemy in life."†

Catherine, indeed, did not content herself with
using her own influence upon the King of Navarre.
The Duke of Nevers, for whom he always entertained the highest esteem, was employed to confer
with him in private and endeavor to bring him
over to the views of the court; and in a letter
from that nobleman to Henry III. we have not

* The account given by Brantome, and copied by Anquetil, of
this affair, is as incorrect as it is absurd; for the defeat of these
regiments did not take place till the conferences between
Catherine and Henry were at an end.

† Perefix.

only a curious account of their conference, but
also a very interesting description of Henry's demeanor at this time. "Such as you have seen
him, Sire," says the Duke, "such is this Prince at
the present moment. Neither years nor troubles
change him in the least. He is still agreeable, still
joyous, still, as he vowed to me a thousand times,
devoted to peace, and your Majesty's service. He
told me in the fulness of his heart, that he only
wished he had forces enough to deliver you in a
single day, from all the authors of the League,
without even obliging you to give your consent.
He would shew you, how very dear your tranquillity
is to him, how nearly your honor touches him, and
how much he wishes to see you as powerful and as
well obeyed as you deserve."

But the arguments of Nevers proved ineffectual to induce Henry of Navarre to change his religion, although the Duke frankly told that monarch,
that he himself would never serve a Protestant Sovereign. Henry replied kindly and openly,
but still demanded liberty of conscience for himself and his friends, security in the exercise of
their own faith, and the execution of the edicts,
which had been granted and revoked, adding, that
there was nothing which he himself desired so
much as to die sword in hand against the Spaniards,
and the League, the only irreconcileable enemies of
France.*

Another sort of death, however, had well nigh

* Mem. de Nevers, tom. i. p. 767.

overtaken Henry, while the conferences were going on.   Having arranged a hunting party, at which the two courts were to be present, his eye was caught by two very beautiful horses, belonging to Bellievre, one of the King's ministers, and after some jesting conversation regarding their speed, he proposed to run the horse on which he was mounted against them.   The ground chosen was bounded on one side by a field of young wheat, and on the other by a hedge, behind which some swine were feeding; and the word being given, the race began.   Before a quarter of the course was finished, the King was considerably in advance of the other riders; but, at that moment, the swine taking fright at the noise, ran across the road and under the feet of his horse, which fell and rolled over upon the King.   He was taken up senseless, with the blood gushing from his mouth and nose, and carried to the chateau of St. Brie, where the Queen-mother testified the greatest grief at the accident.   " But every one," says the narrator, " kept upon his guard for fear of being surprised."   The King soon regained his consciousness, and asked what had happened, replying, when the surgeons asked where he felt the greatest pain, that he felt none at all.   In a few days he had so completely recovered, that not the least inconvenience remained, although the physicians had at first affirmed that he would be obliged to keep his room for the rest of the year.*

* Mem. de Nevers, tom. ii. p. 588.

Immediately after the termination of the conferences at St. Brie, the small towns of Vouvans and
La Fay, were surprised by the Catholics; but Catherine still kept up the appearance of pacific intentions, and though Henry had retired to Rochelle,
sent to require another interview. The council of
the King strongly opposed it, pointing out that the
Queen-mother was only seeking to amuse him, while
she endeavored to seduce his friends, to gain advantages in Poitou, and by the rumors of a peace
industriously spread in Germany and Switzerland,
to arrest the progress of his Protestant allies. It
was soon discovered also, that Henry III. with his
usual weak vacillation, had taken an oath, in a
chapter of the Order of the Holy Ghost, held on the
1st January, 1587, to suffer no religion in France
but the Roman Catholic; and every one represented
to the King of Navarre, that farther discussion
could only produce evil.

Henry was, nevertheless, anxious to leave no effort
unmade to obtain peace; and he accordingly advanced
to Marans, offering to resume the conferences in that
place. Mutual suspicions, however, prevented the
meeting from taking place;* and Turenne, at the
request of the Queen-mother, was sent to Fontenoy
to hear her last resolution. It was found that she

---

* It has been asserted by some English authors that Henry
himself went to Fontenoy, (Browing's Hist. of the Huguenots),
but such was not the case; see Lettre d'un Gentilhomme Francais,
written by an eye-witness at the time.

had nothing in reality to add, to that which she had before proposed; and when she repeated to Turenne that the King was resolved there should for the future be but one religion in France, that bold leader replied ; " We desire it much, Madam, provided it be ours ; otherwise we will fight well for it :" and with these words he retired, breaking off the discussion.*

Thus ended the negotiations commenced at St. Brie ; and the conduct of Catherine, from the beginning to the close, left a strong impression upon the minds of the Protestants, that her sole object was to entangle the King of Navarre in long debates, which would delay the progress of his arms, excite doubts and suspicions amongst his followers, and diminish the zeal of his allies.

* Cayet, tom. i. p. 31.

BOOK VIII.

It is not improbable that Catherine de Medicis might have endeavored to occupy the attention of the King of Navarre for some weeks longer in fruitless conferences, and that Henry himself might have yielded not unwillingly to her schemes, had not other events occurred, in various parts of France, to call for her immediate presence in the capital. We find from one of the letters of the Bourbon Prince, that he had purposely suffered the negotiations to be protracted, long after he knew that they were illusive, in order to give time for the advance of a large body of German forces, which Monsieur de Segur had been busily raising for his service on the banks of the Rhine. Though Catherine, perhaps, divined his intention, she trusted to the activity of the Duke of Guise to impede the progress of the reiters; but early in the year 1587, many motives led her to refuse all concessions to the Protestants, and to hurry back to Paris. The successes of the Duke of Epernon against the Huguenots of Dauphiné, and the threatening aspect of the League, gave her courage and inducement to break off her treaty with those who were considered heretics; and a plot to seize upon the capital, and imprison the King, which was discovered and frustrated on the 21st of February, shewed her the necessity of her presence in the court of her son.

It may be necessary here, before I proceed to trace the course of the war, which was vigorously resumed in Poitou immediately after the termination of the negotiations of St. Brie, to notice briefly the proceedings of the leaders of the League, and the events which had taken place in Paris. The Duke of Mayenne, after having taken Castillon and, to use the words of l'Etoile, "given his army the fine present of rags, and the plague," which was all that was found in the city, perceived that, without supplies of men and money, thwarted by Matignon, abandoned by his Swiss, and with desertion and disease thinning his French forces every day, he could not hope to make any farther progress in Guienne.* The anticipations of Henry of Navarre, regarding the wasting away of the Duke's army in tedious attacks upon well garrisoned fortresses, were by this time fully realized; and Mayenne found, with bitter mortification, that the system of defence, which was at first regarded with contempt, had proved successful against all his efforts to subdue the Protestants of Guienne. He therefore gave up the attempt, and boldly hurrying to Paris, presented himself to

* L'Etoile. Discours de M. de La Chastre. Though La Chastre was a violent partisan of the League, yet his account of the difficulties of Mayenne's army is borne out by every other authority.

Henry, not with the humility of a defeated general, but with the air of a deceived and ill-treated ally. At the same time the pulpit and the confessional were employed with redoubled force to calumniate the King; and the danger of the latter instrument to morals, religion, and government, was never more fully exemplified than on the present occasion. It became a maxim of the priests, which they took care to instil into the minds of the laity, that the penitent who revealed what was said to him by his confessor, was as criminal as the confessor who revealed the secrets of his penitent; and it may be easily conceived what was the use made of such immense means of private influence by daring and unscrupulous men.

We have noticed already the meeting of the Leaguers of Paris, at the College of Fortet, the proceedings at which were at first irregular, and confined principally to wild declamations against the King and the Huguenots; but by the counsels and advice of the Duke of Guise, a regular system of organization was speedily instituted. A council of sixteen was appointed, one being chosen to represent and to manage each of the sixteen quarters of the city, and numerous inferior agents were selected, to act in each quarter both as spies and officers, communicating all that they learnt during the day to the sixteen, and receiving from them intimation of the course to be pursued by the people. The League of Paris thus became distinct from, though subsidiary to the

League of Peronne, and from the number of its leaders, obtained the name of " The Sixteen." Its meetings were held in various places, sometimes at the convent of St. Dominic, sometimes at the Jacobins, sometimes at the Jesuits, and sometimes in private houses ; and as it was more regularly organized than the general League, so was it also more vehement and determined, urging even the family of Lorraine forward to acts which they meditated, but feared to perform without great caution and long delay.

Amongst other projects conceived in their assemblies, the most prominent and the most frequent was that of arresting the King.   Arms were obtained and distributed throughout the whole town ; the Leaguers were formed into bands and instructed as to the part each was to act ; and every movement of the monarch was narrowly watched, especially in coming and going between Vincennes and the Louvre.   Henry, however, was not long without intimation of their designs, for Nicholas Poulain, lieutenant of the Isle of France, who had been engaged deeply in their plots, opened a communication with the court about this time, and thenceforward observed all their proceedings carefully, under the direction of the Chancellor de Chiverny.†   In consequence of the intelligence he thus received, Henry took extraordinary precautions for his own defence, and never rode any distance from his palace

* Procès verbal de Nicolas Poulain. Davila.

without being accompanied by a large train of armed
gentlemen, besides his famous guard of forty-five,
each of whom had been selected for his vigor and
determination.

The arrival of the Duke of Mayenne in Paris,
towards the end of the year 1586, gave new vigor
to the movements of the Sixteen; and numerous
consultations took place between him and the leaders
of the League, in which their vast and treasonable
plans were fully developed to the coldest, most prudent, and least ambitious of the brothers of the
house of Guise.   Mayenne pondered long upon the
state of affairs thus displayed, equally unwilling
to enter fully into such schemes, or to break entirely
with the parties proposing them, and thus to cause
a division in the faction which was his brother's
great support.   In the mean while, the negotiations
between Mayenne and the Sixteen were all communicated to the King; and although his favorite
Villequier, and several others of his council, endeavored to persuade him that the information he
received was false, he used every precaution to guard
against surprise, brought a considerable number
of troops into the immediate neighbourhood of Paris,
doubled the guards about the Louvre, and took
measures for securing the Bastille and the Arsenal.
These steps shewed the faction and the Duke, that
their proceedings had been discovered; and Mayenne, feigning illness, retired into his government of
Burgundy.*

* Davila.   L'Etoile, tom. ii.

Having traced the events which took place at the court thus far, I must go back to the summer of the year 1586, to notice, shortly, the operations of the armies of Epernon and Joyeuse, the assembling of which, in the central provinces of France, I have already mentioned. Epernon, depending wholly upon the favor of the King, and his own personal merit, arrayed himself with the most bitter hostility against the house of Guise. He was friendly to the King of Navarre; but without consideration for either party, he formed a determination, which, had it been vigorously pursued on all occasions by Henry III. himself, would have soon restored tranquillity to France. He resolved to repress, with equal severity and energy, both Protestants and Catholics, who refused to submit to the royal authority; and immediately marched his army, consisting of ten thousand infantry and twelve hundred cavalry, all veteran soldiers, into Provence and Dauphiné. The famous Lesdiguieres, at the head of the Huguenots in those provinces, had lately given a severe defeat to Monsieur De Vins, commanding the forces of the League. The latter, finding that the efforts of the Duke of Guise to gain over Epernon, by offering him his daughter in marriage, had been treated with contempt, resolved to prevent the royalist general from taking possession of Provence, the government of which province had been conferred upon him at the death of the Grand Prior. But Epernon attacked him with skill and vigor, took place after place, till he reduced the power of the League in that quarter to nothing, and then turned his arms against Lesdiguieres. Although it is evident from all accounts, that he pursued the Protestant forces with less success than he obtained against the Leaguers; he, nevertheless, gained many advantages, and reduced them to a situation of great difficulty. But towards the end of the year, finding that innumerable machinations were going on to ruin him at the court, he returned to Paris, leaving his brother La Valette in command of the army.*

Joyeuse, on the contrary, allied to the house of Lorraine by his marriage with the sister of the Queen, and jealous of the Duke of Epernon, forgot all the ties of gratitude which bound him to the King, and daily leaned more and more towards the party of the League. Leading his army into Languedoc, he directed his efforts entirely against the Protestants, forced Chatillon to raise the siege of Compierre; and taking five or six considerable places by the way, he at length arrived at Toulouse, which was under the government of his father. He there passed some time in unfruitful military display, while his credit daily decreased at the court, and that of Epernon augmented.

In the meanwhile, the Duke of Guise, whom the King had left without occupation, upon the pretence of holding him in readiness to oppose the entrance

* Girard. Vie du Duc d'Epernon. Davila.

of the Germans into France, determined to act upon his own account, and turned his arms against the towns held by the Duke of Bouillon, on the frontiers of Champagne. Rocroi was soon forced to capitulate, not without suspicion of treachery on the part of the governor; and then, without paying the slightest attention to the remonstrances of Bouillon, or to the commands of the King, Guise proceeded to ravage the territories of Sedan and Jamets. His success was not such as might have been expected from his reputation and undoubted military skill. Douzy was taken, but not without a loss of four hundred men; and, though the troops of the chief of the League approached to the very walls of Sedan, his forces were not sufficient to lay regular siege to that important place. In a skirmish near Daigny, the party of the Duke of Guise was defeated by Bouillon in person; and the Lorrainese prince himself escaped with difficulty, leaving his mantle in the hands of one of the enemy who had seized him.*

His army, having by this time exhausted the provisions of the neighbouring country, was glad to obtain a truce of fourteen days; and Guise retired into Champagne to recruit. But shortly after, a battle took place under the walls of Jamets, in which the troops of the League were once more defeated; and the Duke of Bouillon, believing his officers to be perfectly competent to resist all the efforts of the enemy, proceeded into Germany for

* Peyran, Histoire de Sedan.

the purpose of leading the Protestant levies from the
borders of the Rhine, to join the armies of the
Prince de Condé and the King of Navarre.

Where the junction was to take place had not been
decided; but important events had occurred in Poitou, after the conferences of St. Brie had come to an
unsuccessful termination. No sooner was Catherine
de Medicis on the way to Paris, than the King of
Navarre recommenced the war, by pushing forward
against the various fortresses which were held by
the Papists in the neighbourhood of Rochelle.
The first place attacked was Talmont, which was
at that time a considerable town, lying between
Britanny and Aunis. The distance from Rochelle
by sea was short, and the Duke of La Trimouille
was despatched against it with twelve hundred foot,
two hundred horse, and three pieces of artillery.
The town, destitute of regular defences, was seized
at once; but the castle, which was well fortified,
held out in the hope of immediate aid : and the Protestant force being found insufficient to reduce it,
Sully was sent back to the King of Navarre, who
now embarked in person with two thousand men, to
carry on the siege more vigorously. The weather
proved unfavorable; a violent tempest overtook the
King in his passage; and during two days, which
were occupied by a voyage usually performed in a
few hours, the whole party, crowded into three small
vessels, were several times in imminent danger of
perishing. On their arrival, however, the garrison
surrendered without farther resistance; and Henry

led his forces to the attack of Chizay. The defence here was more obstinate, although one piece of artillery was all that the place possessed ; and Fayolle, the governor, held out till all his provisions were exhausted, and famine stared him in the face.* Sansay was stormed, and St. Maixent capitulated almost as soon as the Huguenot forces appeared. The more important town of Fontenoy was attacked, as soon as La Rochefoucault and the Prince de Condé had joined the King of Navarre ; and the great suburb, called *les Loges*, was taken by assault during the night. The sap was then employed against the walls of the place, and was carried on with such activity, that before the garrison were aware of their danger, the voices of the soldiers on the walls were heard by Henry himself in the mine. He immediately called to them to surrender, giving his name ; and so great was the consternation produced by this unexpected sound, that the governor at once entered into a parley, when the terms were arranged in a few minutes. No formal capitulation was drawn up between the Catholic troops and the King of Navarre; " the security of his word being so well known," says the historian, " that the garrison did not require any writing." All his promises were punctually kept ; and the Papist force marched out with the honors of war.† The city was pre-

---

* Such is the account of Sully, who was at the attack of Chizay. Aubigné, who does not mention that he was present, gives a different statement, and represents the defence as feeble.

† Sully. Discours de la Guerre.

served from pillage ; and the King of Navarre, advancing rapidly, made himself master of several other towns ; so that, through a wide circle round Rochelle, no place of any importance, except Brouage, remained in the hands of the Roman Catholics.

Henry's intention, at this time, was undoubtedly to hurry forward, with all the forces he could collect, to meet the army of foreign auxiliaries, which was now in movement upon the eastern frontier of the kingdom,* though the measures of precaution taken by the League rendered the enterprise extremely perilous. But early in June, 1587, intelligence reached the head-quarters of the Navarrese monarch, that the King of France had commanded Joyeuse, at the head of a powerful army, to take the field against him in Poitou ; and the nearer approach of that nobleman, followed by a large body of courtiers, and a force consisting of six thousand arquebusiers and two thousand horse, induced Henry to determine upon quitting the open field, and leaving the places he had taken, to break the strength of the new wave that was thus poured upon his head. His plan, it would seem, was to strengthen the town of St. Maixent, to throw into it a considerable part of his army, and to retire himself with the rest upon Sainctonge ; and no sooner was he informed of the rapid marches with which Joyeuse was advancing from Tours, than he hastened to the town he had resolved to fortify. Conducting all the operations

* Lettres Missives, tom. 2.

in person, he so completely exhausted himself, that on the way back to Rochelle he was obliged to cast himself into a cart drawn by bullocks ; and there, giving way to fatigue, slept as soundly as in a bed of state.

All his precautions, however, were not sufficient to save St. Maixent, though, always in activity, he is said, by one contemporary* writer, to have surprised and cut to pieces several of the enemies' detachments ; but his officers, less prudent, and less energetic than their leader, suffered themselves, on more than one occasion, to be attacked unprepared. Doubtful as to where the first blow might be struck, and unwilling to consume the stores of the fortified towns, Henry of Navarre had placed two regiments in La Motte St. Eloy, at a short distance from St. Maixent, with orders to throw themselves into the latter place in case Joyeuse advanced against it. The officers in command, however, neglected to take the most necessary precautions ; and by a night march the Duke reached La Motte, and was actually in the open streets of the place, before the Huguenots were aware of his proximity. A gallant defence was made by the two regiments in some houses which they seized upon ; and they contrived to set the whole army of Joyeuse at defiance for two days, at the end of which time, being destitute of provisions and ammunition, they were forced to yield. Whether any terms were agreed to or not, is not clearly

* Chappuis.

known; some authors saying that they were assured
of safety, others, that they surrendered at discretion;
but, whatever were the conditions, they were slaughtered to a man in cold blood.* St. Maixent was
then besieged, and capitulated after a resistance of
only fifteen days, much to the surprise and indignation of the King of Navarre. The Protestant clergyman of the place was hanged; but no other butchery
took place; and Joyeuse, after having threatened
Marans, turned upon Tonnay Charente, which immediately surrendered. His next enterprise was
the surprise of a company of foot within sight of
Rochelle, where the same acts of sanguinary fury
were perpetrated as at La Motte; and then, after
retaking Tonnay, which had been recovered by the
Prince de Condé, the Duke commenced his retreat,
followed by the forces which the King of Navarre
had called rapidly together from all quarters, and
losing several detachments by the way.

Joyeuse paused, however, to attack Maillezais,
which was unable to offer any effectual resistance,
and thence retired to Niort, with an army daily
weakened by desertion, fatigue, and pestilence.
Henry of Navarre was by this time treading close
upon his steps; the Protestant forces daily cut off
parties of stragglers; and tidings from Paris shewed
Joyeuse that the King, aware of his communications
with the League, had withdrawn from him that favor

* Aubigné. Discours de la Guerre. L'Etoile. The latter
states that the Duke violated the terms of capitulation.

by which he had risen to power and distinction. At Niort he was visited by Sully, to arrange the terms of a combat, proposed between a party of the Duke's light troops, and a small body of Scottish gentlemen in the service of the King of Navarre. Joyeuse would not suffer this pass of arms to take place; but Sully found him sombre and desponding; and divining from all that occurred during their interview, that the Catholic general was about to leave his army, and to hurry to Paris, he carried the intelligence to the King of Navarre, who seized the opportunity of falling upon the disorganised force, left under the guidance of his former friend, Lavardin, and, attacking it in detail, cut to pieces several corps of cavalry. He then pursued Lavardin and the main body into Touraine, where he kept that officer shut up during five days in La Haye; but having brought neither cannon nor infantry with him, in his rapid pursuit of the enemy, he was at length obliged to retire.*

In the meanwhile, Joyeuse, having reached Paris, was received with the utmost enthusiasm by the people, and by the young nobility of the court, who had been captivated by his chivalrous spirit and profuse generosity; but from the King he met nothing but insult.† Henry plainly told him that he was looked upon as a coward, and that he would not easily remove the stain from his name. Yet Joyeuse found no difficulty in recruiting his

* Discours de la Guerre.   Aubigné.   Sully.   † Davila.

forces; multitudes of the brilliant nobles of the court, enlisted under his banners; several of the adherents of the League joined him; and the Duke of Mercœur promised to meet him on the Loire, with a large reinforcement.

Henry of Navarre had not neglected any means, during the absence of Joyeuse, to increase his strength; and intelligence that the German auxiliaries, having received a large sum of money from the Queen of England, were marching towards the frontiers of France, although as yet he had no certain information of their route,* induced him to call all his friends around him, even at the risk of leaving some important points but feebly defended. He also held communications with his cousin, the Count de Soissons, who had long secretly favored his party, and obtained a promise from that Prince that he would join him with all speed on the Loire. Early in September, having collected a considerable force, Henry advanced to Monsoreau, in order to favor the passage of the Count de Soissons, who was hurrying forward with a small corps between the army of Joyeuse, and the troops which the Duke of Mercœur was leading to the aid of the Catholic general. To support his young and inexperienced cousin, the King of Navarre directed the Viscount de Turenne to cross the river and advance

* A gentleman sent from Germany with verbal intelligence, was killed at the King's side, under the walls of Chizay, before he could pronounce more than the first two or three words of his message. Sully, liv. 2.

to meet the Count on the other bank ; but in per-
forming this operation the forces of Turenne encountered those of Mercœur ; and a combat immediately
commenced, in which the Huguenots were completely
victorious, the rich baggage of the Duke falling into
their hands.*

The same day, the Count de Soissons himself
appeared, and on the following morning passed the
Loire, bringing to Henry the welcome intelligence
that the Germans were advancing rapidly. But the
pleasure produced by such tidings was mingled with
no slight anxiety, when the King of Navarre found
that great difference of opinion existed amongst the
leaders of the auxiliaries, as to the point at which
they should enter France, and the course they should
pursue. New measures now became necessary, and
Henry resolved to march as speedily as possible to
meet his fellow Protestants from Germany ;† but
his army was not yet prepared for so long and dangerous an expedition ; and farther tidings obtained
from the prisoners taken at Monsoreau, shewed him
that Joyeuse was nearer than he had imagined, and
was advancing with the express commands of the
King of France to risk a battle.

The secret motives which induced Henry III. to
issue such commands, have been doubtful to all
historians ; but, in considering his conduct we must

* Aubigné. Discours de la Guerre.

† See a very interesting letter from Henry to the Queen of
England on this subject, in which he expresses the strongest de-
termination to force his way across the country to meet the
Germans. Lettres Missives, tom. ii. page 305.

recollect that he was now threatened by numerous
dangers.   The League was, undoubtedly, the enemy
he most feared; but at the same time, the march of
so large a body of foreign troops, as was now approaching the heart of his dominions, was necessarily
regarded by him as both perilous to himself, and
destructive to his country.   Their junction with the
King of Navarre, would have rendered that Prince
master of the destinies of France; and Henry III.,
whether he threw himself into the hands of the Protestants, or gave himself up to the League, would
have been powerless in his own kingdom.   His plans
then seem to have been to oppose Joyeuse and his
army, which he now looked upon as a part of the
League, to Henry of Navarre, so as to impede the
movements of that Prince; to leave the Duke of
Guise with an inferior force to break the first shock
of the Germans; and then in person, at the head of
his own forces and with the counsels of Epernon
and Nevers, to meet the foreigners on the banks
of the Loire, with a view of preventing them from
passing that river.   Whether Henry of Navarre or
Joyeuse obtained the victory, the French monarch
gained an object; if the Duke were successful, the
Protestants of France would be cut off from the
Germans; and if Henry, on the contrary, won the
day, his forces must be weakened, and his movements
retarded by a battle, while, at the same time, one of
the armies of the League would be destroyed.
That such were the views taken by Henry III. and
his counsellors is clear, from a letter of the Duke

of Nevers, which I shall have to cite hereafter, but which has been unaccountably overlooked by most, if not all historians.

The intelligence which Henry of Navarre received, regarding the movements of the enemy, caused him immediately to retire to Rochelle, in order to make further efforts to call the scattered Protestants to his standard, and to put his army into a better state of preparation; but, notwithstanding every exertion, it remained still greatly inferior to that of the Duke of Joyeuse,* which was increased by the arrival of various reinforcements at Ruffec.†

Finding that the Catholic forces were rapidly approaching St. Maixent, Henry took his departure from Rochelle, on the 14th of October, and passing through Taillebourg, with all the artillery he had been able to collect, joined the main body of his army at Pons,‡ intending to open a way for himself by Guienne, Languedoc, and the Lyonnais, towards the source of the Loire, in the hope of effecting his junction with the German auxiliaries. It would appear that he expected to be able to outmarch the Duke of Joyeuse, and he did indeed somewhat gain upon him. Had Joyeuse, as there was every reason to believe he would, waited for the junction of the

---

* Sully.   † Aubigné.

‡ Discours de la Guerre. It will be found that in regard to the dates of these movements, I have differed from all other writers; but I have been induced to do so by the accounts of Henry's household expenses, which mark with precision the places where he dined and slept during all the events referred to in the text.

strong corps of Marshal Matignon, the object of
Henry would have been effected, and he would
have been enabled to place the Isle as well as the
Drogne, between himself and the enemy. But
Joyeuse perceiving his intention, hastened forward
by forced marches, and came up with him in the
neighbourhood of Montlieu and Montguyon. The
object of both generals was now to seize upon the
town and castle of Coutras, situated near the junction of the Isle and Drogne; and on the morning
of the 19th of October, the royal army was at
La Rochechalais, about four leagues and a half
from Coutras, while Henry was marching up from
the side of Montguyon. Lavardin was thrown forward by Joyeuse, with a small body of men to take
possession of Coutras; but the Duke of La Trimouille coming up with a superior force, and fording
the Drogne, obliged Lavardin to retreat, and leave
the little town in the hands of the Protestants.*

Thinking that he should be able to pass the Isle
before Joyeuse arrived from La Rochechalais, Henry
caused some of his officers the same night to cross
with the artillery and a body of arquebusiers.
Before morning, however, some prisoners were
brought in; and from them the monarch learned
that the Duke had ordered his drums to beat at ten
o'clock at night, and was actually marching upon
Coutras. It now became evident that the whole
of the Protestant army could not pass the river; and
orders were sent in haste to recall the artillery and

* Aubigné. Discours de la Guerre. Sully.

the regiments which had already crossed, while Henry, after having pointed out where the three cannon, which were all that he possessed, were to be placed, drew up his forces in order of battle. With the rapid glance of genius, which Sully assures us that Henry possessed above any general of his age, the position of his artillery was chosen in a manner that decided the fate of the battle ; and the disposition of his forces was not less skilful, although the unfortunate attempt to pass the river, prevented several regiments from arriving on the ground till the combat had actually commenced.

The Protestant army was drawn up on a small plain, having to its left the Drogne, with the town of Coutras behind it ; and on the right, a copse of low wood, advancing somewhat into the plain, and strengthened by a ditch. On this side were placed the principal force of arquebusiers, the regiments that were absent taking place in their rear as they came up. These were supported by La Trimouille, with two hundred light horse, and another company of arquebusiers. Towards the centre was Turenne, with his Gascon cavalry ; and farther on the left appeared the Prince de Condé. On his left, again, was stationed, the King of Navarre ; while a little in advance of both, but still to the left, was the Count de Soissons, with two hundred men at arms.* The whole position took the form of a

---

* It is generally stated by historians, following De Thou, that the Count de Soissons commanded the left wing of Henry's forces, and Condé the right ; but in the absence of any despatch

crescent, of which the left of Turenne, and the right of Condé were the centre. Each body of cavalry was accompanied by a small party of arquebusiers, five deep; the first line lying down, the second on the knee, the third stooping, and only the fourth and fifth upright. These were ordered not to fire till the enemy's forces were within twenty yards.

Before the arrangements were completed, the army of Joyeuse appeared, and began to take up its position in haste, debouching from several narrow roads. Henry has been accused of want of skill for not attacking the enemy in this difficult operation; but it must be recollected, that a considerable body of his troops was still on the other side of the river; and that his artillery, on which so much depended, had not yet taken up its position.

The first body of the army of Joyeuse that became visible, was a battalion, consisting of two regiments of heavy cavalry, forming a thousand men, the flower of the army, supported by eighteen hundred arquebusiers. On their right were four hundred chosen lances. Next came five hundred more; and, soon after, towards the river, was seen the cornet of Joyeuse himself, with ten companies magnificently caparisoned; amongst which appeared a hundred and

from Henry himself upon the subject, I have thought it best to follow the statement of those whom we have every reason to believe were present at the battle. The Discours de la Guerre, which, as I have before observed, is a contemporary record, and was probably written by an eye-witness, perfectly coincides with Aubigné in regard to the disposition of theProtestant army.

twenty volunteers, each followed by a troop raised at his own expense, making in the whole twelve hundred lances, the first rank of which consisted entirely of nobility. The vacant space was soon filled up with arquebusiers, horse and foot. The Duke's artillery, was at first placed in a low ground where it could have no effect at all, and, though afterwards removed, proved of very little service during the day. The Papist force presented nothing but shining arms, gold, and waving scarfs; while that of the Protestants offered a front of rusty iron, stained buff coats, and tattered banners; but the youth and freshness of the one, was well compensated by the veteran hardihood of the other, gained in a thousand fields, and strengthened by the habit of strife and endurance.

A different spirit, too, animated each force, and each commander. Joyeuse, vain, presumptuous, and inexperienced, looked upon his victory as certain; and he is said, with the cold-blooded ferocity of his religion and party, to have given orders that no quarter should be granted, even to the King of Navarre himself. On the night before the battle, he exclaimed, "We hold the enemy between two rivers; he cannot now escape us." The same presumption reigned throughout his troops; and it was scarcely possible to keep up any thing like discipline amongst them, the officers, almost as much without experience as the men, having but little authority over them, so that much time was lost in taking up their position.

The King of Navarre, on the contrary, though full of confidence, knew well that nothing must be neglected to insure success; and every measure was taken to give his inferior force the advantage of position and preparation. The Protestants felt, too, that the battle was for life or death ; that their fortunes, their homes, their families, their religion, were all staked on the issue of the approaching strife. Rivalries and jealousies had existed among them, but they were all forgotten in the hour of danger and of battle ; the troops were obedient to officers on whose judgment they had full reliance, and all looked to the great general who commanded them, with the memory of the successes he had obtained, the enterprises he had executed, and the great achievements he had performed with the smallest and most insignificant means.

The conduct and demeanor of Henry himself, was well calculated to raise the hopes and ex-pectations of his army. Calm cheerfulness appeared upon his countenance, and all his words and move-ments were full of confidence but not presumption. As he sat gazing upon the brilliant battalions of the enemy, while they deployed before him, some one called his attention to the splendor of their arms: but Henry replied with a gay smile, " We shall have the better aim when the fight begins." And as soon as he found that the commencement of the battle was approaching, he addressed the gentlemen who surrounded him, in a tone which well expressed the feelings of a generous and beneficent prince, mingled

with those of a gallant and determined soldier.   He
spoke in touching language of the evils of war ; he
lamented almost with tears the state to which
France had been reduced by civil contentions ; he
called on all who heard him, to witness what efforts
he had made to avoid the recourse to arms, which
had been forced upon him ; and, solemnly declaring
that he only drew the sword in defence of his rights
and religion, he exclaimed, "Let them perish who
are the authors of this war ; and may the blood shed
this day rest upon them alone."   Then turning to
the Prince de Condé, and the Count de Soissons, he
added in a gayer tone: " To you I shall say nothing,
but that you are of the house of Bourbon ; and,
please God, I will shew you this day that I am
your elder."*

Another act, however, which he performed immediately before the battle, tended still more to
secure the love and confidence of his troops.   The
famous Du Plessis Mornay, advanced to the King's
side, and boldly reminded him that he had deeply
injured a respectable citizen of Rochelle, by se-
ducing his daughter, and that God could not be
expected to favor the arms of one who left such an
offence unrepaired.   The King at once dismounted
from his horse, and in the face of the whole army,

* There are various accounts given of the King's address to
his soldiers, by Le Grain, Pierre Matthieu, and others, but as I
find the above expressions generally attributed to him, by the
best authorities, I am inclined to believe that they must, at all
events, render the substance of his address.

avowed his sincere grief for what he had done; called upon all to witness that he publicly asked pardon of the family he had injured; and promised to repair, as far as possible, the fault he had committed. The troops were then called to prayers by the ministers Chandieu and d'Amours; and each man fell upon his knees in the ranks, asking the God of victories for protection and success.

At the sight of the kneeling host of his enemies, Joyeuse exclaimed, " The King of Navarre is frightened; look—he kneels!" But Lavardin, who was standing behind him, replied, " Do not fancy such a thing, Sir; these men only do so when they are resolved to conquer or die."*

The Roman Catholic infantry now advanced to gain possession of the ditch which defended the wood; but just at that moment, the artillery of the Huguenots opened its fire upon the adverse line, from the high ground on which Henry had placed it; and nothing could exceed the execution which the three cannon did amongst the ranks of Joyeuse. Every shot, we are assured by Sully, swept down twelve, fifteen, and sometimes twenty-five men;† while the guns of the Duke could not be sufficiently elevated to carry the balls amongst the Protestants, and spent their force in a sandy hill. An effort was then made to remove the artillery of the Leaguers, but with little effect; and the battle becoming fierce between

* The words are given variously by different authors, but the substance of the Duke's observations is the same in all.

† Sully. Le Grain. Discours de la Guerre.

the arquebusiers of the two parties, for possession
of the little wood, Lavardin charged at the head of
a body of five hundred horse, under his own cornet,
and that of a Captain Mercure.*   They were met
by the light horse of La Trimouille and Arambure;
but so severe was the shock, that the Protestant
cavalry, in that part of the field, gave way, and was
driven in confusion back upon Coutras.   The squadron of Turenne was also broken by the charge of
Monsieur de Montigni.   Mercure forced his way
into the town itself; and the Catholics, seeing the
centre of the enemy in disarray, imagined the battle
won, and began to shout, "Victory."

Turenne and La Trimouille, however, rallied behind the corps of Lavardin, and with what men they
could collect, joined the division of the Prince de
Condé.   At the same moment, a body of four hundred and fifty Protestant arquebusiers, which had
been detached on the left, to hold in check a part of
the Catholic force, hearing the Leaguers' cries of triumph, suddenly abandoned the defensive, drove back
the enemy, and on one of their commanders exclaiming, "Let us die in the midst of that battalion:"
they rushed upon the regiments in front, and, dis-
charging their pieces almost within arm's length
of their adversaries, took to the sword, and routed
all who opposed them.   The battle was now going
on upon both wings, the centre of the Huguenots
broken, but the advantage turning to the side of
their infantry; while the three strong squadrons of

* Or Mercœur.

cavalry under the Bourbon Princes remained un-
moved, ready to meet the advancing forces of Joyeuse,
and the artillery thundered from the heights.

The Duke's cavalry was formed in line; and
Aubigné seems to suppose, that, from the position
which Joyeuse occupied, he could not see the exact
disposition of the troops of Navarre; but the horse
of the Protestant army was formed in squadrons,
and from the high ground on which the King himself was placed, the whole field was discernible.
The news was quickly carried to the Roman Catholic commander, that Lavardin had routed Turenne and Trimouille; and, advancing before his
own guard, covered with armour of silver and
enamel, he ordered the whole line to charge, " as
if to victory rather than battle." His immensely
superior cavalry then came forward at full speed,
with the banderols of their lances shading the ground;
but as they reached the top of a little elevation which
ran across the field, some confusion took place when
they found that three bodies of cavalry were before
them instead of one. Their line, too, was in disorder, from the length of way they had galloped
and the eagerness of some to get before the rest;
so that much disarray was apparent in their ranks
before they came near the forces of the Protestants.

Henry, on his part, as soon as he saw them in
motion, prepared to meet them; and exclaiming
aloud—" My companions, we fight for the glory of
God—for honor and our lives! To safety and to
victory, the road is before us! On, in the name of

God, for whom we draw the sword!"—he took his helmet, covered with white plumes, and put his lance in the rest.* Some of his friends now sought to place themselves before him, in order to break the shock of the enemy, but he would not permit them so to do; saying, "To your places—to your places; do not hide me; I would be seen!"† and led on his squadrons to meet Joyeuse. At first they advanced at a walk, then at a quick trot, and then the arque-busiers, whom Henry had placed beside each body of men-at-arms, having fired at twenty yards' dis-tance, so as to shake the first rank of the enemy, the Bourbon Princes, and their veteran soldiers, clad in grey iron, swept the glittering host of Joyeuse before them, like the wind driving the dust.

The only troop of the Huguenot cavalry that wavered, was that of the Count de Soissons; but it was speedily rallied by Fabas, and all were soon engaged. The horses of the Protestants, neither tired by a long march, nor panting with the exer-tion of a charge of nearly half a mile, met those of the Catholics, fresh and vigorous; but still the nobles of the royalist army, shewed all the courage for which French gentlemen have ever been renowned. Though broken and routed, they fought in small par-ties to the last. The Prince de Condé was thrown to the ground, and his horse killed by St. Luc, the governor of Brouage, who, seeing his own host defeated, took the moment of this success to surrender to the Prince. The charger of Turenne

---

* Aubigné.   † Perefix.

was also slain ; and the white plumes, and plain iron
armour of Henry of Navarre, were seen wherever
the fight was most fierce.   In the crisis of the battle,
he was engaged hand to hand with two of the enemy
at once, but one of his opponents having been killed
by a Protestant officer who came up, Henry seized
the other, named Chateau-renard, exclaiming, with
the gay tone which did not even then abandon him,
" Yield, Philistine, yield !"

The Protestant arquebusiers were now making
great progress on either wing, and the rout of the
cavalry soon decided the fate of the Catholic infantry.   The Huguenot foot took up the cry of
" La Motte !" in memory of the cruel butchery of
Joyeuse at that town ; and little quarter was given
to the regiment of Picardy, which was opposed to
those corps who had suffered most severely in the
cold-blooded slaughter that there took place.   Joyeuse himself was killed, as well as his brother ;
but whether after surrender, as some have said,*
or in a gallant effort to win renown even in death,†
as others have asserted, cannot be clearly ascertained.

The rout of the Catholic forces, however, was

* Aubigné.   There is a curious mistake in the notes upon the
edition of Sully, published 1822, where it is said, that Joyeuse
was killed in cold blood by La Mothe St. Heray.   The words
of Aubigné are, that Bourdeaux and Centier, his two assailants,
"knowing him well by La Motte St. Heray," meaning by the
massacre he had committed in that place, " gave him a pistol
shot," &c.

† Brantome.   I am inclined to believe that the latter authority is the best upon this point.

complete, when a small body of two hundred lances, in compact order, was seen advancing behind the fugitives; and one of the Protestant officers remarked to Henry of Navarre, that it must be the head of Matignon's army. "Well, my friends," cried the King, with an unconcerned air, "this will be what was never before seen: two battles in the same day."

But this small corps soon took flight with the rest, and the pursuit was carried on for three hours, during which, a great number of the infantry were slain. It was remarked, on the contrary, that almost all the cavalry who fell, sold their lives dearly on the field of battle.* All the principal officers of the army of Joyeuse were killed, with the exception of Lavardin and Mercure, who made their escape towards the close of the day; and there was scarcely a noble family in France that had not to reckon one of its members amongst the dead. The prisoners were equally numerous, and equally distinguished. Of the slain, four hundred were gentlemen of rank; and three thousand foot fell in the fight or the pursuit. The number of prisoners is not given, but it was very large; so that not more than one-fourth part of the brilliant army of Joyeuse escaped from the field of Coutras.

The successful issue of this battle is entirely attributable to the dispositions of the King of Navarre.

---

* Aubigné says, that not more than ten gentlemen were killed, or made prisoners, beyond the actual limits of the field of battle.

The position chosen for the whole army, which gave so much advantage to his arquebusiers, the situation in which he placed his artillery, and the formation of his cavalry in squadrons rather than in line, as was then customary, as well as the union of a small body of arquebusiers with each troop of horse, compensated fully for the inferiority of his numbers ; and the gallantry and determination of himself and his soldiers, as well as some want of discipline amongst the ranks of Joyeuse, effected the rest.

A skilful movement, too, ordered in the beginning of the day by the King of Navarre, remedied the chief defect in the position of the Huguenots. Just as the battle began, a large vacancy was perceived at the left of their line, which was menaced by a strong body of Catholics, under M. de Cluseau. It was judged dangerous, however, to march any considerable infantry force from the right, in face of the enemy, while the distance from the rear was too great to render such an operation practicable in time. In these circumstances, Henry, after having thrown out two hundred skirmishers in that direction, brought, under cover of their fire, five separate parties from different regiments, to the weak point of his line, on which the skirmishers also fell back, forming with the draughts from the regiments a body of nearly five hundred men. This manœuvre is said to have greatly contributed to the victory of the Huguenots.

I must not omit to mention in this place an anecdote of an old Protestant officer, who, seeing the Prince de Condé about to charge the light horse of

Lavardin, just as the cavalry of Joyeuse was advancing, caught him by the bridle, exclaiming, "That is no game for you;" and pointing to the heavy men-at-arms of the Duke, he added, "but here it comes."

The King of Navarre himself, during the space of an hour, which was all the time that the battle actually occupied, was continually engaged hand to hand with the soldiers of the enemy, killing several with his own arm, without receiving the slightest wound, though his armour was covered with blows; and, at one period, while grasping a Roman Catholic officer with one hand, he shot with a pistol another assailant, who came to the rescue of his prisoner.

Nevertheless, he did not follow the enemy far in person; but, after having carried on the pursuit for a quarter of a league, he returned to the field of battle, and joined in a solemn act of thanksgiving, which was performed by the Protestant ministers on the scene of this great victory. He then retired to the chateau of Coutras, to which he caused the bodies of Joyeuse and his brother to be carried, and there gave orders for burying the dead, and taking care of the wounded.

In the hour of victory he shewed the same moderation which has distinguished all great men before and since, and which is, in fact, the strongest— perhaps the only proof of real greatness. He expressed no feeling of triumph as standard after standard, taken from the enemy, was brought into the hall where he sat at supper; and neither harsh-

ness nor exultation gave an additional bitterness to
the cup of captivity, as one noble prisoner after
another was presented to him by their captors.
Amongst the rest, his former tutor, Sautrai, who
had abandoned him in the hour of adversity, and
had shewed himself one of his bitterest enemies for
some years, was now brought before him; but
Henry, as if to mark particularly his readiness to
forgive all personal injuries, ordered him to be set
free without ransom, contrary to the urgent remonstrances of several of his friends.

It was at this time, that, in the midst of fifty-six
standards of the enemies' infantry, and twenty-two
banners of the horse, and at the end of the first
pitched battle that had ever been gained by the
French Protestants, some one asked him what terms
of peace he would now demand, after so glorious a
victory.

" The same as before," replied the King; and
the next day he sent off one of his officers to solicit
peace at the hands of Henry III.

It has been generally asserted that the greatest
advantages might have been derived from the victory of Coutras, and that the Protestant party might
have obtained that power in France which would
have secured to Henry of Navarre the unopposed succession to the crown. No other benefit, however, resulted, than the removal of a false notion which had
been previously entertained, both by Protestants and
Catholics, that though the Huguenots were invinci-
ble in skirmishes and desultory warfare, they were

incapable of winning a regular battle.   Henry remained inactive; his victorious troops were dispersed;
the Prince de Condé proceeded to lead the forces of
Poitou and Sainctonge towards the banks of the
Charente and the Loire; Turenne marched with his
Gascons to besiege the small town of Sarlat; and at
the feet of the Countess de Grammont were laid the
banners of Coutras, by the conqueror who should
have been leading his hardy soldiers to fresh achievements.* I am not inclined to deny that Henry, to all
appearance, neglected opportunity; but various causes
have been assigned for the error thus committed,
and it is necessary to state them.   It is true, great
differences of opinion existed in the monarch's council, and great dissensions amongst the noblemen who

* Certain it is that Henry of Navarre did visit the Countess
of Grammont before he quitted Guienne; but he did not fly to
her with that haste, which the statements of Sully and Aubigné
would lead their readers to suppose. This is proved beyond all
doubt, by the manuscript accounts of his household expenses,
which shew that he remained two days at Coutras after the
battle; that he subsequently spent three days at St. Foy, three days
at Clairac, and five at Nerac, and did not reach Pau till the 6th
of November, 17 days after his victory. It is to be remarked
also, that several of the towns he visited, were out of his way
towards Pau, and that no hostile force is known to have prevented his pursuing a more direct course, so that there is every
reason to suppose, some motives of great weight—though unknown to us—led him to visit Nerac and the Agenois. It is
very easy to find fault with great men, especially when we do
not know all the circumstances in which they acted; and it unfortunately happens, that human malignity too frequently induces
us to attribute to weakness, that which was perhaps inevitable.

gave him their voluntary support.   Condé and
Turenne were in open enmity; the former seeking
to erect several of the western provinces of France
into a separate principality, the latter entertaining
views as treasonable and at the bottom as ambitious.
It is true, that Henry of Navarre did not wish to
render the breach between himself and the King
of France irreparable; it is true, that Matignon and
his army were ready to follow him on his march;
and that Henry III. himself, at the head of a very
large force, was before him on the Loire; it is true,
that very great difficulties might have presented
themselves, if he had attempted to induce the troops
who had followed him to Coutras, to pursue their
course across the whole of France, in order to meet
the German army, which had now entered the kingdom and was making its way slowly forward; and
it is also certain, that the line of conduct adopted,
was determined upon in the council, over the deci-
sions of which Henry had no other control than that
afforded by his moral influence.   Nevertheless, there
can be little doubt, that influence, after this victory,
would have been sufficient, if vigorously exerted, to
prevent the Protestant force from separating; and
that it was his duty to the great cause which he
supported, not to suffer the immense advantage he
had obtained to pass away without some fruit, if
there was a possibility of avoiding such a result.

The only causes for not marching to join the German army, which we can suppose to have had any
real weight with his mind, were, first, the great

chance that existed of a collision with the King
himself; secondly, the uncertainty of the course
which his foreign allies would take; and thirdly, his
inability to pay the sums which the auxiliaries expected to receive immediately.   He had always
professed not to draw the sword against Henry III.,
but only against the leaders of the League; and
he knew that the monarch was now at the head of
his own forces, somewhere between him and the
Germans.   Of the exact position of the latter, he
had no intimation;* he neither knew their difficulties nor their line of march; and under these circumstances it was scarcely possible for him to advance to meet them, without being encountered by
the King.   At the same time, he felt keenly the want
of those pecuniary resources, without which it was
impossible for him to supply the German troops
with the money that was required even for their
support.   But the Protestants of France failed to
furnish him with funds, at the very moment they
were most needed.   Two letters from the monarch
to the town of Nismes, and to M. de Scorbiac, shew
the extreme distress of Henry's mind, at the obstacles
which the remissness of various towns in paying
their quota, threw in the way of his junction with
the auxiliaries, and afford strong grounds for believing that the emptiness of his treasury, contributed
more than any thing else to deprive him of the
fruits of his victory.

A great error is, nevertheless, generally allowed

* Discours de la Guerre.

to have been committed, in not making some effort
to derive permanent advantage from the battle of
Coutras, especially if Condé, as we are informed by
De Thou, professed his willingness to march to
join the Germans, and urged Henry to do so. Sully
indeed declares that such was not the case; but the
assertion of De Thou is confirmed by the fact that
the Prince remained in Sainctonge, waiting some
time for the coming of the King of Navarre, in
order to make a forward movement to support their
allies.*

One fact however is certain, that such an advance would have been altogether fruitless; for before the Huguenot forces could have arrived on the
banks of the Loire, the Swiss, who formed no incon-
siderable part of the army of auxiliaries, were already treating with Henry III., the whole force was
in a state of confusion, and the first intelligence of
the battle of Coutras, reached the Duke of Nevers
in the midst of the Swiss camp.† The King of
Navarre, on the day of his victory, was, by the short-
est route he could have followed, at the distance of
more than a hundred and twenty leagues from the
head-quarters of the Germans; while an army,
at least four times as strong as his own, in point
of numbers, lay between him and them; so that the
course he must have pursued to reach his allies
would have been still longer. He had every reason to believe, that instead of following the directions
he had sent, they were endeavoring to force their

* Discours de la Guerre.   † Mem de Nevers, tom. i. p. 773.

way across the Loire, into Beauce, so that, had he proceeded, according to his original plan, by Guienne and Languedoc, there was every probability, even if the Germans succeeded at all in passing the river without a battle, that the want of combination would frustrate his purpose, their march counter-vail his, and the relative position of the two allied forces remain the same, with the army of the King between them. But, before eight days were over, after the battle of Coutras, the Germans were attacked by Guise, at Vimory,* and a severe skirmish took place, in which the Protestants suffered considerably.

From that period forward, nothing but dissension, loss, and disorder occurred amongst the body of auxiliaries, although their numbers would at any time have justified them in risking a general engagement with the troops of Henry III. and Guise combined. After the junction of all the reinforcements which arrived during their march through France, the force they had at command amounted to thirty-five thousand men and nineteen pieces of

---

* On the 27th October. Pierre Matthieu. We have no means of ascertaining precisely how soon the news of the defeat of the Germans reached Henry of Navarre. The first letter in which we find it mentioned by that monarch is without date; but M. de Xivrey places it about the middle of November. It is more than probable, however, that the intelligence of their first disaster at Vimory, must have arrived while Henry was at Nerac, where he remained till the afternoon of the 3d November, or at Pau, in which town he slept on the 6th.

artillery; but they were led by commanders of little
experience, harassed by want and sickness, continually attacked by Epernon and Guise, or led into
negotiations which spread hesitation and doubt
amongst them,* till at length, surprised in Auneau†
by the Duke of Guise, a more serious disaster befel
them than that which occurred at Vimory. The
loss indeed was not severe,‡ but the consternation
was great, and was never tranquillized.

The conduct of Henry III., in the whole of these
transactions, is well worthy of some consideration.
In this moment of the utmost difficulty and danger,
he shewed a degree of decision and judgment, which,
had it been lasting, would have soon quelled the
factions which convulsed his kingdom ; but it passed
away with the occasion to which it owed its existence,
and did not revive, till new perils, equally menacing,
called forth once more his latent energies.

In the early part of the year 1587, he received
daily intimations of the Protestant levies in Germany, and he himself knew that a large body of
Swiss had, in consequence of his negotiations with
Sully, been raised under an indefinite understanding, that they were called into the field for his own
service, as well as that of the King of Navarre. The
union of the Swiss and the Germans, however,
alarmed him. Their junction with nearly six thou-

* Vie du Duc d'Epernon. Discours de la Guerre. Mem. de Nevers.
† 24th November.
‡ The loss, according to Pasquier, Livre XI., Lettre 15,
amounted to fifteen hundred men.

sand French Huguenots, under different leaders. excited still more that jealousy which was one of his chief weaknesses; and the double policy in which he had been brought up, at once prompted him to oppose the arms of deceit and treachery, to the various factions which threatened to overwhelm him in their struggle. His mind was incapable of placing confidence in the King of Navarre; towards the house of Guise, he entertained feelings of both dread and hatred; but the Duke of Lorraine, when he found the Protestant auxiliaries advancing towards his territories, besought aid in a tone more peremptory than that of a petitioner, and Guise, without waiting for command or permission, hurried with the troops of the League to the assistance of his relation. Taking advantage of the King's professions, however, in order to advance his own purposes, the Duke sent messengers to Henry, requiring him to despatch to his support, all the forces which that monarch had lately called into the field.

But Henry better counselled, determined to put himself at the head of the large army he had collected; and leaving Guise to defend Lorraine and Champagne, he prepared with wonderful vigor to oppose the passage of the Loire, as willing to see the Leaguers kept in doubt regarding his intentions, and to place them in a situation in which they ran the risk of a defeat, as to prevent the junction of the allied army with the King of Navarre. By the advice of the Duke of Nevers, he brought to his aid all the troops which could be mustered, and rejecting the insidious suggestions of the partisans of the League in his council, he took measures for calling out in case of need the ban and arriere-ban of France, and set out from Paris once more, to lead his forces in person. The sight of the King at the head of his troops, was far more unpalatable to the faction than to the King of Navarre ; and it is evident that Guise and his brethren were greatly embarrassed as well as surprised by this decision.

In these circumstances not only the Duke but his party also, greatly lost in reputation. While Henry found himself surrounded by one of the finest armies which had been brought into the field since the commencement of the civil wars, while he boldly planted himself on the banks of the Loire, destroyed the fords upon that river, seized upon La Charité in face of the Germans, and prepared to give them battle if they should effect a passage, Guise, with all his influence, had not been able to collect sufficient troops to prevent them from entering Lorraine, and thence advancing into France. He made no effort, indeed, to check them and is severely blamed by many historians for suffering them to pass the Vosges unopposed.* Certain it is, that at the time of their first appearance in Lorraine, they were comparatively weak in numbers, not having been yet

---

* If the account of Aubigné is correct, the army of the Duke of Guise must have been equal to that of the Germans when they entered Lorraine, and before they had been joined by the Swiss.

joined by the Swiss, or any of the many reinforcements which reached them on their march, that
in the gorges of the mountains a small army might
have attempted to bar the way with success, and
that nothing like vigor was displayed by the Princes
of Lorraine, either in opposing the advance of the
Germans, preventing their junction with their
allies, or cutting off any of the bodies of Protestant
troops which were hurrying across the country from
every quarter to swell the army of auxiliaries.
In regard to the latter point, there can be no doubt
that Guise committed a great error ; and though
the brilliant enterprises of Vimory and Auneau
displayed high courage and activity in the partisan
leader, and were found sufficient to keep up his
credit with the League, yet through the whole campaign he shewed but little skill as a general, and
little energy as the chief of a great party.

The dissipation of the confederate forces must be
chiefly attributed to the firm and decided conduct
of the King, and to the military skill with which he
guarded the passages of the Loire. To these were
added, the means of negotiation and deceit. The
Swiss were persuaded that Henry had never authorized their enrolment for his service, and were bribed
to desist from an enterprise which they saw was
hopeless. The Germans were also treated with,
and deluded by promises ; but it is only just to say,
that Henry III. kept his own engagements with
them punctually ; and that the passports which he
offered them to secure, as far as possible, their safe

return to their own country, were delivered before their departure.

His rebellious subjects of the League, however, paid no attention to the King's wishes and commands. The retreating bodies of Germans were pursued by Guise and his companions with the utmost fury, followed even into the neighbouring countries, and slaughtered wherever they could be found. The three French leaders by whom they were accompanied, and who had quitted them in the midst of their negotiations with the King, effected their escape from the enemy, though not without great difficulty. The Duke of Bouillon arrived at Geneva, where fatigue and grief terminated his life, within a few days after he had left the territory of France. The Prince de Conti, with a few servants, fled through by-ways, concealing his rank and name ;* but Chatillon, who had rejected all passports, and refused to surrender his banner to any one but the King of Navarre, from whom he had received it, opened a way for himself with the sword into Languedoc, and then placed himself in safety in the Vivarez, giving, on more than one occasion, a shameful defeat to those who opposed him with vastly superior forces.

* Anquetil, with his usual inaccuracy, represents the Prince de Conti as taking part in the battle of Coutras, and is consequently obliged to make more mistakes to bring him to the head of the reiters. He might have seen, in any contemporary historian, that when the Count de Soissons joined Henry on the Loire, he left Conti to effect a junction with the Germans as best he might.

Thus was dissipated and nearly destroyed, one of the largest foreign armies that had ever taken the field to support the Protestant cause in France ; and if Henry III., who, before the Germans began their retreat, had collected under his own command a force of nearly thirty thousand men, which he might easily have swelled to between forty and fifty thousand, by calling to his aid the troops of the Duke of Montpensier, had determined to act vigorously against the League, he might have crushed that faction with very little difficulty, without even accepting any assistance from the Protestants under the King of Navarre.

Returning to Paris, however, where he was at first received with joyous acclamations,* he once more relapsed into indolence and frivolity, and left the Duke of Guise to attribute to himself all the glory of the campaign, of which the very smallest part was really his due. While the preachers of Paris were lauding the conduct of the popular leader to the skies, and the priests in the confessional were exhorting the people to do that which the doctors of the Sorbonne declared to be justifiable and to snatch the royal authority from the hands of the King, Guise himself, after pursuing the Germans to the county of Montbeliard and committing the most frightful barbarities in that state, hastened secretly to Rome, to hold a conference with the Pope and with Cardinal Peléve.† Of the particulars of

---

* Pasquier.   † Mem. de la Ligue. L'Etoile.

their interview we are not aware; but Guise only remained three days in the ancient capital of the world, and then returned with all speed to Nancy, in order to direct the operations of his party against the King. An assembly of the family of Lorraine, and all the principal leaders of their faction, was held at that city in the month of January; and it was there determined to present a memorial to Henry III., requiring him to put himself openly at the head of the League, to dismiss all persons from his service who should be pointed out as obnoxious by the princes of that party, to cause the publication of the decrees of the council of Trent, to establish the inquisition, to command the church to re-purchase its alienated property, to give up to the Leaguers such cities as they should demand, fortified and garrisoned according to their pleasure, and to keep up an army on the frontiers of Lorraine to prevent the return of the Germans. It was also determined to take possession of the duchy of Bouillon, and to besiege Jamets and Sedan.

The memorial of the League was presented to the King, who gave a vague, but conciliatory answer to demands which he should have treated at once as treasonable ; and, while Guise hurried to Soissons to confer with the Cardinal de Bourbon, the "Sixteen" carried on their intrigues in Paris, and prepared for a decisive effort to seize upon the person of the King. They kept up a continual communication with the Duke and his brothers, pressing Guise to come to Paris and put himself at

their head. Although, not yielding immediately
to their solicitations, the Duke encouraged them to
proceed, gave them directions for conducting their
enterprise upon a more regular and skilful plan
than they had themselves devised, and sent them
five of his captains to lead the five battalions,
into which he advised them to divide their forces.
Nicholas Poulain, however, who still continued
to act as the spy of the court, revealed to Henry,
that it was the intention of the " Sixteen," to arrest him and the Duke of Epernon, during one of
the processions, at which he was accustomed to be
present, during Lent. He offered even to conduct
the King's officers to the spot where the conspirators
were discussing their plans, so that they might be
apprehended with their treason on their lips. But
Henry was dissuaded from pursuing so vigorous a
course ; and he contented himself with keeping
away from the procession, bringing the Swiss troops
into the neighbourhood of Paris, and by means of
the Duke of Epernon, fortifying the royalist party
in Normandy and the Orleanois. At the same time,
he collected arms, and strengthened the guard at the
Louvre ; and, shortly after, brought a body of Swiss
into Paris for his defence.

Although the " Sixteen" now clearly perceived
that their treason was discovered, they proceeded
more and more boldly every hour, sent messenger
after messenger to Guise, and with the aid of his
sister, Madame de Montpensier, laid a new plot
for seizing upon the monarch's person, as he re-

turned from Vincennes. This, however, was likewise revealed to the King by Poulain, and once
more the scheme was frustrated. In the mean
while, Guise had advanced from Soissons to Go-
nesse; but hearing the precautions of the King,
he retired, and applied for permission to come to
Paris and justify himself. Madame de Montpensier,
who, though she had received repeated orders to quit
the capital, still continued to frequent the court of
the Queen-mother, zealously supported the Duke's
demand, and kept up a constant communication with
the "Sixteen." Villequier, who, there is every
reason to suppose, had been gained by the party of
the Duke of Guise, added to the hesitation which
reigned in the King's council, by maintaining that
the danger was imaginary; and the Queen-mother
encouraging the same idea, Henry fell back into indolence, from which he was only roused by the news
that Guise was actually about to set out for Paris.
He then despatched Bellievre in haste to forbid his
approach; but Guise sent back the messenger to his
Sovereign, requiring assurances in regard to his
own honor and the safety of his Catholic friends
in Paris, and, in the mean while, continued his
advance upon the capital. The King immediately
wrote to the Duke, granting him all that he required,
and promising to give him further intimation of his
pleasure, but still forbade his approach. The letter was either lost, or Guise concealed that he had
received it; and after a short delay, during which
he seems to have entertained some apprehensions of

the result, the Duke hurried suddenly to Paris, where he arrived on the 9th of May, accompanied by only eight attendants. He had taken care, how-ever, beforehand, to introduce a number of armed men, in small parties, into the capital ; and if he experienced any fears for his personal safety, they were dissipated by the reception he met with from the populace. Thousands upon thousands fol-lowed him through the streets ; the windows were filled with ladies, who showered flowers upon his head ; the people held out their rosaries to touch him as he passed, as if some holy influence ema-nated from his person ; and voices were heard to cry, " Welcome, welcome, great Duke ; now you are come, we are safe."

Without stopping at his own house, Guise pro-ceeded at once to the Convent of the Penitents, where the Queen-mother was then residing, and was immediately introduced to her presence. She was pale and trembling, and greeted him in ambiguous terms, saying, that although she was glad to see him, she would rather have done so at another time. The Duke replied, with a courteous air, but in a determined tone, that being a good servant of the King, and having heard the calumnies circulated against himself, as well as the designs which were entertained against some of the wisest and best of the people, he had come to remedy this evil, and to justify himself. Catherine then despatched Davila, the father of the historian, to inform the

King of the Duke's arrival, and to say, that she would bring him speedily to the Louvre. Henry was dreadfully agitated at this intelligence, and demanded of Alphonso Ornano, a resolute Corsican officer, who was with him, what he would do in his place.

" Do you look upon him as a friend or an enemy ?" asked Ornano. The King only replied by a gesture of anger and indignation ; and Ornano continued, " Well, then, if you but give me the order, I will bring his head to you this day without your taking any farther trouble in the matter." But Henry was persuaded by Villequier and others, to pursue a less violent course ; and while they were still in discussion, intelligence was brought that the Queen-mother and the Duke were approaching. Immediate orders were given for the guards to line the way ; and Henry prepared to receive his ambitious subject with some shew of dignity.

Catherine was carried in her chair, with the Duke walking by her side, and the acclamations of the people, as well as the affability with which Guise noticed every one, as he passed bareheaded amongst them, must have taught the politic Queen the full extent of his dangerous popularity, and the means which he took to secure it. On arriving at the Louvre, however, Catherine and the Duke had to pass between a double line of guards ; and Guise saluted them as he went by. But Crillon, who was at their head, made no movement in return for this act of courtesy; and it was remarked, that the Duke turned somewhat pale. Beyond the French guards, at the bottom of the great staircase, were the Swiss, the archers of the guard in the hall above, and the gentlemen of the chamber lining the other rooms through which Guise passed, till at length he reached the apartment of the Queen-consort, which Henry had appointed for his reception. The moment he approached, the King addressed him with a heavy frown, saying, "I warned you not to come;" to which Guise replied, in a calm and respectful tone, that he was there to cast himself into the arms of his Majesty, to demand justice, and to reply to the calumnies of his enemies. He then went on to say, that he should not have disobeyed, if the King's commands had been more explicitly conveyed to him. Some discussion then commenced between the Duke and Bellievre; but the King interrupted them, and dismissed Guise, saying, "It is by your conduct that you will justify yourself, and by the results I shall judge of your intentions."

After this abrupt termination of their interview, the Duke retired to his own hotel, where all the nobility of his party soon assembled round him, and the courts and the neighbouring streets, were crowded with a dense multitude of Parisians ready to shed their blood in his defence. The next morning, Henry published a proclamation, commanding all persons not regularly domiciled in Paris, to quit the city without loss of time; and the royal officers were directed to see that it was obeyed; but the order was not rigorously executed; and those who were driven out of one quarter of the town, took refuge in another, or found shelter at the Hotel de Guise itself.

On the 12th of the month, early in the morning, the Parisians remarked the entrance of several regiments of Swiss and French soldiers, with Marshal Biron at their head; and immediately after, a number of important posts were occupied by the royal forces, while Crillon, with a party of the guard, approached the Place Maubert, to secure which was of consequence, as it commanded the quarter of the university. But the order was given too late; a party of Parisians, principally composed of boatmen and students, defended the ground as the guards advanced; and at the very moment that Crillon was directing his men to charge, he received an express prohibition from the King to shed blood on any account.

Finding that the important post which he had been commanded to occupy was lost, that officer attempted to retreat towards the Louvre; but by this time the inhabitants were in arms; and even those who wished well to the royal cause, disgusted with the weak indifference which the King had shewn, abandoned him at a moment when he had recourse to measures, which threatened to deluge the streets of the capital with gore, but which might easily have been rendered unnecessary by timely firmness, and a due assertion of the royal authority.

It is curious to remark, how, in all ages, similar weakness on the part of rulers is followed by the same result, notwithstanding the difference of times and circumstances; but sad to perceive, that history, which is the experience of States, has no effect upon statesmen, as if fools and knaves returned in cycles to commit the same errors and crimes, and produce the same disasters at their appointed seasons.

The Duke of Guise was soon informed of what was taking place in the town; and without shewing himself in the affair at once, he directed his officers to go forth and counsel the people in their resistance to the troops. The first suggestion of barricading the streets is said to have been made by Brissac. Chains were stretched across from corner to corner with the greatest rapidity; barrels were procured, and filled with stones and earth; the organised bands of the Parisians took post behind them, armed with pikes and arquebuses; barricade after barricade, was pushed forward almost to the gates of the Louvre; and the posts of the royalists, forbidden to make use of their weapons to impede the progress of the enemy, were, in an incredibly short space of time, surrounded by forts garrisoned by the furious population of the capital.

Guise still affected to have no share in these occurrences. Towards midday he walked out for a few minutes; but he was unarmed, and soon returned to his hotel; and though persons were coming and going continually between him and the leaders of the revolt, their conferences were always held in secret, so that no one knew the orders that he gave but the bearer, and the persons to whom they were addressed.

The officers in command of the King's troops, in the mean time, sent messengers to the Louvre, as long as any were suffered to pass, requiring permission to oppose the proceedings of the people; but consternation and uncertainty reigned at the court. The traitor Villequier, and the Queen-mother, urged Henry to go forth and shew himself, but to this the King would not consent; and at length Catherine herself undertook the task of negotiating with Guise and endeavoring to persuade him to quit the capital. Her carriage, however, was stopped at the barricades, and she was obliged to alight, and proceed in her chair, a sufficient space being left open for her train to pass. Her attempt proved vain. Guise steadily refused to quit Paris, but falsely declared that he had no part in the insurrection; and she returned to the Louvre without success. An order was then sent to recall the troops from their dangerous posts; but it arrived too late; it was impossible for the soldiers to return; and a gun having shortly after been fired near the new market, in which the Swiss were quartered, an attack was made upon the unfortunate foreigners from the windows and roofs of the surrounding houses, during which a number were killed, and the rest threw down their arms. At that moment,

Brissac arrived in haste, and causing the carnage to cease, ordered the Swiss to take refuge in the slaughter-house of the market.

On one of the bridges the French guards were likewise attacked; but on receiving intelligence that bloodshed had begun, Guise himself, with no arms but the sword which he usually wore, and with a cane in his hand, went out on horseback, and proceeded from quarter to quarter, exhorting the people to abstain from violence. Every where he was greeted with the loudest acclamations, and everywhere his commands were promptly obeyed. The royalist troops laid down their arms at his desire; and after having, in some degree, calmed the storm he had raised, he caused the French and Swiss guards to pass before him on their way to the Louvre. At the head of the former, he placed one of his adherents, named St. Paul, with a wand in his hand, while Brissac, with a similar emblem of peaceful authority, conducted the Swiss; and thus the two corps were led back unmolested to the palace, through the innumerable barricades which crossed the streets. A distinction, however, was made between the French soldiers and the foreigners, in order to fix a politic mark of disgrace upon those who opposed their factious countrymen. The former were ordered to lower their arms, and march bareheaded, while the Swiss were allowed to proceed in their usual military array.

The succeeding night passed in much agitation on all parts: news arrived at the Louvre that strict watch was kept at all the barricades; and it was found that Guise visited the principal posts more than once during the period of darkness. All communication between the palace and the town was cut off; and although arms had been laid up in plenty to resist a sudden attack, no provisions had been accumulated to enable the Louvre to stand a siege. At the same time, intelligence was received that a design was entertained of investing the King the next day in the palace, and that forces had been prepared for the enterprise. Under these circumstances, several members of the council strongly advised Henry to quit the capital; but the suggestions of Villequier, and the entreaties of the Queen-mother, induced him to pause while she made a last attempt to negotiate with the Duke of Guise.

Early on the following day Catherine set out; but her efforts on this occasion were as unsuccessful as before. Guise appeared sterner and more decided than he had shewn himself at their former interview. He was even discourteous, and suffered his conference with the mother of his sovereign, to be interrupted continually by private audiences demanded by, and granted to, the rebellious citizens of the capital. She saw that he would be King, if not in name, in reality. But Catherine had a consolation under the endurance of these insults, of which Guise was not aware. She knew that while he was indulging in dreams of authority, and laying down the terms on which he would grant tolerance to his King, the golden opportunity was slipping away from him. He had committed one error in the course of successful treason, and it had been seized.

While she detained him in negotiation, Henry, in consequence of warnings she had sent him, was making his escape. As soon as she had perceived the actual state of the public mind as she passed along, and had received the various intimations of coming events, which reached her directly and indirectly on her way to the conference, she sent back Pinart, the Secretary of State, to inform the King that his only chance of safety was in quitting Paris without loss of time. Henry followed her advice at once. The regiments of Swiss and French guards were immediately marched out of Paris, while the King's attendants spread the report that this sacrifice was made to satisfy the people. The monarch then went out in an ordinary walking dress, proceeded to the garden of the Tuileries, or the Queen's garden, as it was then called, at the back of which lay the royal stables. His air was easy and unconcerned, his pace slow, and he spoke to several persons as he walked along; but the moment he reached the stables the doors were closed. He drew on a pair of riding boots, and mounting a strong horse, passed the Porte Neuve, and rode on at full speed towards Chartres, accompanied by sixteen gentlemen and twelve servants.

He was received with acclamations by the people of that city. His faithful guards arrived a few hours after; and, delivered from imminent peril by the neglect of the Duke of Guise in not securing the gate at the back of the palace, he once more breathed at liberty. As he quitted Paris, however, the guard at the Porte de Nesle, had the insolence to fire upon him; and Henry is said to have sworn, that he would never re-enter his rebellious capital but by the breach.

When the tidings of the King's escape were carried to the Duke of Guise, he became extremely agitated; and turning angrily to the Queen-mother, he exclaimed, " Madam, you amuse me to my ruin!" But Catherine assured him that she knew nothing of her son's intentions, and took her departure as soon as possible. Guise immediately wrote letters to various persons in order to justify his conduct, and to shew that the King had misconstrued his actions, which he pretended had been conducted with all loyalty; but previous letters are still in existence, which prove that his design was certainly to seize the monarch, and probably to depose him. In one of these epistles he says, " I hold the Louvre so closely invested, that I will give a good account of those who are therein;" and he presses his friends to send him armed assistance without loss of time.

To remedy the mistake which had been committed, as far as possible, the Duke made every effort to secure Paris against attack, and acted in the capital as if he had been actually sovereign, while he continued to protest his loyalty and affection towards the King. He made many attempts, at the same time, to induce Henry to return; the most blasphe-

mous processions were sent to the King,* in order
to suit his peculiar notions of religion ; a deputation
from the Parliament of Paris visited him ; and it is
evident that Guise felt all the magnitude of the error
into which he had fallen, in suffering the monarch,
once in his hands, to escape him.

Henry steadily refused to return ; but in every
other respect, he acted with his usual feebleness. He
strove to conciliate, instead of preparing to punish ;
he began to negotiate without taking measures for
defence; he dismissed Epernon and La Valette; and
abandoned his friends and faithful servants to please
the house of Guise and his open enemies. Intrigue
followed intrigue, and negotiation negotiation, till the
simple question became, what was the price which the
Duke and the League would take for a new interval of
apparent amity. That price was not ascertained without difficulty ; but at length the bargain was concluded ; and by a decree of the nineteenth of July,
1588, called the Decree of Re-union, Henry granted
to the League every thing it could demand, except
his crown : that the King should place himself at
the head of the faction ; that he should never lay
down his arms against the Protestants ; that he
would induce all his subjects to promise the same
on oath ; that he would bind them by a vow to exclude all persons even suspected of heresy from the

* In one of these a Capuchin (it is doubtful, whether Henry de
Joyeuse, brother of the deceased Duke, or another) represented
our Saviour going to Calvary, with circumstances which I shall
beg leave to omit.

succession; that the decrees of the council of Trent should be received in France; that the towns held by the League should continue in their hands six years; that four others should be added; that Guise should be appointed Generalissimo by letters patent; that all the rebellious acts of the League should be forgiven, and their late nominations to offices confirmed; and that the States-general should assemble in October following, solemnly to ratify all these stipulations. By several secret articles to the treaty, of which this edict was the expression, other concessions were made; and the King, having returned from Rouen, where it was signed, to Chartres, received the Duke of Guise with open arms, and testified the same admiration and respect towards him, which had been displayed by Charles IX. towards the Admiral de Coligni a few hours before his assassination.*

* I have not thought fit, in giving this account of what is called the day of the barricades, and the events which followed, to affix to each minute particular the authority on which I have relied, as by so doing I should have had to multiply notes to little purpose; and in many instances I might have had to enter into long discussions of why I preferred one author's statement to another, as each person saw the transactions of the period with very different eyes, and gave different particulars as they struck him most forcibly. It may be sufficient to say, that all the facts mentioned by me will be found in De Thou, the Life of the Duke of Guise, the Memoires de la Ligue, Cayet, Davila, L'Etoile, the notes of the Satyre Menippée, and the Procés verbal de Nicolas Poulain. The letters of the Duke of Guise, which I have mentioned, are to be found in that very valuable little collection called Discours de la Guerre, and one in Aubigné.

BOOK VIII.

WHATEVER were the motives of the King of Navarre, and it is probable, as I have shewn, that he was moved by very many and very cogent reasons, to refrain from pushing his advantage after Coutras, he remained if not in a state of absolute inactivity, at all events without any display of those energies which every one knew him to possess. From Coutras he turned his steps to Bearn, accompanied by his cousin, the Count de Soissons, with the intention of bestowing the hand of his sister upon that Prince. But he soon had cause to regret that he had listened to the solicitations of the Count, and discovered the true character of that vain and perfidious Prince. Intimations from all quarters poured in upon him, of the wild designs entertained by Soissons, and he found that the plan which his cousin had laid out for himself, was to found upon his marriage with Catherine of Navarre and upon the papal bull of deprivation against her brother, a title to the whole territories of Bearn and Albret, not without some hope, however extravagant, of succeeding also to the throne of France itself. As soon as Henry became convinced that such were the views of the Count, his decision was taken.   He first delayed the marriage of his sister, and then broke off the engagement; and the Count shortly after left him to join the King of France, filled with chimerical expectations of advancement and success.   Before he went, however, he did not scruple to seduce several of Henry's officers from his service; but the King of Navarre took care to send some of his tried friends with him, to watch his proceedings, and to frustrate his iniquitous schemes.*

While in Bearn, Henry with the small force at his command took measures for securing that principality, in which several towns were still held by the Roman Catholics, while many of the castles and strongholds that filled the mountain passes, were occupied by bands of robbers, who had greatly increased in numbers and audacity during the civil war.   He obtained possession of Tarbes, retook the town of Aire, and swept the country of the troops of marauders which infested it.   His council then brought before his notice the fact, that if the Duke of Mayenne, instead of wasting his time on the banks of the Dordogne, had pushed on at once into Bearn, he could have made himself master of the town of Pau, and of the whole country at the foot of the Pyrenees, there being no place of any strength to oppose his progress.   Henry accordingly gave orders for fortifying several of the passes, both on the side of France and Spain, and provided various

* Sully.

cities both in Bearn and Albret with strong garrisons, arms and ammunition.*

Such operations were interrupted by one of the
most distressing events of the time, which not
only deeply affected Henry at the moment, but
entangled him in dark and painful proceedings
against one of his near connections.   On the 3rd
of March 1588, the Prince de Condé was taken
ill in the town of St. Jean d'Angeli, and after suffering violent torture for two days, expired on the
5th of the same month, with great suspicion of
poison.   The body was immediately opened by five
physicians and surgeons, several of whom had attended him during his illness ; and a report was
drawn up, of the symptoms by which he had been
afflicted before death, and the appearances presented
by the body on dissection.   From this paper it appears
that Condé was seized with violent pain and continual
vomiting an hour and a half after his supper,
together with intense thirst, followed by great difficulty of breathing.   No remedies which the physicians could apply produced the slightest effect ; and
at three o'clock on the 5th of March he died in great
agony, foaming at the mouth.   The autopsy was
performed the following day, early in the morning,
and indubitable traces of poison were found in the
stomach and intestines.†   Immediate investigations

* Cayet.

† Discours de la Guerre, in which we have a copy of the report
of the surgeons.   The particulars of the transaction and the
papers concerning it are found with difficulty, having afterwards
been suppressed by royal command.

were made for the purpose of discovering the assassins; messengers were sent to the King of Navarre; and rumors spread rapidly, attaching the
guilt to the Princess de Condé, whose fidelity to
her husband was not without suspicion, to a page
named Belcastel, and to several other domestics of
the deceased Prince. The page effected his escape, it
is said with money furnished to him by the Princess;
and a report was circulated that she had been induced
to commit the act in order to conceal from Condé her
pregnancy by Belcastel, at a time when the Prince
was absent.* But this report was evidently false,
as Conde had been at St. Jean d'Angeli for several
months before his death. One of the servants,
however, was tried, condemned, and torn to pieces
by four horses.

The trial of the Princess, she having been found
pregnant, was ordered to be delayed till after the
birth of the child; but in the mean time, she was
kept a close prisoner by order of the King of Navarre.
The cause was afterwards proceeded in by judges assembled at St. Jean, when she likewise was condemned.
She appealed, however, to the Court of Peers, in
right of her rank; and in consequence of various
irregularities having been shewn in the proceedings
against her, she was ultimately acquitted by the
higher tribunal, after long delay, notwithstanding the
opposition of her husband's brothers. It may be as
well here to remark, that a gross and absurd falsehood regarding this Princess and the son which she

* L'Etoile.

bore in the month of September following, was widely circulated and has obtained credit with persons who should have been better informed. It was asserted that the young Prince was born thirteen months after Condé's death; but there is no foundation for such a statement, only six months having elapsed between the assassination of the Prince, and the delivery of his wife; and not the slightest cause exists, except the rumored incontinence of that Princess, for supposing that her son was not the child of her husband.

Henry of Navarre was greatly affected by the death of his cousin, and gave way to bitter lamentations when the news was communicated to him, declaring that he had lost his right hand. Hurrying to St. Jean, he immediately despatched messengers to the court of Henry III. to require that the page, Belcastel, should be arrested and sent back to Poitou, if he could be found in Paris; and although it is reported that he was personally attached to the Princess, he caused the proceedings against her to be carried on with considerable rigor, and evidently felt convinced that she was guilty of the crime with which she was charged. He would not suffer her to be set at liberty till the year 1595, and the decree of Parliament pronouncing her innocent was not obtained till 1596.*

* Several of Henry's letters upon this subject are very curious and interesting. From them we find that two horses had been placed in the stables of an inn in the suburbs of St Jean d'Angeli,

The Protestant party in Poitou, being left by the death of Condé without any leader of sufficient rank to command the obedience of all, Henry set out as soon as possible for Rochelle, where his presence was very much needed. Scarcely were the eyes of the Prince closed, when Lavardin, who was making head with the Leaguers in that district, seized upon the isle of Marans, which had been so often taken and retaken during the civil wars, and laid close siege to the town, which was compelled to surrender shortly after by the want of provisions, notwithstanding

by a favorite domestic of the Princess de Condé, named Brillant, fourteen days before the death of the Prince, and that on them the page and his accomplice made their escape. Brillant declared on examination that he had placed the horses there, and had given a thousand crowns to the page, by order of the Princess. The accomplice of the page was afterwards entrapped, and upon him were found diamonds and pearls supposed to have belonged to the Princess. In consequence of the destruction of all the records of the trial, the principal facts on which reliance can be placed, are derived from the letters of Henry IV. which leave little doubt of the lady's guilt. It would seem also that at the same time, a number of villains were engaged to assassinate the King of Navarre. He himself states that twenty-four persons had undertaken to perpetrate that crime. Only one, however, was taken ; and he confessed the fact. Henry also asserts that the Roman Catholic priests rejoiced with indecent exultation at the death of Condé, and exhorted their flocks to attempt a similar act in his own case. "The Romish preachers," he says, on the 17th March, "preach aloud in the neighbouring towns, that there is only one more to be had; they canonize this fine act, and admonish all good Catholics to follow the example of such a christian enterprise."—Lettres Missives, tom. 2, page 349.

some gallant efforts made by the Rochellois to give it succor. The citadel, however, held out; and in the mean time the King of Navarre arrived at Rochelle; but having preceded his troops by several days, he was not able to bring such a force into the field as would have enabled him to relieve the place; and after resisting for some time longer the castle also surrendered.*

This important town did not remain long in the hands of the enemy, for having gathered a considerable body of men together, and restored confidence and order in the neighbouring districts, Henry suddenly appeared before Marans; and notwithstanding all the preparations which had been made by the Papists for its defence, he carried the town with scarcely any resistance, and forced the castle to surrender at discretion. Although the governor, who had been left by the Catholics in Marans, was accused of having committed various brutal and barbarous acts during the civil wars, Henry would not suffer any punishment to be inflicted upon him. He kept him indeed, for some time, in Rochelle as a prisoner on parole, and only allowed him at length to be liberated, on his taking an oath never to join the League again. Henry then proceeded to put all the fortresses, which the Protestants held in Poitou, into a state of preparation to resist the fresh enter-

* Henry arrived on the isle de Marans before the 21st March, and made various gallant but unsuccessful attempts to succor the citadel. Lettres Missives.

prises of the League with which he was now menaced; and then finding that the Duke de Mercœur governor of Brittany, was about to attack his
town of Montaigu, he collected a small force, and set
out from Rochelle in the beginning of August, for the
purpose of succoring that place.   Before he arrived,
Mercœur had appeared in the environs of Montaigu,
and a severe skirmish had taken place under the walls,
between his troops and the garrison.   The following
day, however, the Duke hearing that Henry had left
Rochelle to attack him, took fright at his very
name, and determined, without waiting to inquire
the strength of his enemy, to retire from the siege
before it was regularly commenced.   He himself fled
with such expedition that he reached Nantes three
days before the King of Navarre arrived at Montaigu, but he left behind him the regiment of Gersay,
to cover his retreat.

Gathering troops by the way, Henry pursued with
the utmost speed, and overtook the regiment of
Gersay within a short distance of Nantes, charged
the enemy and completely defeated them, taking four
hundred and fifty prisoners, with all the baggage of
Mercœur's army.   He then amused himself with
shooting partridges for a day, under the very walls of
Nantes, to shew his contempt of his adversary: but
having learned that the Duke of Epernon, who
had on various occasions proved himself personally
friendly towards him, had been treacherously
attacked by the Leaguers, in the chateau of Angou-

leme, (to which place he had retired after having been driven from the court) Henry set out without loss of time to deliver him. Epernon, however, assisted only by his servants and a few friends, made a most gallant and determined defence; and, after having supported for more than two days the constant attacks of the people, and for forty hours endured hunger, thirst, and want of sleep, succor having arrived from various quarters, he succeeded in concluding a convention with the citizens, by which they agreed to return to their duty towards him as governor. He even reserved to himself the right of punishing the ringleaders,* but with greater magnanimity than could have been expected at his hands, he freely pardoned all after their submission, and gave up the body of the Mayor, who had been mortally wounded in attempting to assassinate him, to be buried by his friends.

The officers of the League, who had entered the town and stirred up the inhabitants against the Duke, were suffered to retire unmolested; and Henry of Navarre, learning that Epernon was safe, halted on his march at the town of St. George's, where he was joined by La Trimouille with several regiments of horse and foot. He then attacked and took Beauvais sur Mer,† and several other

---

* Vie du Duc d'Epernon.

† Henry gives several of the details of this siege in letters to Madame de Guiche, and to M. de Vivans. It was then considered strong and of great importance. The walls were more than ten feet thick, flanked with large towers of great solidity, and de-

places; but having learned that the Duke of Nevers, at the head of a large army of royalists, was advancing into Poitou, he abandoned the offensive, and hurried from fortress to fortress, preparing every where against attack. Early in November he returned to Rochelle, to meet the general assembly of deputies from the Protestant church of France, which he had called to hold its sittings, while the States-general of the kingdom were in session at Blois.

The Duke of Nevers, in the mean time, made progress in Poitou, having under his orders one of two large armies which had been raised according to the terms of the treaty of re-union, agreed upon between the Duke of Guise and Henry III. in July. By that treaty it was stipulated, that the command of one of the royal hosts should be conferred upon the Duke of Mayenne, and that it should march immediately into Dauphiné. The King himself was permitted by the League to nominate the general, who was to lead the other into Poitou; and Henry at once fixed upon the Duke of Nevers. The choice was highly displeasing to the League, and not without reason; for not only had Nevers separated himself from the faction, but, we find, that in his correspondence with Henry he always spoke of

fended by a ditch, sixty paces broad, filled with water from the sea. The siege lasted three weeks, during a continual storm of rain and wind; but on the 20th October, Henry, "after having prayed," caused the garrison to be summoned at the extraordinary hour of ten at night, upon which the governor consented to parley, and the terms of capitulation were arranged by the next morning.

the house of Guise and its partisans, as the chief enemies of the monarchy, deplored the state to which they had reduced the royal authority, and even congratulated his sovereign upon the victory of Henry of Navarre at Coutras, as upon a triumph obtained by the King of France himself. It is not to be wondered at then, that Nevers advanced into Poitou, determined to treat the Protestants with the utmost lenity, or that the faction of the League took care that his forces should be deprived of all that was necessary to carry on the war with rapidity and success. The reputation of the general, indeed, induced many of the French nobles to serve as volunteers under his command; and it had been arranged that in point of numbers, his army and that of Mayenne, were to be equal; but we find, from a letter written by one of his officers, that many of the infantry regiments at the end of a month, were without doublets, and without shoes, and the whole force without pay, without money, and without any provisions, but the scanty portion which they could exact from the peasantry on their line of march.

Nevertheless the conduct of the army under the Duke, and the regulations which he enforced, were more like those observed in regular warfare, than had been seen in any of the campaigns of religion. The officers worked together in harmony, and obedience to their leader; strict discipline was kept up in the ranks; the goods found in captured places were sold, and the produce divided equally, one half being applied to the general support of the army, the other made over to the captors. A well conducted hospital for the sick and wounded was established; and, as far as possible, a general system was adopted for the commissariat.

The progress of Nevers however was slow. He took thirty-six fortified places and castles it is true, but most of these were perfectly insignificant. Mauleon was the first town attacked; and as it was incapable of defence, a capitulation was immediately signed. A party of the Catholic force broke in while the terms were under discussion; and before Nevers could interpose, a number of the garrison were slaughtered. Montaigu was afterwards besieged; and fifteen days were spent in skirmishes and approaches, while the greater part of the artillery of Nevers was on the way. During that time Colombières the governor, began to shew signs of hesitation, and after a few cannon shot had been fired, surrendered the town by capitulation, much to his own disgrace, and to the regret of a large portion of the garrison. Henry of Navarre, when he heard of this act, was on the eve of commencing his march from Rochelle, to relieve the place, though, from the first, it had been part of his plan, to suffer the army of Nevers to melt away with fatigue and the inclemency of a rainy season, before he ventured with his small force to meet it in the field.[*]

* It is proved by one of the letters of Henry to the Countess de Guiche (or Grammont) that his intention was to march to

The surrender of Montaigu was immediately followed by the siege of Garnache, a small town badly fortified, at the distance of seven leagues from the former place.   The determination of the gover-nor, one of the family of Du Plessis, compensated for the weakness of the defences, and rendered this the only regular siege which Nevers undertook, during the course of his campaign in Poitou.   No sooner did his movements prove to the garrison, that the next attack was to be directed against themselves, than Du Plessis sent to inform the King of Navarre, of the state of the fortress, and of the little chance there existed of his being able to maintain it long, against so large a force as that which the Duke could still bring around it.   He expressed his willingness to defend it to the last, however, if the monarch would send

the relief of Montaigu.   He says, " I am calling in all my troops, and hope if the said place (Montaigu) can but hold out fifteen days, to strike a good stroke there."   He was however at this time sadly straitened for money, and was obliged to borrow from many of his private friends, the sums necessary to support his army.   One letter upon this subject, written on the 25th October, 1588, to M. de Launey d'Entraigues, who had been wounded by his side at Coutras, is so characteristic that I cannot refrain from extracting a part.   " Without doubt you have not failed," the King says, " to sell your woods of Mezilac and Cuze, as you told Mornay, and they must have produced some thou-sand pistoles.   Should it be so, do not omit to bring me all that you can, for in my life I never was in such need.   I know not when, nor how, if ever, I can repay you : but I promise you plenty of honour and glory ; and money is not diet for gentlemen such as you and me."

2 A 2

him aid ; and Henry lost not a moment in despatch-
ing Vignoles, St. George, Aubigné, and Robiniere,
with reinforcements, arms, and ammunition, as well
as Monsieur de Ruffigni and his company of arquebusiers.   All parties labored hard to strengthen the
fortifications ; and provisions were obtained, though
not in abundance, from the neighbouring villages.
The sharp frosts, which came on during the course
of the siege, deprived the garrison of the defence
afforded by a deep ditch and a neighbouring mo-
rass, and enabled Nevers to bring his cannon from
Montaigu without difficulty.   On the 16th of December the enemy appeared before the town ; and,
after a gallant struggle, the suburb of St Leo-
nard was carried, the Protestants meeting with a
severe loss in the death of the Baron de Ruffigni.
On the last day of December, the artillery opened
upon the place; and the besieged attempted to
throw up entrenchments within the walls; but the
earth was frozen so hard, that an hour's labor
scarcely sufficed to move a cubic foot of earth.
After having commenced the cannonade, Nevers, as
an indication of his resolution not to quit the siege
without success, sent a herald to summon the garrison,
announcing himself as the King's Lieutenant.   But
Du Plessis replied, that they recognised no Lieutenant for the King, whose faithful subjects they
were, but the King of Navarre ; and that without
his express orders they would not surrender the
town to any one.   Two more attempts were made

to parley with the governor ; but he refused to receive the herald; and the siege began in form.

The same day, however, a Walloon soldier ran from the camp towards the walls, crying, " Navarre, Navarre! The Duke of Guise is dead! Niort is taken!" He was instantly admitted into the town, and assured the garrison that his report was true ; but they could not help doubting the reality of such tidings, from the firm aspect of Nevers, who carried on the siege without giving the Protestants a moment's repose. At length, having sustained and repulsed with great gallantry an assault upon two practicable breaches, Du Plessis was induced to meet the Baron de Palvau,* who had sent to inform him that he had important intelligence to communicate. In consequence of the information he then received, the governor agreed to the terms offered, which were that, if not succored by the King of Navarre or one of his lieutenants, the garrison should march out at the end of eight days, with their arms and baggage, and should be escorted in safety, whithersoever they thought fit to go.

Ere I proceed to notice the events which had taken place in other parts of France, and which were communicated to Du Plessis by Palvau, it may be necessary to relate the proceedings of the King of Navarre, who had not been forgetful of his faithful friends at Garnache, and had resolved even to risk an unequal battle to give them relief, if the same object could not be effected by other means.

* Or Paluau.

Before having recourse however to so hazardous an
expedient, he attempted to divert the enemy, from
the attack of that place, by an enterprise upon a city
of much greater importance.   He had long had his
eye upon the rich town of Niort, which had formerly
been held for years, as one of the strongholds of
the Protestants, but had since gone completely over
to the faction of the League, and had shewn itself
foremost in the persecution of the Huguenots.   His
plan it would seem was, to send a party to surprise
the town by night, and then to march to besiege the
citadel himself; but the bold confidence of the
inhabitants was so great, and the skill with which
the surprise was managed so remarkable, that the
assailants were on the walls, the gates blown open
with petards, and the commanders marching
through the streets, before any one but a sentinel
was aware of their presence.   The citadel also was
quite unprepared for defence, and surrendered at
the first summons, the only condition exacted being,
that Malicorne the governor should be permitted to
give it up to the King of Navarre in person.

That Prince hurried thither without loss of time
from St. Jean d'Angeli, where he had awaited the
event.   No act of cruelty whatsoever took place ;
Henry suffered his old and inveterate enemy Malicorne, to bear off all his property from the chateau;
and even the dead body of the lieutenant, one of the
most violent Leaguers of the country, which had
been carried to a gibbet to be hung as a mark of
disgrace, for many barbarous deeds which he had

committed, was saved from what was then considered as a stain upon a whole family, and delivered to his relations. The League, however, did not fail to publish an account of the monstrous cruelties perpetrated by the heretics at Niort; and though it is proved that not one word of the accusation was true, there were persons found to give it credit.

Knowing well that this sudden and unexpected success would not induce Nevers to abandon the siege of Garnache, Henry hastened from Niort, in order to give battle to that general, or to force his way into the town ;* but the rapidity with which he marched, and the fatigue which he endured in a most rigorous season, affected even his frame of iron ; and as he approached the small town of St. Péré, a sudden and violent coldness seized him. Not willing to yield to the first sensation of illness, he dismounted and proceeded on foot, hoping to warm himself by that means; but shiverings followed, succeeded by so severe an attack of fever, that he was compelled to suffer himself to be carried to the neighbouring chateau of La Mothe Frelon, where the

* Henry had long been collecting all the troops he could gather together, for the purpose of fighting Nevers, and his letters at this time breathe nothing but anticipations of success. On the 17th December, 1588, he says, " If Monsieur de Nevers amuses himself with attacking any thing, I am resolved to give him battle ;" and in a letter to Du Farget, " The enemies are near us ; Monsieur de Nevers is resolved to be beaten." In another to Madame de Guiche, he writes, " I am going to St. Jean to collect my troops, to visit M. de Nevers, and perhaps to do him a signal displeasure, not in his person, but in his command."

symptoms of pleurisy soon displayed themselves;
and for some days his life was despaired of. He
did not however neglect the besieged garrison of
Garnache, but writing to Du Plessis informed him
of his state, and at the same time he sent La Trimouille, at the head of his army, to attempt the
relief of the place.

That nobleman found Nevers so strongly en-
trenched, that he dared not risk an engagement
with a superior army ; and Du Plessis, who, having
learned that the news of the Duke of Guise's death
was true, and that Henry III. entertained thoughts
of calling the King of Navarre to his aid, had
signed terms of capitulation, as we have seen, surrendered the place according to his word, and
marched out with arms and baggage.   The Duke
of Nevers admiring the courage and devotion of the
Protestant troops, treated them not only with courtesy, but with kindness.   He met them at the gates
in person, with a small train, lent them waggons to
convey their goods and their wounded, caused the
arquebusiers to re-light their matches, as a mark of
honor to brave men; and, to those who were too severely
injured to quit the town at the time, he paid every
generous attention, and assured them tendance and
protection. *

In the meanwhile, the news of Henry's dangerous

* The details of the war in Poitou, during the campaign of
the Duke of Nevers, are to be found in his letters, in the Discours
de la Guerre, and Aubigné, with some particulars in Sully, though
not so ample as might be wished.

illness reached Rochelle at night, on the 13th of
January, 1589 ; and now were displayed, in a remarkable manner, the love and confidence he had
inspired amongst all classes of a turbulent, though
warm-hearted population.   The tidings spread like
lightning through the town ; and, though the hour
was so unusual, the bells of all the churches were
rang, to call the inhabitants to pray for their defender.
Men, women, children, masters and servants, poured
forth in multitudes ; the churches were filled, so
that many could not gain admission, and, in the
words of one who was present, returned home very
sad, to add their private petitions to those which
were offered up in public, with tears and mourning.
Extraordinary prayers were continued each day ;
and the whole place presented the aspect of grief
and terror ; till, at length, news of the diminution
of Henry's disease brought relief, and rejoicings
succeeded to sorrow.   A rumor of his death was
soon spread in many places, and reached the court
of the King, where it caused much consternation ;
but shortly after came intelligence of his recovery ;
and the party of the League saw their malevolent
expectations disappointed.

It is necessary now to turn once more to the
court of Henry III., and to give a brief account of
the important events which followed the publication of the Edict of Reunion, and the apparent reconciliation of the King and the Duke of Guise.
All the promises which Henry had made on that

occasion were fulfilled, without difficulty or delay. Guise received the appointment of Generalissimo, in connection with that of Grand-Master, which he already held; two large armies, as we have shewn, were raised, and the command bestowed upon Mayenne and Nevers; the Cardinal de Bourbon was declared by letters patent, first Prince of the blood, and heir-presumptive of the crown; and the States-General were called to meet at Blois, in the month of October. The favors and emoluments of the court seemed entirely at the disposal of the Duke and his friends; his word was law with the King; and nothing shewed the rankling memory of former injuries, or the apprehension of future aggressions, but a few accidental words regarding the barricades, and the pertinacity with which Henry refused to visit the capital.

The King and the Duke, however, looked forward to the States of Blois with expectation of great events; and the measures that both took, as the day of meeting approached, shew that each meditated some design against the other. The Duke of Guise sent letters into every province, instructing his partisans to make use of all the intrigues which they knew so well how to employ, for the purpose of ensuring the election of deputies, who would be the mere creatures of his will. In many of these letters, indeed, he speaks of the King as perfectly won over to his faction, and almost entirely at his mercy; and his confidence seems

to have been so great, as to have excited the
anger of many of his own friends.   The tragedy of
St. Bartholomew's day was not so remote as to be
removed from the minds of many of the party of
the League ; and the share that Henry himself had
taken therein was fresh in the minds of some, who
had been fellow-actors with him in that horrible
transaction.   His behavior, also, was too like that
of Charles IX. during the few months which preceded the massacre, not to strike every one.   Those
he formerly loved were treated with neglect, or disgraced; favors of every kind, offices, and honors, were
showered upon those who had taken part against
him, who had set his commands at nought, and
treated his person with contempt.   He held long
and secret conferences with the various leaders of
the League ; and he honored the Duke of Guise,
in public and in private, as if he looked upon the
acts which he had done, as the greatest services
which could be rendered to the crown.   But Guise
probably felt greater confidence in his own position,
from a knowledge of the designs which were concealed from his friends.   He was well aware that
treasonable ambition must be constantly progressive,
ever to be safe ; that security is only to be found
for those who arm themselves against authority,
when they have made that authority their own ; and
that in the struggle for power, impunity is obtained
only when the supreme power is reached.   He
might say to himself, Coligni stopped and hesi-

tated; I go on: and in the consciousness that he was aiming at more, he might think the elevation which he had attained deprived of its perils.

One of those who gave him the most direct and plain warning of his danger, was the famous Leaguer, Hubert de Vins, whom we have seen struggling with the Huguenots in Dauphiné, and who, on receiving letters from the Duke, full of the confidence which he felt, exclaimed, in his coarse style, "Curses on the Lorraine, has he so little judgment as to believe, that a king with whom he has dissembled so long, in order to take from him his crown, will not dissemble with him in order to take from him his life." The sister of the same officer, when she found that Guise was about to accompany the King to Blois, observed, "Since they are so near each other, you will soon hear that one or the other has killed his companion." These convictions were fully expressed to the Duke by De Vins; but Guise replied, "that though he put no confidence in any thing the King said, knowing well he was false and revengeful; yet he trusted for safety, not to his virtue, but to his good sense; because he believed that Henry had wit enough to perceive if he attempted any thing against him, it would cost him his throne and his life."*

* Pasquier, who gathered with great care and discrimination the rumors of the day, informs his son, (in the 8th letter of the 13th book,) that the Cardinal de Bourbon, in speaking to Catherine de Medicis, after the death of the Duke of Guise, had

The court set out for Blois in the beginning of September, and the designs of the two parties now began to develope themselves. Guise, on the one hand, had deep cunning, great decision of character, an immense body of partisans amongst the deputies, and the devoted love of a great portion of the people, for his support in the enterprises which he meditated. Henry, on the other, had nothing to rely upon but profound dissimulation, the remnants of the royal authority, and a small troop of brave, zealous, and determined friends.

The object of the King seems to have been, so to entangle the factious leaders of the League, by various acts and professions, as, either to bar their further efforts against the crown, and force them to take measures which would tend to the dissolution of the bonds that held the faction together, or to afford him a just and full motive for executing a design which he had evidently long entertained in secret, of inflicting upon them a signal punishment.

On the other hand, there is every reason to believe, that the course which Guise intended to pursue, was, by daily courting favor with the people and the states; by putting himself forward as the zealous and bigoted defender of the Roman Catholic religion,

made it a matter of reproach to that Princess that she had plighted her word for the safety of the Duke and himself, notwithstanding which, Guise had been assassinated, and he imprisoned. The Cardinal added, that without her word, neither would have visited Blois, which would seem to prove, that the Duke had not reposed only on the good sense of the King.

as the most furious enemy of the Huguenots, and as
the advocate for the suppression of all onerous taxes
and obnoxious offices; by representing the King as
incapable; and by shewing him unworthy of confidence, to cause himself to be declared, not by the
Monarch, but by the States, Lieutenant-General
of the kingdom; by which the authority of Henry
would be reduced to nothing, his own power secured upon a permanent basis, and a way opened
for him, first to the station of Mayor of the Palace,
and then to the throne itself, by the exclusion of all
the Bourbon Princes from the succession, except the
old Cardinal, whose age and infirmities promised
soon to remove him.   At all events such were the
designs generally attributed to him at the time; and
his own friends and family gave the strongest countenance to the report, by the constant calumnies
which they poured forth upon the head of the King,
by the means they took to familiarize the public
mind with the idea of confining him in a monastery,
and by their frequent allusions to the example of
Childeric, and to the great benefits which had ensued to France, from the bold assumption of the
crown by the race of Charles Martel.

From the first opening of the States, the two
parties appeared in half-concealed collision, and ostentatious, but insincere co-operation.   The speech
of the King was full of eloquence and vigor, and was
delivered with the utmost grace and dignity; but in
it, he did not fail to refer to the rebellion and ambition of the leaders of the League, declaring that he

would long before have extirpated heresies from his
dominions, if he had not been impeded by the intrigues of many of his nobles. He immediately ordered this oration to be printed; but the faction of
Lorraine had the impudence to stop the press, while
they went to remonstrate with the monarch, upon the
expressions he had used; and Henry consented that
some passages should be suppressed.* It was also
remarked, that before the opening of the States, he
had dismissed several of his principal ministers, and
no longer suffered the Queen-mother, though she
accompanied him to Blois, to exercise that influence
over him which she had hitherto possessed.
Amongst the officers disgraced were the Chancellor, Villeroi, Bellievre, Brullard, and Pinart, all
of whom had the reputation either of favoring the
League, or revealing all that passed in the King's
cabinet to Catherine de Medicis. In place of the
Chancellor he sent to Paris for Francis Montholon,
a celebrated jurisconsult, but so retiring and
moderate a man, that when introduced into the
King's cabinet to receive the seals, he was obliged
to ask which was the monarch, never having seen
him.† The other offices were filled up by gentlemen of no great name, but against whom no ob-
jection could be offered; and Henry, resolved to
avoid past errors, kept his secrets to his own breast,
and concealed his bitter determination to the last.
After a solemn procession which took place soon upon

* Pasquier, liv. xiii. let 1. † Pasquier.

his arrival at Blois, he received the sacrament with the Duke of Guise, whether with a view to deceive, or to bind that nobleman, it is impossible to say. But, step by step, the pretensions of Guise became more clear, and his intrigues to influence the deputies less decently concealed. He still more openly advocated the diminution of the taxes, the reception of the Council of Trent, and the exclusion of the King of Navarre, with every other person *suspected* of heresy, from the succession to the crown; by which proceeding he at once conciliated the people, bound to his cause the bigoted Papists, and opened the way for himself to power. He found some difficulty, however, in accomplishing the latter object; for none of the orders assembled in the States would carry the exclusion farther than the King of Navarre himself; and a protest, drawn up by that Prince, gave Henry III. an opportunity of delaying for some time the publication of the edict against his brother-in-law, while he made efforts to obtain from Rome, the absolution of the Count de Soissons and the Prince de Conti, by which the designs of Guise were in a great degree frustrated.

In the meanwhile the Duke of Savoy seized upon the territories of the crown of France beyond the Alps; and Henry dexterously availed himself of this aggression, on the part of one of the Princes of the League, to cast odium upon the Duke of Guise, and to turn the indignation of the States against the foreign enemies of France. But Guise, with as much skill, cast back the imputation of exciting the Duke of Savoy to the daring course he had pursued, upon his enemies, and proposed to the States, that his brother, the Duke of Mayenne, should immediately march from Dauphiné against that Prince.

It were needless to follow all the intrigues which agitated the court, during the long sittings of the States. Suffice it to say, that almost every thing which was proposed in the assembly, was in the first instance discussed in the apartments of the Duke of Guise, while tumults took place and blood was shed between the attendants and pages, who were divided, like their masters, into the two classes of Royalists and Guisards. Daily, however, Guise gained a greater and greater ascendancy in the States, and it was even suggested that their acts should be published without the examination and sanction of the King. This daring attempt upon the royal authority was frustrated; but the very idea was naturally looked upon by the monarch as an insult, and he had no difficulty in tracing the proposal to its right source. With whatever designs the King had opened the assembly of Blois, the object of the Duke of Guise now became so clear, that he could no longer doubt the struggle between them was for existence. He saw also, that if any effort was to be made for the purpose of saving himself, it must be speedy, in order to prevent the Duke from so completely guarding against surprise, as to leave no opportunity of arresting or putting him to death.

Guise boldly demanded a body of guards as Lieutenant General, and urged as a reason that the same privilege had been formerly accorded to the King's brother while he held that office. He had filled the town and the neighbouring villages with his armed adherents, * and the danger to the King's person became imminent. It was also necessary to act as quickly as decidedly, in order not to be out-run by the operations of the faction, which were evidently tending to some bold stroke. Intimations that a plot against him was about to be carried into execution, poured in upon Henry daily; and if he had entertained any doubt that such was really the case, during the first sittings of the States, that doubt was removed by the warnings he received from near relations of Guise himself. The Duke of Mayenne sent the monarch notice by a gentleman from Lyons,† that he must look to his own safety, for that Guise meditated designs against him ; and the Duchess of Aumale was dispatched by her husband from Paris, to inform the King that he was in extreme peril. The Duke of Epernon gained intelligence of the intrigues that were taking place, and of their object, and gave full information thereof to the King.

* Nevers de la prise d'armes.

† This gentleman is said to have been Alphonso Ornano. The King in his declaration against Mayenne, Feb. 1589, asserts these facts. Nevers repeats them in his manifesto addressed to the Pope; and they were never contradicted by the parties.

The acts of the house of Guise, were not only treasonable, but in direct violation of the oaths they had taken at the opening of the States, and it was reasonable, to conclude that no bonds would bind that family from new aggressions, and just, to punish them for offences clearly committed.* Two courses were open before the monarch : to arrest and try for high treason the principal conspirators, or to put them to death without trial, for which he had but too many precedents. The question of what line of conduct should be pursued, we are assured by those who had many opportunities of learning the truth, was agitated in a secret council held by the King. D'Aumont and others proposed to seize the Duke and his accomplices, and try them according to the common forms of law; but it was shewn, that in that case, no tribunal in the land would be found bold enough to condemn them; that Guise must be taken to Paris, and brought before the court of Peers ; and that no prison in the capital would hold him for an hour; that every part of France would

---

* The King and the Duke, early in December, had sworn on the sacrament perfect friendship and oblivion of the past ; but Nevers cites papers, found amongst those of the Duke of Guise after his death, which proved, that notwithstanding his oath to abandon all leagues within or without the realm, he had entered into engagements with the King of Spain, with the Prince of Parma, with the Duke of Savoy, and with the Governor of Cambray, and had received large sums from foreign powers.

rise to deliver him; and that the attempt would but set him on the throne, towards which he was advancing with gigantic strides. It was then resolved to slay him on the simple authority of the King; but to carry out this plan was difficult, for he was usually surrounded by so many armed adherents, that any open attack must end in a battle rather than an execution. Neither was it easy to find a man of such resolution, skill, valor, and devotion to the royal cause, as to render him fit for the task of effecting secretly the great, but perilous object which Henry had in view.

The first whom the monarch fixed upon was Crillon, the bravest of the brave; but on the design being communicated to him by Henry in person, he replied that he was a soldier and a gentleman devoted to his King, and that if his Majesty commanded it, he would immediately challenge the Duke to single combat, and do his best to kill him; but that he was not an executioner, and that post did not become his rank or his character. The King then warned him to keep the secret; to which Crillon answered that he was a faithful subject and servant, and never revealed the counsels of his Sovereign.

The next person applied to was Monpezat de Laugnac, * commander of the famous guard of Forty-five, attached to the King and the Duke of

* I find this name written in various manners by the authors the day as Longnac, Loignac, and Lognac.

Epernon, bold, unscrupulous and skilful. No difficulties were made by him; and he at once undertook to perform the task, as soon as an opportunity should be afforded him. At first it was proposed to put the Duke to death at a grand entertainment given by the Archbishop of Lyons; but many considerations prevented this plan from being followed, and the execution of the scheme was delayed for several days, during which Henry himself arranged the whole details, and carried on with wonderful dissimulation the delusion which he practised upon the Duke. Not long before, on the occasion of some sharp disputes which had taken place between them, several of the nobles had interfered, and a reconciliation had to all appearance been effected, in confirmation of which the monarch and his powerful subject had received the sacrament together, and vowed oblivion of the past and perfect union for the future.* But there can be little doubt, that at the very time when the King received the emblems of divine mercy, and took the pledge of forgiveness and peace, he meditated the destruction of his enemy; while his fellow communicant revolved the means of dethroning his King. Such frauds, however, were perfectly consistent with the religious notions which they both entertained. Henry followed up this act by several concessions to the Duke, and crowned it with another piece of hypocrisy. He pretended to be anxious to prepare himself for the solemn rejoicings of Christmas, by visiting the chapel of Notre Dame

* L'Etoile.

de Clery, between Blois and Orleans, and appointed the morning of the 23d December, for holding a council, to conclude all business of a pressing kind before the festival. The Duke of Guise and the Cardinal his brother were summoned with other counsellors; and every preparation was made for carrying into execution the bloody deed that was about to be performed.

In the meantime, the secret had not been so well kept as to prevent suspicions and rumors, proceeding no one knew whence, from floating about the court in regard to the approaching catastrophe. Note after note, warning him to beware, was placed in the hands of the Duke; and under his napkin at dinner he found a scrap of paper, bearing the words, "Take care what you do. They are about to destroy you!" The Duke immediately wrote below the caution, "They dare not;" and threw the paper under the table.

Schomberg, one of his most sincere friends, likewise spoke to him on the subject of his dangerous position; but Guise treated his opinion with careless indifference, saying, that he had been born and brought up in the midst of the clang of arms, so that he regarded death without apprehension, adding, "I do not know that man on earth, who, hand to hand with me, would not have his full share of fear. Besides, I am always so well attended, that it would not be easy to find me off my guard."

Nevertheless, reports of a design upon his life reached his partizans also, and a conference between the leaders of the faction was held in the Duke's apartment, to consider what was best to be done. The persons present are said to have been the Duke, the Cardinal de Guise, the Archbishop of Lyons, the President de Neuilly, the Prevôt des Marchands, Chapelle Marteau, and Monsieur de Mandreville. The opinions expressed by the various speakers are reported differently by contemporary writers; but it is clear that some advised Guise to fly, while others declared that it would be both dangerous and disgraceful so to do, and that the Duke himself cut the conference short, by saying, "Affairs are now in such a state, that if I saw death coming in at that window, I would not seek to avoid it by going out at the door."

One more effort is said to have been made, the Marchioness of Noirmoutier, famous for her intrigues as Madame de Sauves, having come to Blois on the 22nd December, to pass the night with the Duke, for the express purpose of persuading him not to trust himself in the King's power. Guise, however, would listen to no remonstrance; and the fatal morning of the 23rd dawned, without any of the repeated warnings he had received having produced the slightest effect.

Everything was prepared before daylight for the execution of the King's will. In order to blind the victim in regard to the number of soldiers who were congregated round the door of the council chamber, Henry III. had directed Larchant, the captain of

the guard, whom he had admitted to his confidence,
to make some excuse to the Duke; and that officer,
on the 22nd, had given Guise notice that he would,
on the following day, present him a petition at the
head of his corps, praying the payment of their arrears.   Thus the military array in the halls of the
castle did not strike the Duke as extraordinary.
The keys of the castle, which were usually brought
to him every night, in his quality of Grand-Master,
had not been delivered, and though we hear of no
apology having been offered for the omission, Guise
himself does not seem to have remarked that it
took place.   When he had entered the council-hall,
however, it is generally stated that a sensation of
faintness seized him, and that, complaining of cold,
he asked for some sweetmeats, when St. Prie, one of
the King's valets-de-chambre, brought him a box of
dried plums.   News of his danger meanwhile
reached the ear of his secretary, Pericart, who immediately sought a handkerchief, and folding up a
note in it, sent it by a page to the Duke, as if he
had forgotten to take one with him; but the boy
arrived too late, the guards were drawn up across
the top of the staircase leading to the council-
chamber, and no one was permitted to enter.

A few minutes after, Revol, the Secretary of State,
appeared, and requested the Duke to accompany him,
to speak with the King in his cabinet.   Guise without hesitation rose and followed.   There falls the
curtain upon all certain history. and every different

writer has given a different account of the events that succeeded. As the King openly avowed and justified the deed, we must reject the statement of the Memoirs of the League, which represent the death of the Duke as more the result of an accidental rencontre with Laugnac, than of a preconcerted plan. Davila, however, probably heard the particulars from his father, who, we have every reason to believe, was with the Queen-mother, even if he did not witness some of the events; and I shall therefore follow his narrative, which does not differ in any important particular from that of Miron, the King's physician.

At an early hour of the morning, and while it was yet dark, the monarch called the persons he had selected for the execution of his scheme around him, and arranged them himself. He retained in his own cabinet three of the most determined, Revol, Alphonso Ornano, and de la Bastide. Monsieur de Termes was in a small room opposite, and Laugnac, with eight of the Forty-five, in the anteroom; which, from other accounts, we find had a short passage between it and the council-chamber. On entering the ante-room Guise found Laugnac and the eight guards; but the former continuing to keep his seat, and the soldiers not moving to raise the tapestry* which covered the door of the cabinet, Guise put out his hand to draw it back himself. At the same moment he received a

---

* Miron calls it a "portiere de velours."

blow from a poniard in the throat,* and the guards springing upon him, inflicted several severe wounds. The unhappy Prince endeavored to draw his sword, and threw himself furiously upon Laugnac; but that officer, who had remained seated on a coffer in the window, pushed him backward as he came staggering towards him, and Guise fell dead before the door of the wardrobe.

Some authors assert that he never spoke a word during the whole of this terrible scene; but others, that he cried aloud, "Ah, traitor!" when he received the first blow; and others, that he exclaimed, "Oh my God, I am killed; have pity upon me; my sins have caused this!"†

The noise and confusion in the antechamber of the King's apartments, reached the council hall, and the Cardinal de Guise with the Archbishop of Lyons, rose and ran towards the door, as if to aid the Duke; but Marshals d'Aumont and de Retz interposed, and drawing their swords, made them resume their seats, crying, "Let no man stir, on pain of death!" A few minutes after, some of the King's officers entered and arrested the Cardinal and the Archbishop, who were conducted by a back staircase to a small chamber, and there detained for several hours without knowing their fate.‡   All the

* Miron declares that the first blow was struck by M. de Montsery; De Thou and others by St. Malines.

† Journal de Henri III.

‡ In the original MS. of De Thou's History, it is stated that De Retz was not acquainted with the King's design, and only drew his sword "from a ridiculous vanity."

leaders of the faction who had apartments in the castle were likewise apprehended; among whom were the Cardinal de Bourbon, the Duke of Nemours, the Duchess his mother, widow of Francis Duke of Guise, the Duke d'Elbeuf, and the Prince de Joinville, the son of him who had just fallen by his own ambition. In the apartments of the Duke of Guise were arrested M. de Hautefort, Pericart the Duke's secretary, with Bernadin his valet de chambre; and the whole of his papers were seized, displaying a mass of treasonable correspondence and treaties with foreign powers, against his sovereign and the state, which would have well justified the application of the extreme penalty of the law, had it been inflicted after trial, and which afforded sufficient excuse in the eyes of many wise and good men, even for the act which had been committed. The Cardinal de Guise equally guilty with his brother, and but little less dangerous, was put to death in prison on the following day by a party of the guard, dying with the utmost firmness, and only requiring time to repeat a short prayer, at the end of which he covered his head with his mantle, and bade the guards execute their commission.*

After the assassination of the Duke, Henry who

---

* De Thou states that the Cardinal, in his conversation with his fellow prisoner, the Archbishop of Lyons, let fall several menaces against the King, which proved the cause of his death. That great writer had his account of this part of the tragedy of Blois from the Archbishop himself.

had waited in a neighbouring chamber, came forth, and is said to have spurned the corpse with his foot, as Guise himself had spurned the body of the great Coligni, exclaiming in the very words which the dead man had used on that occasion, " Venomous beast, thou shalt cast forth no more venom ;" and then gazing at him attentively, he added, " Good God, how tall he is ! He seems taller dead than when he was living." The bodies of the two brothers were subsequently ordered to be consumed in quick-lime, and their bones buried secretly, " in order to prevent the Leaguers making relics of them."

Measures were instantly taken to arrest several other members of the faction in the town of Blois, and to communicate the intelligence of the death of Guise to the friends of the King, in various parts of France, before it reached the monarch's enemies ; for which purpose the gates of the city were kept closed till mid-day. Nevertheless the Leaguers found means to give intimation of the fact to their confederates without ; and a scene of indescribable confusion took place in their flight from the neighbourhood of Blois.

The King himself carried the news of what he had done to Catherine de Medicis, who was lying ill in the chamber immediately beneath that in which the deed was committed. On first entering, he asked how she felt. The Queen replied that she was better than she had been ; to which Henry rejoined, " So am I, for this morning I have rendered myself

King of France, having put to death the King of
Paris."

" Take care," exclaimed his mother, " that you
are not soon King of Nothing! Two things are
now absolutely necessary for you, diligence, and resolution."

From the secrecy which had been observed towards
her, however, she judged that her influence over
Henry was at an end ; and, though she rallied for
a single day, gradually sank, till, on the fifth of
January 1589, she expired in her seventieth year,
after a long, troublous, criminal and disastrous life.

Henry III. now cast off his inactivity ; but his
want of firmness and resolution still remained. Instead of retaining in prison, and bringing to trial the
traitors whom he had caused to be apprehended, he set
several of them free after a short imprisonment, and
left them to join the ranks of the rebels, who were
immediately in arms against him. This weakness
was his ruin ; for had he proceeded to try and punish
the most culpable, as they deserved, the example
must have struck far more terror into the hearts
of the faction than the death of the two brothers
of Guise, which the League looked upon and represented, merely as a private assassination, rather than
an act of justice.

In other respects Henry displayed more vigor.
The Duke of Nevers was commanded to bring his
army to the support of the King,* with all possible

* Mem. de Nevers.

despatch; and Epernon was directed to raise all
the forces that he could, and be ready to join his
Sovereign when called for.* But Henry's first
and most important act was to send Alphonso
Ornano to Lyons, with orders to arrest the Duke
of Mayenne, and supersede him in his command.
Ornano, however, was imprudently detained for
some time, while a manifesto was prepared by
Henry himself, which states at large the causes
that induced him to put the Duke and Cardinal
of Guise to death. The first draft not having been
satisfactory, it would seem, a second and more detailed statement was drawn up, in which the monarch
asserts, not only that he had received intelligence
from persons connected with the house of Guise,
that the two brothers were conspiring against his
authority, but that he had obtained positive proof
of their having meditated his death, and that he
only anticipated them by three days: the very meeting places of their friends having been appointed
at the three gates of the city, for the execution
of their design.† Ornano did not set out till the
24th, and in consequence of this fatal delay, news
of the death of his two brothers, reached Mayenne
a few hours before the officer sent to arrest him
arrived in Lyons. Mounting on horseback as
speedily as possible, the Duke rode out by one gate
of the city, while Ornano entered by the other, and

* Vie du Duc d'Epernon.
† Journal de Henry III. preuves.

hurrying without loss of time into Burgundy, and thence, after securing that province, to Paris, he put himself at once at the head of the League.*

The press now groaned under manifestoes from both parties. On the one hand, the act of the King was declared a base and tyrannical murder, and it was insinuated that Henry had merely put the Princes of Lorraine to death in order to favor the Huguenots; while on the other, the monarch, both in declarations to his people and in letters to neighbouring Princes,† set forth the treason of the house of Guise, and the real causes of his conduct towards the Duke and the Cardinal. He tried to mollify the Pope also in regard to the violence he had committed upon the person of one of the Princes of the church, and he sent the Legate Morosini to endeavor to persuade Mayenne to lay down his arms. At the same time his proclamations breathed nothing but punishment to those who should persist in rebellious leagues and conspiracies, and peace and immunity to all who would desist from such practices and return to obedience.

All these measures, however, were vain ; the Pope was highly exasperated at the death of the Cardinal,

---

* The news of the death of the Duke of Guise had reached Henry IV. before the 1st January, 1589, and with it intelligence of the King's having sent to arrest Mayenne at Lyons. He was, however, ignorant of the death of the Cardinal, which clearly fixes the departure of Ornano on the morning of the 24th.

† See instructions given by Henry, to M. de Maisse allant trouver le duc de Ferrare. Tours, 23 Mars, 1589.

and announced his condemnation of the act in more and more vehement terms each day, as fresh solicitations came upon him from the League. Morosini had no success with the Duke of Mayenne, and ultimately quitted France to avoid the painful task of mediating between two parties whose deeds he equally disapproved. The Sorbonne published a decree,* by which the Doctors pronounced all the King's subjects freed from their allegiance and justified their taking arms against him; and the clergy declared from the pulpit that he was no longer King, and threatened to refuse communion, absolution, and burial in holy ground, to every one who yielded obedience to " the perfidious apostate and tyrant Henry of Valois."†

Neither were efforts in arms wanting. Paris set the example of rebellion; Lyons, Toulouse, Rouen, and many other towns followed; and in the space of a few weeks one half of the principal cities of France had declared for the League.

The first that openly resisted the royal troops was Orleans, which, from its various advantages, had been called the citadel of France. The news of the death of the Duke of Guise was carried to that city in the evening of the 23rd December, by Bassompierre and Breton, adherents of his faction, who fled thither from Blois, and the citizens with one consent rose to secure the town

* 7th January, 1589.
† Traité de la prise d'armes par M. le Duc de Nevers.

against the King. Long and troublesome negotiations had been going on for some weeks in regard to
the possession of Orleans, as it had been placed in
the list of those cities which were to be given up
to the League by the treaty of Rouen. Henry declared that the name was inserted by a mistake of
the secretary, and that it was well known to both
parties, that Dourlans had been intended. Guise
never retreated from any point he had gained; but
at the time of his death, the troops of Entragues, the
governor for the King, held the citadel, and by it the
town, against the claims of the League. The inhabitants now threw up entrenchments against the
castle, which was unprepared to offer a vigorous
resistance ; the place was closely invested, and
Entragues, having been sent from Blois by the King,
was prevented from entering. A party of Parisians, however, coming to the assistance of the Or-
leannois, were totally defeated, and Marshal d'Aumont was subsequently despatched with all the
troops Henry could spare, to attack the city. But
the Chevalier d'Aumale, one of the most furious
and corrupt of the Leaguers, had previously forced
his way in ; and Mayenne himself, marching to support the citizens, d'Aumont was compelled to retreat in haste, after which the citadel surrendered,
and was razed to the ground. Chartres also re-
belled, notwithstanding the popularity of the King
in that town ; but it will be remarked, that the
lightest persuasions, or the slightest offences were

sufficient at any moment to induce cities and nobles to throw off their loyalty with a levity equally disgusting and instructive.*

The great evil of suffering for a length of time, any seditious or treasonable resistance of legitimate rule, is not so much that we thereby encourage men to persist in a particular course of aggression which may require strife and bloodshed to cut it short, as that we engender a general contempt in the people towards lawful authority, and teach them to suppose that obedience to the government depends upon the will and pleasure of individuals and parties, rather than upon duty and respect for the law. The tolerance of that which is clearly illegal and wrong, has never produced any but one result.

Le Mans followed the example of Chartres; and, finding the insurrection spreading from town to town around him, with extraordinary rapidity, Henry, whose force in Blois was very small, retreated first to Amboise and then to Tours, where he was joined by the army of the Duke of Nevers. That army, however, had been greatly weakened by desertion; for though the personal character of the general, and the respect with which he was regarded by his officers, were sufficient to retain all the

* In speaking of Orleans and Chartres, I have followed the account of the Chancellor Chéverny, who, as the governor of the district, was more likely to be acquainted with the real course of events than any other author. Mem. de Chéverny, Tom. i. p. 175.

nobles of the League who accompanied him, till Garnache had surrendered, the moment the siege of that
place was concluded, he found himself abandoned by
a number of leaders, who did all in their power to
seduce the soldiery from the service of the King.*

In the meanwhile, before the arrival of Mayenne
in Paris, that city had displayed all the horrors of
anarchy. The houses of the royalists, and the
Louvre itself, were pillaged, persons suspected of
disaffection to the League were pointed out by the
preachers from the pulpit. The first president was
insulted in the church by one of the priests ; and
afterwards, on shewing a disposition to resist the
lawless proceedings of the faction, he was conveyed
to the Bastille, with all the most honest and upright
members of the parliament ; while Barnabé Brisson,
a less resolute and conscientious man, was elected
in his stead. The Duke of Aumale took upon
himself the government of Paris at the request of
the Sixteen, and appointed a council of forty to
superintend the affairs of the League, into which
body many of the lowest and most incompetent
people of the capital were introduced.†

Letters were sent to Mayenne, beseeching him

* Mem. de Nevers.

† De Thou asserts that this council was appointed by the Duke
of Mayenne, but Victor Cayet assures us that it was called into
existence by Aumale, and there is reason to believe that in this
statement he is correct, as Mayenne, immediately after his arrival,
is found to have changed the constitution of this body.

to hasten to Paris with all speed; and his sister, the
Duchess of Montpensier, set out to join him at
Dijon, to which place he first retreated from Lyons.

It would seem that Mayenne did not require
much persuasion to induce him to put himself at
the head of the faction. He was no longer obscured
by the more brilliant qualities of his brothers, and
though calmer, slower, and more deliberate in his
proceedings, he was not less ambitious or less resolute. Gathering strength as he advanced, after
having secured a great number of towns in Burgundy, Champagne, and the Orleanois, the Duke
marched from Chartres to Paris with a body of
nearly five thousand men, and immediately took
upon himself the command of the League. His entrance into the capital was in the form of a triumph;
his picture was exposed to the people with a crown
upon his head; and the chair prepared for him, bore
every resemblance to a royal throne. There can
indeed be but little doubt, that had his energy
been equal to his ambition, he might have caused
himself to be declared King, not only by the Council
of the League, but also by the Parliament, which
had been dismembered of all those persons who were
strongly and resolutely attached to the institutions
of the country. But Mayenne hesitated to take so
daring a step, probably knowing that, if he yielded
to the temptation, he would thereby deprive himself
of the support of all foreign princes. The moment
for executing such a scheme soon passed away; the

enthusiasm of the people subsided in a great degree; and the Sixteen resumed their original projects, which tended more to the establishment of a Republic, than to the elevation of a new race to the throne. Mayenne contented himself with the title of Lieutenant-General of the state and crown of France, which was first conferred upon him by the council of the Union, and then confirmed by the imaginary parliament, under the direction of the League. He took the oaths required on the 13th of March, and on the same day two new public seals were ordered to be prepared, each bearing the words, Seal of the Kingdom of France. But a term was fixed for the duration of the anomalous authority conferred upon the Lieutenant-General, which was only granted till the meeting of the States-General, convoked for the 25th of the month of July.* This limitation was a severe mortification to Mayenne; and he immediately endeavored to emancipate himself from the restraint of the council, and upon the pretence of giving authority to its decrees, introduced into that body a number of more respectable persons than those of whom it was already constituted. Several members of the captive parliament too were released by his order; and at the same time he prepared to force the way by military success to a position of still greater power and authority.†

* De Thou says that the States were summoned for the 15th of July.

† Cayet. Vie du Duc de Mayenne. L'Etoile.

In the meanwhile Henry III. had shewn various symptoms of his usual vacillation. As soon as he found that Ornano had failed in arresting Mayenne at Lyons, and that the latter had assumed a menacing aspect at Dijon, he sent him a letter full of flattering professions of regard, which the leader of the League treated with the cold contempt they merited. After the Duke had actually taken arms against the crown, however, Henry employed a firmer tone, and declared the seat of the parliament transferred from Paris to Tours. He likewise published a declaration, pronouncing Mayenne, as well as the Duke and the Chevalier d'Aumale, and all who should aid and abet them, guilty of high treason, which was followed by another directed against the towns that adhered to their party. Nearly at the same time, he sent letters to the governors of different cities and provinces in whom he thought he could confide, commanding them to call out the ban and arriere ban for his service against the insurgents. But these orders were but inefficiently carried into effect ; and shortly after Mayenne taking the field at the head of eighteen thousand men, amongst whom were some of the best troops of France, advanced by rapid marches towards Vendome and Tours.

In the midst of the difficulties that surrounded Henry III. one or two more favorable events occurred, which promised to give a better turn to his affairs, if he could but rally sufficient forces to make a great effort. In the first place the town of

Chalons, which had been so long the head-quarters of the League, no sooner heard of the death of Guise than the inhabitants rose and expelled the governor whom he had placed therein, declaring their determination to maintain inviolate their fidelity to the King. The town of Angers too was saved to the royal party by Pichery, who having the command of the citadel, refused to receive the Count de Brissac, and gave admission to Marshal d'Aumont; and Rennes, the capital of Britanny, after having been won for the party of the League by the Duke de Mercœur, revolted against the officer to whom he had assigned the government of the place, as soon as the inhabitants had time for consideration; and, calling in some royalist forces, that important city remained ever afterwards faithful to its sovereign.

During these transactions the eyes of all parties in France were turned from time to time to the King of Navarre, to see what course he would follow in the midst of the dissensions which had arisen amongst the Papists. The news of the death of the Duke of Guise reached him at St. Jean d'Angeli,* while preparing for the attack upon Niort; but instead of displaying any joy at an event which delivered him from one of his greatest enemies, he

---

* The assassination or execution of the Duke of Guise took place on the 23d December, and the last morning that Henry spent at St. Jean d'Angeli before he visited Niort, was that of the 29th. He did not hear of the death of the Cardinal till after the 1st January.

shewed deep grief at the lamentable circumstances under which he perished, and declared, that France had great cause to regret the loss of such a valiant nobleman, notwithstanding his ill-directed ambition.* The King of Navarre added, however, that he doubted not Henry III. must have had just and important motives for the act he had committed; and shortly after, he published a declaration addressed to the three estates of France, which produced an extraordinary impression upon the minds of the people, and proved highly favorable to the cause of the King. This declaration is too important to be passed over without particular notice, and the first paragraph after the exordium, is so characteristic of the man who wrote it, that I may be permitted to give it in his own words.

* Such is the statement of those about him at the time when the intelligence reached his ears, and in the only letter in which Henry enters into any details regarding the assassination of the Duke of Guise, he certainly expresses no joy, though he displays no regret. His feelings, however, were very different towards the Queen-mother, whom he had long regarded as the great promoter of all the discord that afflicted the realm. Thus, in a note to Segur, dated the 25th December, 1588, he says, " I have just seen some letters which a courier was carrying, and in which he who wrote them stated, that he had left the Queen-mother dying. I will speak as a Christian: God do his will with her." And again, on the first of January, 1589, he writes to Madame de Guiche, "I am waiting for the happiness of hearing that they have sent to strangle the Queen of Navarre. That, with the death of her mother, might well make me sing the Canticle of Simeon."—Lettres Missives, tom. ii. page 418.

"Had it pleased God," he says, addressing the three orders of the people, "to touch the heart of the King my lord, and yours, and that I had been called to the assembly of the deputies at Blois, as certainly it appears to me I ought to have been, and that I had been permitted freely to propose what I might think would prove of benefit to the state, I should have shewn that I had not only the desire at my heart, and the words in my mouth, but also the results in my hand, and that I had neither covert designs, conditions to make for my own advantage, nor fine speeches, to which I would not bind myself, but on the contrary, good resolutions and affection towards the King and the kingdom, as great as it is possible to have, even to my own detriment; and that when every one is so disposed, there will be no necessity of treating or capitulating with me, my conscience assuring me that regard for its dictates and for my honor have proved the only difficulty with me.   That not having been done, however— which, perhaps, France will one day reckon amongst its errors, there being no such good physician as one who loves his patient—I am resolved, then, at this late hour to explain to you that which I believe to be my own duty, and that which I look upon as necessary for the service of God, of the King my sovereign, and of this kingdom; in order that all the subjects of this crown may know it, and that all, for my exculpation, may be informed of my intentions, and by my intentions of my innocence."

The King then goes on to speak at large of his own condition, and of his own acts, with the frank boldness of the soldier but the humility of the Christian; pointing out, that in ten years he had seen ten royal armies led against him and his cause, but that all of them had been dispersed, not by his own valor, for he had in reality fought only one, but by the hand of God; and he asks, what good end has been served by the loss of a million of human beings, and the expense of mines of gold, but the ruin of France? He proceeds to express himself as desirous of peace as ever, and to declare, that he and his fellow Protestants are ever ready to submit to the decrees of a free council, though they cannot be driven to sacrifice their conscientious convictions by the dagger at their throats. He asks what would be thought of him by any but hypocrites, if, for the sake of gaining a crown, he were suddenly, and uninstructed in the doctrines of another church, to yield his religion to brute force; and he exclaims, "No! this shall never be done by the King of Navarre, were thirty thrones to be gained thereby.—Instruct me! I am not obstinate.—Take the means of conviction! You would gain infinitely more; for if you shew me another verity than that in which I now believe, I will yield to it. I will do more; for I think that I should leave no one in my party who would not yield to it also."

He next shews the fallacy of the arguments used

to persuade the people that if possessed of the
crown of France he would oppress the Catholics
in the exercise of their religion ; and then com-
ments on the lamentable fact, that in the discussions at Blois no one had ventured to pronounce
the holy name of peace, declaring that peace is the
only remedy for the innumerable ills under which
France still groaned.   After having, in a powerful
burst of eloquence, exhorted all classes to seek tranquillity, and abandon the unjust enormities to which
they had given themselves up for so many years,
he speaks with tenderness and esteem of the
house of Guise, and with deep regret at the fatal
end of their rebellion, but with still more regret, at
the perversion of their high qualities to such lawless
objects as they had followed.   At the same time,
he contrasts his own successes with the disasters
of his enemies ; but declares his conviction, that if
once he were to quit the path of rectitude and honor,
God would withdraw his blessing and overwhelm
him likewise ; and he beseeches all those who have
adhered to the party of the League, to have recourse
to the mercy of the King, which is graciously offered
to them.   He then proceeds to point out, that the
King has no choice but to make peace with all his
subjects ; or, if that be impossible, from the incor-
rigible sedition of one party, to unite himself with
those who are most willing to shew obedience ; and
he paints, in striking colors, the abyss towards
which the current of civil war is hurrying on the

state. He urges the King not to turn his arms against the League alone, but against all or any who should refuse a reasonable peace ; and he professes himself more ready and willing than ever, to lay down his arms, or to employ them for the service of the state, calling God to witness, that, whatever happens, as a good servant of the King, a French subject, and first Prince of the blood, though all the world should vow the ruin of France, he for one, at the risk of ten thousand lives, would endeavor to avert it. He appeals to all, of every class, who have the same object at heart, to join him ; declares his determination to re-establish, throughout all those districts in which he has influence, the rule of the law, and to enforce obedience to the sovereign, saving his own faith and honor ; and protests, that, as he would never suffer his own conscience to be constrained by force, so will he never allow any violence to be used against the Roman Catholics in the free exercise of their religion.

This paper was signed on the 4th March, 1589 ; but between the period of the assassination of the Duke of Guise and the publication of his Declaration, Henry of Bourbon had carried on the war against the League with great vigor and success. St. Maixent and Maillezais had been taken before the 1st of January ; Chatellerault, Loudun, Lisle Bouchard, Mirebeau, and Vivonne followed ; and shortly after, the town of Argenton, in Berri, sent to demand aid from the King of Navarre, in expelling

from the citadel the governor who had been placed
therein by the virulent and licentious Duchess of
Montpensier.   Immediate reinforcements were expected by that officer from the rebel garrison of
Orleans ; but Henry, with his usual energetic activity, set out at once with a small body of troops,
on the 14th or 15th of March, and before the 18th
of the same month* had forced the castle of Argenton to surrender. This was the last movement of the
King of Navarre, before the formal commencement
of negotiations for the union of his forces with those
of Henry III., although overtures had already been
made, which paved the way for that most important
event.

* We find from the itinerary of the King's movements, furnished
by M. Berger de Xivrey, that Henry was at Chatellerault on the
morning of the 14th March, in Berri on the 16th, and had
returned to Chatellerault on the 18th, which data give us, as
nearly as can be wished, the period of Henry's expedition to
Argenton, which is not mentioned by other authorities.

BOOK IX.

THE evil consequences of folly are often more permanent than those of crime; and the act of vigor which Henry III. had performed in putting to death the Duke and Cardinal of Guise was ineffectual to remedy the mischief which his weakness and indolence had produced. The influence of the Duke of Guise survived him, and he found a fitting successor in Mayenne; but a greater evil still remained, which his death did nothing to remove, and which, though he had undoubtedly fomented it for the attainment of his own objects, was principally to be attributed to the feebleness of character displayed by Henry III. I speak of the utter want of respect for the royal authority which had been superadded under that monarch, to the factious turbulence which had arisen in the reigns of his two brothers. This was the chief of many causes that rendered the period immediately succeeding the death of the Duke of Guise, the most embarrassing, the vicious King of France had hitherto encountered. The monarch was despised; a part of the contempt with which he was regarded, fell upon the crown itself; an act, probably done in self-defence, and which wanted nothing of justice but the forms, was looked upon as murder; the Sovereign's commands

were treated with scorn in every quarter of France ;
large forces were openly levied against him; town
after town declared for his enemies; and although
every day, fresh parties of the nobility went to join
his standard, the troops that they brought to support
him in the approaching struggle with Mayenne
were comparatively few.   Epernon, indeed, lost no
time in collecting all the loyal soldiers that could be
found in Angoumois; and having opened a negotiation with the King of Navarre, which was afterwards conducted to a conclusion by the Duchess of
Angouleme and others, he advanced to Henry's assistance with a body of four thousand five hundred
foot and eight hundred horse.

The movements of Mayenne, however, threatened equally Blois, Vendome, and Tours; and
the King despatched orders to his favorite, to cast
himself into the former city and defend it to the
last, while he himself gathered what forces he
could in the capital of Touraine.   Although the
service was one of great danger, Blois being
destitute of all regular fortifications, Epernon hesitated not a moment; and without pausing even to
visit the King, he hurried on with three thousand
foot and a small body of cavalry, sending the rest
of his troops to the assistance of his master, under
Monsieur de Moncassin.   He arrived at Blois
while Mayenne was still on the march towards it,
and commenced the construction of such defences
as the shortness of the time would permit, throwing
a part of his force into the small and indefensible

town of St. Ouen,* with orders to impede the advance of the enemy at any risk, for the purpose of giving the King time to prepare against attack in Tours. This plan was eminently successful; for Mayenne was detained before St. Ouen during four days, which, as I shall speedily have to shew, was of the utmost importance to Henry III. at that moment. The General of the League, however, avoided Blois; and advancing rapidly upon Vendome, into which town he was admitted by his partisans in the place, made the greater part of the King's council prisoners, and then marched at once upon Tours.

A number of Henry's adherents had been despatched into various parts of France to levy troops for the monarch's service, and few if any had returned. But by this time all the preliminaries had been arranged, for the union of the forces of Henry III. with those of the King of Navarre. The Duchess of Angouleme had been the principal negotiator; and Du Plessis Mornay and Sully had both some share in bringing about that desirable result. Each of the two last took the credit to themselves; but history attributes the result to her who put in on claim.† Henry of Bourbon after struggling with

* Written as frequently St. Ouin. I do not find this place in any modern map that I possess.

† Sully, liv. 3. Du Plessis, liv. 1. For the part taken by the Duchess we rest upon almost every independent writer, Cayet, Gerard, Vie du Duc d'Epernon, Aubigné, Davila. The Duchess of Angouleme was a natural daughter of Henry II., and a woman of great talent; and there is every reason to believe that the claims of Sully and Du Plessis rest upon a slighter foundation than her own.

doubts in regard to his brother-in-law's sincerity,
agreed to march to the aid of his sovereign, on the
sole condition of receiving for his security one of the
various towns or castles which commanded a passage
over the lower Loire.   The Pont de Cé was first
offered, but the governor, who was in communication with the League, refused to give it up ; and as
no time was to be lost, the far more important city
of Saumur was granted to the King of Navarre:
compensation having been first made to the commander of the place.   No sooner was the arrangement concluded, and Saumur placed in the hands
of the Bourbon Prince, than, setting out with a
small body of troops, and leaving the rest of his
army to follow, he advanced rapidly to confer with
Henry III. who was then at the ancient palace of
the Kings of France, better known by the description of the great novelist than by the records of the
historian, and called Plessis les Tours.   The French
monarch met his brother-in-law, whom he had not
seen for years, at a short distance from his place of
residence ; but the King of Navarre had not risked
his person in the power of one who had caused the
death of so many by whom he had been trusted,
without warnings to beware, and perhaps some
misgivings.   His cautious friends pointed out, that
Henry III. desired nothing so much as to reconcile
himself with the Pope ; and that no offering would
be so acceptable, as the blood of a heretic Prince.*

* Perefix.

Sully reports, that at two leagues from Plessis Henry halted, and once more consulted his companions; but after a few moments reflection he exclaimed, "Let us go! let us go! the resolution is taken; there is no use of further thought;"* and l'Etoile declares that the King of Navarre, before crossing the river, answered those who would have dissuaded him, much in the same terms which he employed in writing to Du Plessis Mornay, "God has said that I shall pass, and that I shall see," he replied; "and it is not in the power of man to prevent me; for God guides me and goes with me. I am assured of that; and thus he will cause me to see my King with satisfaction, and to find favor with him."†

At length the small body of Huguenots perceived the King of France advancing along one of the long avenues of Plessis les Tours, accompanied by an immense multitude of the inhabitants of the neighboring city on horseback and on foot; but if Henry of Navarre had felt anything like apprehension it had passed away. Frank and open joy was upon his countenance, as he rode on to greet the monarch; and every one remarked the difference between the meeting of the two Kings and that of Henry III. and the Duke of Guise after the barricades.‡ The satisfaction and enthusiasm of the multitude were beyond description: Mayenne was already almost at the

---

* Sully, liv. 3.   † L'Etoile.

‡ Pasquier, lettre xiii. liv. 13.   He was present.

gates ; they expected to see Tours forced each hour,
but the very sight of Henry of Navarre brought back
confidence to every heart ; order could not be maintained by all the efforts of the King's officers ; the two
sovereigns stretched out their arms to each other, but
for many minutes the deliverer and the delivered
could not meet for the press, while acclamations of
" Long live the Kings! Long live the King of
Navarre ! Long live the King !" rent the air. At
length, when they could approach, they cast themselves into each other's arms, and both shed tears,
in which we may well suppose that many strange
emotions were mingled.*

Henry of Navarre only passed one night in Tours,
and then returned to the head-quarters of his army,
which were at Maillé. Mayenne, hearing of his
absence, and trusting to some intelligence which he
had in Tours, made, between the seventh and eighth
of May, an extraordinary march of eleven leagues.
On the very morning of his arrival he was supposed
to be at such a distance, that Henry III. had ridden
out, with but with few attendants, beyond the suburb
of St. Syphorien ; and it is generally supposed that
he had been treacherously induced to do so by some
of his courtiers, who intended to deliver him into
the hands of Mayenne ; but a miller of the neighborhood, who had seen the advancing troops of
the enemy, warned the King of his danger, and he

---

* L'Etoile. I give this scene exactly as I find it described,
without any ornament whatever.

had time to retreat into the town. Messengers were immediately despatched to call the King of Navarre to the relief of Tours; but before he arrived, Mayenne had appeared upon the heights, and made a furious attack upon the suburbs, which were defended by nothing but a weak barricade.* Crillon and Gersay, with a body of the guards and arquebusiers, hastened to meet him at the end of the hollow way, but were soon driven back by the superior numbers of the enemy,† and Crillon, caught in the gate of the suburb, was for some time exposed alone to the whole fury of the enemy. A party of Protestant gentlemen, however, who had remained in Tours to aid the King, at the head of whom were La Trimouille and Chatillon, crossed the bridge, under the fire of seven thousand arquebusiers, who now covered the heights which crown the rocks in the neighborhood of that city. As soon as the white scarfs of Navarre were seen mingling with the troops of the court, the Leaguers shouted aloud to them to retire, saying, "Brave Huguenots! men of honor, it is not you that we seek; it is that traitor who has betrayed you so often, and will betray you again;" and some one perceiving Chatillon, the son of the murdered Coligni, exclaimed, "Retire, Chatillon; we do not wish to injure you, but the murderers of your father."

Chatillon replied in a loud tone, "You are all

* Sully.   † Aubigné.

traitors to your country! I cast away all desire of private vengeance where the service of my King and the state is concerned." *

The struggle for the suburb now became terrible; but in the midst, the King of Navarre, with a considerable reinforcement, reached Tours, and at once hastened to the scene of combat. He found Henry III. displaying no longer weakness, indolence, and irresolution. That monarch seemed in a manner to have resumed all the vigor and resolution of his early days, exposing himself like the meanest soldier. Seven pieces of artillery were subsequently brought to the heights, commanding the bridge and the gate; but regiment after regiment of the Huguenots passed over at a slow pace, refreshing the troops who were defending the suburb, till at length the Leaguers finding that their fire would never succeed in dislodging them, had recourse to the masses of rock that were scattered about amongst the vineyards, which being rolled down the steep upon the tops of the houses, soon compelled the royalists to retreat into the isle, where the defence was renewed by the King of Navarre. After remaining at the barricades for several hours, that Prince was joined by Henry III., who, pushing over one of the gabions with his foot, remained exposed for some time to the whole fire. The King of Navarre endeavored to dissuade him

* L'Etoile. Aubigné.

from such rashness; but Henry replied, "You have been here all day, and are still safe; such may be my case." * He continued in the same position till evening, when the fire becoming slack, and the enemy shewing symptoms of an inclination to retreat, he returned into the town with his brother-in-law, assuming the white scarf of Navarre as a mark of his admiration of the gallantry which the Huguenot army had displayed. The bridge was left under the guard of Chatillon; but the suburb remained in the hands of the Chevalier D'Aumale, who had much distinguished himself, on the part of the League. During the evening, he and the soldiers under his command, committed every excess that it is possible to imagine, breaking into the monasteries, and plundering the churches, so as to afford sufficient proof that the pretence of religion, with which they covered their rebellion, was mere hypocrisy of the most impudent kind. †

At four in the morning of the ninth, Mayenne, abandoning all hope of forcing his way to Tours, commenced his retreat, setting fire to the suburb, and destroying two arches of the bridge to embarrass the operations of the enemy ‡ Means were immediately taken to extinguish the fire, and a small force was sent to pursue the Duke, and gain intelligence of his proceedings. The tidings brought back, were to the effect that he had advanced so

* Mem. de Nevers.   † Davila. L'Etoile.   ‡ Cayet.

far on the way to Chateau du Loir, it would be
hopeless to follow him; and we find, from another
source, that he again made a march of eleven
leagues that day, an instance of activity which
is rare in his history.   In the suburbs, and the
gardens above, he left a number of wounded, and
the unburied bodies of the dead; but Henry
III., with more charity than might have been
expected from him, caused those who were still
living to be carried into the hospitals and treated
with the utmost kindness, while the dead were
interred with decency and respect.

It may be unnecessary to follow the course of
the negotiatious carried on with Rome, by the
League on the one hand, and by the King on the
other.   Suffice it to say, that, if the march of Mayenne upon Tours effected no other object, it produced a result favorable to his cause, by forcing
Henry to call the King of Navarre to his aid, and consequently to exasperate the Pope still more.   Henry
of Navarre, it must be recollected, was in the eyes
of the Holy See an excommunicated heretic ; and,
consequently, although the treaty between him and
the King of France extended to nothing but a
truce, and not a regular treaty of peace, yet the
co-operation of the Most Christian King with a
personage under anathema, was regarded as a daring
insult to the authority of the Catholic church.   The
legate, in consequence, retired from France, and a
monitory was published on the 24th of May, and

ordered to be affixed to the public places of several
towns, warning Henry of Valois to set at liberty the
Cardinal de Bourbon, and the Archbishop of Lyons,
within two days, under pain of excommunication.
By the same instrument he was ordered to appear
within sixty days at Rome, to shew cause why
he should not be excommunicated for putting
to death the Cardinal de Guise, and why his subjects should not be set free from the oath of allegiance, which they had taken. The age was not
one, however, in which such idle thunder could
have any great effect upon the consciences of men,
and we do not find that many of the King's party
were at all troubled by the threatenings of the
Vatican.

At the same time, various events had occurred in
other parts of France which were favorable to the
royal cause. The Duke of Montpensier had been sent
into Normandy shortly after the death of the Duke of
Guise, in order to provide against the dangers arising
from the revolt of several of the most important
towns in that province. On his arrival at Alençon,
he was joined by a number of the noblemen of Normandy, and marching in haste upon Falaise, he
laid siege to that city ; but ere he had been before
it for many days, he was obliged to abandon the
attempt, on receiving intelligence that the Count de
Brissac, having put himself at the head of a body
of peasantry, which had been long in revolt, on
account of the heavy taxation of the times, was

marching against him with the aid of about three
hundred gentlemen, and their neighbors.   The
whole force under Brissac amounted to between five
and six thousand men ; but they were surprised
by the troops of Montpensier in three villages, in
the neighborhood of Argentan, where they were
completely routed and cut to pieces, with a loss
of near three thousand men killed, and from a thousand to twelve hundred prisoners.   More than
thirty gentlemen of distinction were amongst the
prisoners, and Brissac himself escaped with difficulty.*   At the same time a truce was concluded in
Dauphiné between Ornano and Lesdiguieres, which
secured for a time the peace of that part of the
country.

Having now chosen his part, after the vacillation
of a lifetime, Henry resolved to make a vigorous
effort to crush the League at once.   Embassies
were sent early in the year to require aid of
various sovereigns.   Elizabeth of England was
requested to give men and money for the support of the royal cause in France ; the German
Princes were desired to furnish, as usual, a body of
mercenary troops ; and the Grand Duke of Tuscany was applied to for a loan.   Of these three
Princes, the latter was the only one who forthwith
complied with the request of the King of France.
Elizabeth was at the time embarrassed by a war with
Spain, and the German Princes shewed themselves
slow in risking their troops once more, in a land

* Cayet.

which had been already fatal to so many armies ;
but the Grand Duke of Tuscany immediately contributed a considerable sum of money for the support of the King's army ; and one generous individual, at his own expense, and by his own influence,
raised in Switzerland a body of ten thousand men
for the service of his sovereign.   Nicholas de
Harlay, Baron de Sancy, a gentleman brought up to
the profession of the law, and at that time *maitre des
requétes*, being present at a council, which was held
to consider the state of the King's affairs, shortly
after the death of the Princes of Lorraine, pronounced a long and powerful oration, recommending
an immediate levy of a large body of foreign troops,
as the only means of saving the monarchy; and
pointing out Switzerland, amongst the cantons of
which he himself had resided for some years, as the
only country where there existed a great probability of success.   Every one agreed to his views,
but every one spoke of the bankruptcy of the treasury, and asked who would be the generous or the
happy Frenchman who would raise an army with
nothing but the letters of the King.   Sancy, whose
character was one of the most extraordinary of
that age, full of generous emotions, but also full
of weak facilities, almost always guided by rectitude and honor, when he acted on the first im-
pulse, but often deviating from the right path, by
ill-regulated enthusiasm, and the desire to please
those, whom either situation or genius induced him

to respect, replied with some contempt for the persons around him, " It ought not to be my task; but, nevertheless, it shall be mine." He accordingly accepted the commission, and hurried into Switzerland, where, after difficulties innumerable, and the opposition of the Roman Catholic cantons, he succeeded in raising a splendid force, entirely at his own expense, pledging his estates for the payment of the troops, and leading them to the aid of the King, with the skill and vigor of an experienced commander.*

Before the news of this successful effort in his favor, however, reached Henry III., he met with a severe mortification, in consequence, it would seem, of one of those violations of his word which his necessities more than once induced him to commit. On entering Tours, he had solemnly pledged himself that he would inflict no punishment upon the partisans of the League in that town; but the pressing want of money, arising from the stoppage of all the ordinary sources of revenue, led him to lay a tax upon the Leaguers of Tours. The news of this infraction of his promise soon reached Poitiers, with which city he had made the same engagement, and the parties therein being nearly balanced, an advantage was given to his opponents, which they did not fail to make use of for the purpose of bringing over the citizens to the union. The loyalists besought the King to hasten to their

* Le Laboureur.

aid after the retreat of Mayenne; but, although he acceded to their wish, and called Marshal Biron with his troops from Guienne to join him in that city, the Leaguers, before his arrival, had gained the ascendancy; the gates were closed against him; and his forces saluted with a volley of cannon balls as they entered the suburbs.* The King, not venturing to attack a place which would have required a long siege for its reduction, returned to Tours, where he received urgent messages from the King of Navarre, who had advanced to Beaugency, pressing him to march on at once and strike a decisive blow at the enemy.

In the meantime, a gallant effort had been made in the north; and the Duke of Aumale, at the head of an army raised by the Parisians, had been defeated under the walls of Senlis, by the young Duke of Longueville and the devoted La Noue; but to counterbalance this success, Mayenne had taken Alençon and given the party of the League a preponderance in Normandy. The Parisians, however, were thrown into a dreadful state of alarm by the defeat of their governor, whose fugitive troops had been pushed to the very gates by the victors; and a volley of cannon shot falling into one of the markets increased the consternation of the populace. Longueville pursued his way towards Burgundy to meet the Swiss troops now advancing under Sancy; Epernon made himself master of Montereau ou faut Yonne; and Chatillon in a rencontre with the

* Aubigné. Cayet. L'Etoile, notes.

governor of Chartres, defeated his troops with great
slaughter, in spite of an obstinate and well conducted
resistance. Shortly after the King's return from
Poitiers, Henry of Navarre appeared in Tours,
having ridden, it is said, twenty-five leagues to
decide the movements of his brother-in-law, and
induce him to advance at once to Paris,* whither
the march of the Duke of Mayenne was now tending. It would seem that the timidity of Henry's
friends, more than his own want of resolution, had
detained him in Tours; but the presence of the
King of Navarre removed all hesitation, a general
rendezvous was given to the royal forces at Beaugency, and having left the Cardinals of Vendome
and Lenoncourt with some of the members of the
council to keep Tours in obedience, Henry began
his march towards the capital. After having reached
Beaugency, the royal army proceeded to attack the
town of Gergeau, which was garrisoned by the
League.   The first detachment that appeared under
its walls was commanded by the Duke of Epernon,
who immediately took possession of one of the
suburbs. The King of Navarre arrived soon
after, and having been received by the Duke, the
latter, totally unarmed, led him into the midst of
the great square of the suburb, which was commanded by the enemies' works, saying, that he wished
to shew him his housekeeping.   A tremendous
fire was directly opened upon the party of the

* Aubigné. Cayet.

two commanders, by which a cousin of the Duke's, and an attendant were killed on the spot; but Henry and Epernon walked on at a slow pace, within forty paces of the curtain from whence a fire was kept up during the whole way, killing several more of their followers, till they reached a gate that hid them from the enemy. There, Epernon received a message from two officers, who had remained in the square, asking him to return, and he was about to go back as rashly as he had advanced, when the King of Navarre seized him by the collar,* giving him to understand that he had committed folly enough for one day. When Henry III. was made aware of what had taken place, he asked Epernon angrily if he had wished to cause the death of Navarre. A rumor that such was his object, even spread through the army; but Aubigné exculpates him of all sinister designs, and justly attributes his conduct to that vain imprudence which made him believe, that to expose himself unnecessarily was the road to renown.

The town was soon forced to capitulate, but Henry, though he granted favorable terms to the inhabitants and garrison generally, with wise rigor, excepted those who had violated their faith, and, after taking service with him and receiving pay, had gone over to the enemy. These were given up to the executioner, and amongst the rest, as a warning to his commander, was hanged, a gentleman

* Gerard. Cayet.

whom La Chatre had sent into the place from
Orleans. Gien and La Charité submitted to the
King, and having now secured the means of crossing
the Loire at various points, the monarch marched
on and took Pluviers by storm, after which Etampes
was besieged and taken. The Baron de St. Germain,
who had been one of the King's pages, was seized
in attempting to make his escape, and notwithstanding the intercession of his friends, was executed
for treason. From Etampes, the King of Navarre,
at the head of twelve hundred men, made a hasty
excursion to the gates of Paris, attacked and defeated
a party of the Parisians in the suburb of St. Jacques,
and having spread consternation amongst the inhabitants of the capital, returned without loss to
re-join the King of France. Pontoise was next attacked, and after a gallant defence, received an
honorable capitulation; but the Huguenot army
lost before its walls one of the most distinguished
officers of the time, M. de Charbonnieres, who was
mortally wounded while the King of Navarre was
leaning on his shoulder. A number of smaller
places in the neighborhood made submission on the
fall of Pontoise; and Henry, now approaching the
capital, with the intention of besieging it, sent messengers to call all the nobility of Picardy and Normandy, who still remained true to the royal cause,
to join him at Poissy, while Longueville with his
forces having united with Sancy and the Swiss, approached rapidly from the side of Chatillon sur
Seine.

The difficulties that Sancy had encountered were many ; but the services he rendered, even on his march, were great, and his skill and determination, in leading the force he had raised through so great an extent of country, called forth the highest praises from every one but those who were envious of his well-merited renown. The principal danger Sancy had to encounter, lay in the neighborhood of the town of Geneva, which was almost surrounded by territories held by the Duke of Savoy, at that time in actual war with the King of France. But having obtained the levy which he demanded from Berne, Basle, Soleure, the Valais and the Grisons, he skilfully negotiated with the inhabitants of Geneva ; and while he wrote to Lesdiguieres and Ornano to attack the Duke from the side of Dauphiné, he induced the Genevese to take arms against Savoy, and seize upon different small towns and fortresses in the immediate neighborhood of that city. The way having been thus in some degree cleared, and the troops required raised by the cantons, Sancy advanced at their head, took the town of Thouon, captured and burnt the fort of Ripaille, and then, after some negotiations with the cantons, marched towards Langres, dexterously spreading a report that he intended to turn upon Chambery. From Langres he pursued his course to Chalons uninterrupted,* but not without mortification, for he was met on the march by M. de la Guiche, bearing a

* Cayet. Villeroy.

commission to command the army. Sancy, however, treated his authority with contempt, telling
him to keep his paper, and he would keep his men.*
Having been joined by the Duke of Longueville,
he passed the Marne, and reached Conflans, two
leagues distant from Pontoise, where his arrival
spread joy and confidence through the army of
the King.   Henry immediately received him in
his cabinet, but Sancy was surprised to find that
the monarch shed tears while he embraced, and
thanked him for his services ; nor was he without
apprehension that some unforeseen disaster, which
he had not heard of, had lately befallen the King.
But Henry reassured him, saying, " I only weep
from regret that I have nothing but tears and promises to give you in recompence for your devotion.
Nevertheless, if God gives me the means, I will raise
you so high that the greatest in the realm shall
have cause to envy you."

On the 20th of July, the King reviewed the
Swiss army ; and finding his force to amount to
thirty thousand men, with a well equipped park of
artillery, the siege of Paris was determined upon,
after some debate in the council, in which for a
time the King of Navarre, and M. de Givri, stood
alone as the advocates for that bold measure.   The
bridge of St. Cloud was immediately attacked,
and taken ; while Henry of Navarre, pushing forward along the course of the river, occupied Meu-

* Le Laboureur.

don, and all the villages on the bank as far as
Vaugirard, where Chatillon took the command of
the outpost.   Henry III. fixed his abode at St.
Cloud, in a house named the Hotel de Gondy ; and
on the following morning the King of Navarre
advanced towards the gates of Paris, and threw out
skirmishers to engage the posts of the enemy, whose
principal forces were quartered in the suburbs,
under the command of La Chatre and Mayenne.

Although there cannot be the slightest doubt
that the inhabitants of Paris, and even the leaders of
the League were under great apprehensions regarding the result of the siege, a bold countenance
was assumed by the troops, and various gentlemen
issued forth to break a lance with the officers of
the King.   But in the meantime the most detestable
means were employed to deliver the capital from
the dangerous situation in which it was placed.   It
was determined to have recourse to the dagger of
the assassin ; and a young man of the name of
Jacques Clement, a Jacobite monk, was pitched
upon as a fit instrument for the purpose.   He is
represented as a person of a gloomy and ferocious
mind, licentious in his manners, and of a weak and
superstitious character.   He had been several times
punished in his convent for various excesses ; and
on applying for absolution to his priest, he had
been told in general terms, that it could only be
obtained by devoting himself entirely to the service
of God.   The means which were employed to work

upon his mind have been variously stated; but it would appear certain that the chief agent for corrupting the unhappy man, and exciting his imagination to the necessary point, was Father Bourgoing, Prior of the Jacobin convent in the Rue St. Jacques. It is possible that the Duke of Mayenne himself had no share in this infamous transaction, and he afterwards affirmed upon oath that he was innocent of the deed; * but yet some of the events which occurred in Paris, and which could scarcely have taken place without his knowledge and consent, shew that the council of the League in general must have been cognizant of, and participators in, the design. Pithou, too, in his address to the Duke of Mayenne, published under the name of M. D'Aubray, boldly charges him with having seen and encouraged Jacques Clement before he set out from the capital;† and the Parliament of Paris subsequently proceeded against the Duke of Aumale, who had fled, and condemned him to be executed in effigy.‡ The Duchess of Montpensier is likewise supposed to have used every persuasion, and even to have descended to the most degrading prostitution of her person § to induce this weak and superstitious bigot to undertake the destruction of the King.

After the arrival of Henry in the neighborhood

---

* Pierre Matthieu.   † Satyre Menipée, tom. i. p. 145.

‡ Godefroy. La Veritable Fatalité de St. Cloud.

§ Auvigny.

of Paris, the imminent danger in which the city
was placed, and the terror that was generally
entertained by the party of the League, produced
redoubled efforts to confirm the monk in the
determination he had taken, and to hurry him
forward to its execution. The whole transaction is
so obscure, that it is not without hesitation I venture
to give these details; but it is certain that, a few
days before the murder of the King, Henry was
warned of the danger which menaced him, by a
young lady of high family in the capital ;* that on the
27th of July he sent an officer into Paris, to tell the
Duchess of Montpensier he would burn her alive if he
took the city; and that on the day when Jacques
Clement issued forth, to commit the assassination, a
great number of the principal citizens, who were
known to be attached to the royal party, were arrested
and thrown into prison.† Clement also was, beyond
all doubt, informed that this measure was intended for
his protection, and that if he should be taken, the
heads of these prisoners would be made answerable
for his safety. A passport was obtained for him from
the Count de Brienne, one of the loyalist prisoners of
the League, who was deceived into a belief that the
monk had important communications to make to
the King from the first President de Harley, who

* Pasquier, liv. xiv. 5 Aout, 1589.

† L'Etoile. The number is variously given, some authors
saying 300, others 100. See also La Veritable Fatalité de
St. Cloud.

was a captive in the Bastille. A letter, either forged
or procured from that magistrate by similar arts,
was placed in the hands of the assassin ; and some
authors declare that, before he set out, he had an
interview at the Chartreux with the Duke of Mayenne himself.*

Confirmed in his purpose by the exhortations
of the priests, who promised him the rank of cardinal if he survived, and canonization if he fell,
Clement issued forth from Paris, and took his way
to St. Cloud. He was first stopped at Vaugirard,
where his passport being examined, and his pretended errand made known, he was sent forward,
under the guard of two soldiers, towards the quarters
of the King. On the way he was met by La Guesle,
procureur-general, and was given into his hands
by the guards. That officer, after having inquired
his business, cross-examined him strictly, and looked
at the letter from De Harley, which, if it was not
really written by his hand, was so well forged as to
deceive La Guesle. The replies of the monk
were quite satisfactory, and the Procureur led him
to St. Cloud, with the intention of bringing him
immediately to the presence of the King. Henry,
however, was at the time out on horseback, and did
not return till so late that La Guesle detained the
Jacobin at his own lodgings for the night, promising to obtain an audience for him on the following
day. Accordingly, early on the first of August,

* Auvigny. Vie du Duc de Mayenne.

Clement was taken to the Hotel de Gondy, and the Procureur-general, after having caused him to be questioned by Portail, one of the surgeons of Henry, regarding some of his relations in the Bastille, proceeded to the cabinet of the King, whom he informed that there was a monk without bringing intelligence from Paris, which he refused to communicate to any but the monarch himself. Henry ordered him to be admitted immediately, and Jacques Clement was introduced into the cabinet, which at that moment contained only the King, M. de Bellegarde, and La Guesle. It would seem, from the account of La Guesle himself, that the monk, as soon as he entered, approached nearer to the monarch than that officer judged safe; but Clement having given Henry to understand that the secrets he had to communicate were for his ear alone, Bellegarde and the Procureur-general were ordered to withdraw. Clement then took a paper from the sleeve of his gown, and presented it to the King, who began to read it attentively. Instantly seizing the opportunity, the assassin drew forth a knife, and plunged it into the entrails of his victim, who uttered a great cry, and drawing forth the weapon, aimed a blow with it at the head of his murderer, which wounded him above the eye. La Guesle, Bellegarde, and Du Halde, rushed in at the King's voice; and, seeing him wounded, the former, without pausing to consider, passed his sword through the body of the

murderer. Some authors say that he fell dead with
the first blow; others, that Bellegarde and Du
Halde, with some of the guard, despatched him;
but at all events, it is clear that he was killed immediately, without having uttered a word. This
rash haste gave rise to insinuations against La
Guesle himself, put forth by the party of the Union,
and especially by the Jacobins, when, after having
recovered from the phrenzy of the League, they became somewhat ashamed of an act which they lauded
at the time. But we have the authority of Henry IV.
himself for stating, that Jacques Clement had been
instructed, if taken alive, to accuse the Count de
Soissons of having instigated him to commit the
crime.*

The King was immediately undressed, and put
to bed; and for several hours the surgeons saw
no cause to apprehend that the wound was mortal. They even assured him that he would be
able soon to mount his horse; and he dictated
letters to several foreign Princes, and to those noblemen in the various provinces of France who were
the chief supporters of his cause, stating, that an
attack had been made upon his person, but that no
evil result was to be apprehended.†

The news spread quickly through the army.
Amongst the first who arrived at the monarch's bed-
side was the King of Navarre, having galloped from
Meudon at full speed, and he was moved to tears as

* Pierre Matthieu.
† Memoires de la Ligue, tom. iii. Cayet.

he knelt by the couch of the dying King, with whom
he had been so lately reconciled. Henry III. embraced
him tenderly, and assured him that he did not apprehend any danger ; but added, that if the wound
should prove mortal, he left him the crown as his
legitimate successor. He then said :—" If my will
were to have effect, it would be as flourishing upon
your head as it was on that of Charlemagne.
I have commanded all the officers of the crown to
recognize you as King after my death." Having
uttered these words, he directed all the Princes
and officers of state to be called in, and in well
chosen words, interrupted by occasional groans and
sighs, recommended to them union amongst themselves for the preservation of the monarchy ; then,
speaking of the claims of the King of Navarre
to the throne as indubitable, he ordered them to
swear obedience and fidelity to that Prince after his
own death.* No one, we are assured, ventured to
disobey ; and, satisfied with what he had done,
Henry desired to be left alone with his chaplains,
and the officers of his chamber. If the deep and
bitter regret of all who surrounded him ; if tears
sincere, and full of anguish, on the cheeks of those
whom he had befriended ; if the poignant sorrow
of even his successor, whom he had often wronged
and deceived, could soothe the pangs of a dying
man, Henry had that consolation. All his errors,
all his vices, all his crimes, even all his weaknesses,

* Cayet. Aubigné.

were at that moment forgotten, and nothing was remembered by his courtiers but the kind and generous master, the warm hearted and liberal friend.

The active and energetic mind of Henry IV., however, did not permit him to forget, in the sorrow that he felt, the important duties of his situation. Judging that the attempt upon the King's life would be immediately followed by some enterprise in arms upon the part of the enemy, he caused a large body of troops to march towards the city. But no one stirred beyond the walls of the capital, and the whole of the people seemed to wait in awful suspense for the result of the great crime in which so many were accomplices.

Towards evening, the pain which Henry III. experienced, led the surgeons to perceive that his wound was more serious than they had at first supposed, and various symptoms developed themselves towards night, which clearly shewed that his life was drawing to a close. Henry of Navarre had returned late to the Chateau of Meudon, and had just sat down to supper, when M. d'Orthoman arrived in haste to tell him, that if he wished to see the King once more in life, he must set out instantly. While the horses were being prepared, Henry held a hurried consultation with eight of his friends; and, ordering his attendants to arm themselves well, but to conceal their cuirasses under their ordinary clothes, he set out with a party of thirty-three gentlemen, and arrived at St. Cloud a little before day break.* The agitation of his mind, as he rode along towards the spot where Henry III. lay in the agonies of death, the many considerations that pressed for attention, the dangers which presented themselves to his eyes, the difficulties that lay in his path, but the great destiny to which that path was sure to lead, if, with a firm and constant heart, a bold and energetic mind, a clear and powerful judgment, and the blessing of God over all, he trod it to the end, must have rendered that journey one of the most awful hours of his life. " It was not," says Sully, who accompanied him, " the result of a petty negotiation, nor the success of a battle, nor a little kingdom like that of Navarre which was now in question. It was the finest monarchy of Europe. But how many obstacles were to be surmounted to arrive thereat! and by what labors was it to be purchased! All that the King of Navarre had hitherto undergone could be counted for nothing in comparison. How was to be overthrown a party so powerful, and in such repute, that it had caused a monarch already seated on the throne to tremble, and almost to descend therefrom ? This difficulty, already so great, appeared almost insurmountable when one reflected that the death of the King, would at once detach from the person of the King of Navarre the greatest and the principal part of

* Sully. Aubigné.

his forces. He could not reckon upon the Princes of the blood, nor upon the great nobles; and such was his situation, that having need of the succor of every one, he could rely upon no one. I trembled when the thought crossed my mind, that perhaps this sudden and unexpected news was about to produce a revolution, which would leave the King of Navarre with a handful of faithful servants, at the mercy of his ancient enemies, and in a country where he was without any resource."

On the arrival of Henry and his followers at St. Cloud, the first tidings they received were, that the King was better, and the whole party were ordered to give up their swords before entering the royal quarters; but on reaching the Hotel de Gondy, they found the monarch had just expired.

END OF VOL. II.

G. NORMAN, PRINTER, MAIDEN LANE, COVENT GARDEN.

NOW READY,

In 1 Vol. 8vo. with Maps and Woodcuts, price 10s. bound in cloth,

A BRIEF ACCOUNT

OF THE

DISCOVERY OF AMERICA

BY THE NORTHMEN,

In the Tenth Century,

WITH

NOTICES OF THE EARLY SETTLEMENTS OF THE IRISH
IN THE WESTERN HEMISPHERE

BY

NORTH LUDLOW BEAMISH,

FELLOW OF THE ROYAL SOCIETY, AND MEMBER OF THE ROYAL DANISH SOCIETY OF
NORTHERN ANTIQUARIES,
AUTHOR OF THE " HISTORY OF THE GERMAN LEGION," ETC.

LONDON:

T. AND W. BOONE, NEW BOND STREET.

1841.

EXTRACT FROM THE PREFACE.

AMONG the various, valuable, and important publications of the Royal Danish Society of Northern Antiquaries, that which has created the greatest general interest in the literary world, is the able and elaborate work of Professor Rafn, which came out in Copenhagen in the year 1837, under the title of "*Antiquitates, Americanæ sive Scriptores Septentrionales rerum Anti-Columbianarum in America.*"

This interesting publication, the fruit of great literary labour, and extensive research, clearly shews that the eastern coast of North America was discovered and colonized by the Northmen *more than five hundred years* before the reputed discovery of Columbus.

These facts rest upon the authority of antient Icelandic MSS. preserved in the Royal and University Library of Copenhagen, and now, for the first time, translated and made public. Fac-similes of the most important of these documents are given in Professor Rafn's work, together with maps and delineations of antient monuments illustrative of the subject; a Danish and Latin translation follows the Icelandic text, and the whole is accompanied by introductory observations, philological and historical remarks, as well as archæological and geographical disquisitions of high interest and value.

The design of the writer of the following pages is to put before the public, in a cheap and compendious form, those parts of Professor Rafn's work, which he considered were likely to prove most interesting to British readers, the greater part of whom, from the expense and language of the original publication, must necessarily be debarred from its pursual. The translations of the Sagas or Narratives are made substantially from the Danish version, of the correctness of which, coming from the pen of the learned Editor, there could be no doubt; but, in many cases, where the style of this version appeared to the translator to depart from the quaint and simple phraseology of the original, the Icelandic text has been specially referred to, and an effort has been made throughout, to give to the English translation, the homely and unpretending character of the Icelandic Saga. In all cases where it was thought possible that doubts might arise, or where it was considered important to impress some particular fact or statement upon the mind of the reader, the original Icelandic word or expression is given: and free use has been made of the copious and lucid notes and commentaries of the learned Editor, to explain or illustrate the various etymological, historical, and geographical points which call for observation: As an appropriate introduction to the whole, is prefixed a sketch of the rise, eminence, and decline of Icelandic historical literature, from the Danish of Dr. P. E. Müller, Bishop of Zeeland.

This publication forms an indispensable introduction to the celebrated work of Dr. Robertson, who appears to have been totally unacquainted with the early discoveries of the Northmen.

Made in the USA